DATE DUE

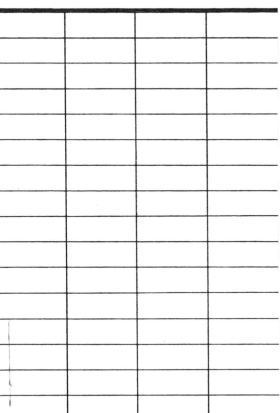

Memoirs of a Judge

By: Hon. Paul I. B. Staniszewski

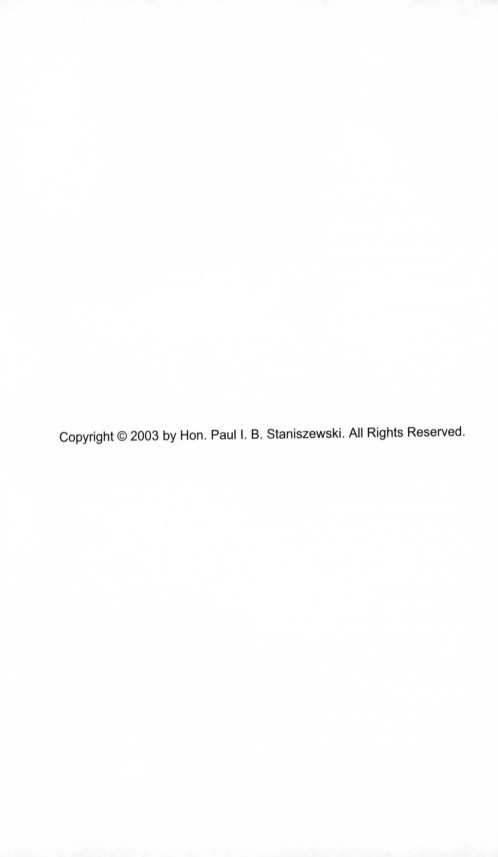

Table of Contents

Dedication

TO THE FAMILY

This is dedicated to my dearest Tevis Marie, Gayle, Camille, Michelle, Andrea, Kurt, and our four grandchildren.

In addition, to infants and children in their multiple needs, including cancer treatments.

Preface

The Hon. Paul Staniszewski is a prince of a man. I first met him and his first wife Wanda, prior to the election of 1957 when I had the dual responsibilities of being the Liberal Party liaison with the various ethnic groups in Toronto's rapidly changing cultural mosaic, and recruiting representatives of the new Toronto to run as candidates for the Liberal Party in the federal election. Paul was one of the bright, young, rising stars of Polish-Canadian origin and a natural for my list. I got in touch with him and asked if he was interested in a career in federal politics.

In principle, he was interested. However, at that time, he and Wanda had a young family and he felt that his responsibility to them and to his law practice had to take precedence. He kept the door open for the future, however, and we remained friends and political collaborators. Meanwhile he wished me well in efforts to recruit Dr. Stanley Haidasz to represent his community in the 1957 contest.

Although he was keenly interested in public affairs, the day came when he had to choose between politics and the judiciary. Justice won and it became one of his cherished causes when he was appointed to the County Court in 1968, just months before his beloved Wanda died. He put heart and soul into his work and this was recognized when all County Court Judges were subsequently promoted to what is now the Superior Court of Ontario. It was around this time that our paths began to diverge and we eventually lost touch.

Years later, I was both astonished and delighted when I received an unexpected telephone call from Paul. We brought each other up to date, he told me about his marriage to Tevis, his struggles, and achievements as a jurist, and that he had retired and was living in Windsor. The reason for the call was that he had read an article in the University College Journal, which mentioned my concern that Canada was losing its independence and that if we didn't do something about it, and soon, we would inevitably wind up as the 51st U.S. state. He shared my concern, and with a passion. He was able to be helpful in many important ways.

He told me that he would like to write a book about his life and the struggles of a young immigrant's son who overcame the inevitable hurdles and achieved much in this promised land of Canada, which I encouraged him to do. I shared his conviction that it was important for his life story to be on the record, not just for his family, but also for all Canadians who want a better understanding of their history.

This, then, is his book. He succinctly and eloquently writes the tale of two very different sides of Canada's legal system as experienced by him. On one side is the champion of law, justice, and truth. On the other is the heartache and suffering of a supplicant and the disappointment and frustration of not seeing justice adequately served. It is a real life story of real life experiences told by a man who has lived many different roles.

While the book may be of special interest to Paul's friends in the Polish-Canadian community, who are aware of his fierce loyalty to his family and his commitment to justice, it is a story that we can all relate to in one way or another.

It reminded me of his early years in Toronto and his involvement in the Polish-Canadian Congress and other associations, which have played such an important role in maintaining the cultural traditions of a great society for the benefit of future generations who would otherwise lose that portion of their identity.

It is also a story of Paul's generosity, almost to a fault, in keeping with the spirit of giving that his loving immigrant parents instilled in him. He and his dear wife Tevis are always thinking of others and they have created several bursaries to assist university students in financial need. All of this in spite of Paul's failing health and his battles with intransigent bureaucracies

His book is a crowning jewel from a man who has given his all to his family, to other people, and only finally, to himself. He deserves to have his name enshrined in the history of his beloved country and to know that his children and grandchildren will be proud to acknowledge his legacy.

Hon. Paul Hellyer
Toronto 2003

Acknowledgements

In writing the autobiography of my life, I have divided this book into four general segments: the first era in Montréal, the second in Toronto, the third in Windsor, and the fourth—retirement, in Tecumseh, a suburb of Windsor.

My inspiration and recollection of events for the Montréal segment were greatly aided by materials from my deceased father (1961) and my mother (1979), my matriarch sister, Eugene Gryszówka, my sister Wanda Rozynska, Ms. Sophie Zurowska, J. Bednarz, F. Matusiewicz, Stanley Rozynski, Mrs. Jenny Dasys (Mikalauskas), and Helen Morin.

In compiling my life experiences, I was greatly assisted by newspaper clippings of the Montréal Star, Toronto Telegram, Globe & Mail, Polish Weekly "Zwiazkowiec," the Windsor Star, and the Youth Congress paper (The Dawn). In addition, by commemorative publications of St. Mary of Czestochowa Church and the Polish White Eagle Society, the Polish Veteran's Association, publications of the Polish Business Men—Toronto, St. Stanislaus Credit Union (1968) publication, Polish Federation booklet (1938), the Holy Trinity Parish (1991) magazine, and the Polish Parish School Association's report.

I would also like to credit as resource materials—letters sent to my father from relatives in Swislocz in the Russian Soviet Republic, family letters from siblings to parents and myself, and letters from Wanda, my wife to be.

The Toronto epoch of my life was entirely inspired by my deceased wife Wanda Marie Staniszewska (1925-1968). Had it not been for our deep love for one another, I most probably would not be writing this book. I also owe much to my now deceased law partner, George G. Bagwell, Q.C. and to a loyal friend, Judge James B. Trotter (deceased). To the late Senator A.W. Roebuck, Q.C., the late Pat Cameron, Q.C., M.P., and his gracious wife. To Engineer Joseph Kicinski (deceased), Mrs. Francis Piorczynski and Mrs. M. Stanley, Mr. Keith Russell, Osgoode Hall classmate C. Vipavec (deceased), the Honourable Mr. Justice Hugh R. Locke, and countless election volunteer workers and voters of High Park in 1959, 1963, and 1967.

In the compilation of the Windsor segment of this autobiography, I am indebted to several lawyers and justices and above all, to my dearest wife, Tevis Marie, who not only encouraged me to write this work, but also, by having a better memory for past events than I have, helped me tremendously.

In my 23 years as a Federal Appointed Judge, I had amassed thousands of pages in numerous Judges' books of my own notes concerning criminal and civil trials, motions, and applications. These invaluable resources aided me greatly in selecting the legal cases, which I have incorporated into this book.

I also would like to acknowledge the assistance of Windsor lawyers: James Ball, Leon Paroian, Q.C., Tulio Meconi, and Greg Monforton's law firm, and the Honourable Mr. Justice Robert M.P. Daudlin, and I am much obliged to the Honourable Madam Justice Karen M. Weiler of the Ontario Court of Appeal for her assistance.

I wish to thank the editor of this book—Tina Petrova. When I first presented my pages of manuscript for her opinion and perusal, I had included in my memoirs—examples of lawsuits on which I had sat in judgment. She advised me that the addition of these cases weighted my story down and detracted from it. In addition, my writing style from my days as a lawyer tended to be on the pedantic side and she edited the telling of my memoirs into a more empathic voice.

I learned a lot through the process of allowing someone to change my voice into a more sincere and direct tale of two very different worlds. As a Judge and Purveyor of Justice—upholding the law, and as a supplicant of the legal system, fighting the long and hard uphill battle of trying to win a judgment when I considered myself wronged by a "Goliath…"

I am greatly indebted to Mrs. Lisa Kelly for her fervent work as to typing the manuscript, copy-editing the manuscript for the final printout, and professionally designing the book. She was a friendly liaison with the printer, and created two PDF files containing the camera-ready documents to be published. Her professional work was outstanding.

My Polish Heritage

Poland's history began in the 9th century, when the *Polians* (meaning dwellers in the fields) established their authority over other Slavic enclaves in the region. Poland had become a powerful monarchy in Europe during the Middle Ages. United with Lithuania, it reached its peak in the 16th century by ruling territories that stretched out across Europe from the Baltic Sea to the Black Sea. In the 18th century, it was weakened by an ineffective system of electing its kings.

The three predatory neighbours, after interfering in Poland's internal affairs, had by 1795 all but erased Poland from Europe's map entirely by their last partition. These lustful "neighbours," Prussia, Austria, and Russia, signed a secret protocol *"to suppress all things Polish from the present and forever."* The English historian Lord Eversley wrote, "The partition of Poland, although remote and indirect, was the essential cause of World War I." The European equilibrium was overthrown and introduced the victory of violence and the principle *"Might is Right."* Polish uprisings were multiple. They fought on Napoleon's side and then rose up in rebellions in 1830, 1863, and 1905.

My parents lived in Tsarist-occupied Poland; they were ethnically Polish. The occupiers had implemented laws to stamp out their languages, history, culture, and religion. At night, my parents, in small groups, were taught the rudiments of their language and history in cellars and barns, which was an underground movement of teachers who were willing to risk their safety and their lives. If a "teacher" were discovered, a Summary Military Court would exile (him or her) to Siberia. The parents of the student (if discovered) would be required to deliver a large quantity of their agricultural produce to the state, in lieu of a monetary fine.

The Armistice of 1918 made Poland free. *Joseph Pilsudski* became the national founder and leader of Poland. In 1919, the Bolsheviks (Communists), having subdued all of the White (Tsarist) Armies, turned on newborn Poland to swallow it up and use it as a path to Pro-Red Germany, igniting and spreading Bolshevism in Western Europe. However, with French supplies and advisers, on August 15th, 1920, Pilsudski counter-attacked from the Wieprz River, cut off the Bolshevik rear flank, and annihilated the Bolshevik invaders. The Red Army lost its first war and peace ensued.

In September 1939, Nazi Germany and Soviet Russia, again by the brute force of modern Blitzkrieg and manpower, partitioned Poland. By sheer determination, with odds of one Pole to thirty Nazis and Communists, Poland fought long and hard for one exhaustive month.

The West was at war with Hitler's Germany and many citizens and allied soldiers ridiculed "The Phoney War" (October 1939–May 1940). During the "Phoney War" about 17,000 Polish high officers and 10,000 civilians (War Prisoners of the Soviet Russians) were blindfolded, hands tied behind them by Russian NKVD officers, shot in the back of their heads, and their limp bodies were pushed into prepared ditches.

The written order by Stalin (circa Spring 1940) still lies in "the Democratic Russia's" files of the NKVD (Russian Secret Police). Only President Boris Yeltsin, of Democratic Russia, admitted that this heinous crime was perpetrated by the Soviet Russians under Stalin. Some neutral sources allege that this was Stalin's revenge for the Bolshevik rout at Warsaw on August 15th, 1920. The military men, captured as prisoners of war by the Soviets in 1939, and executed in 1940, were ninety-five (95%) percent Reservists and intellectuals.

They flouted the Geneva Convention on war prisoners, and with horrific cruelty, they murdered 17,000 Polish officers individually, reminiscent of Genghis Khan. These Soviet murderers were never brought to justice: there was no compensation for their victims, no outcry from the United Nations, or from any other country for that matter.

A Few Distinguished Sons and Daughters of Poland:

M. Kopernik (Copernicus) (1473–1543)

Astronomer who established that the sun was at the centre of the solar system and that the planets circled around it.

General Pulaski (1747–1779)

He trained American cavalry in the U.S.A. War of Independence (1776–1783). He died at the Battle of Savannah (1779) at the age of 47.

General Kosciuszko (1746–1817)

He also trained Americans in their struggle for independence. Led a rebellion with a Peasant army (1794) against "irrevocable partitions of Poland" and only after partial success, was subdued by the enemy alliance.

Frederick Chopin (1810–1849)

Composer, pianist; his music drew inspiration from the romance and melancholia of traditional Polish dance music. He refused to play for the then Tsar of Russia. His music has survived for over 151 years and is exceedingly popular to this day.

Ignacy Paderewski (1860–1941)

Composer and statesman, and was the first President of Poland.

Adam Mickiewicz (1798 — 1855)

He was the greatest Polish poet and romanticist. In 1962, his epic *"Pan Tadeusz,"* a poem that generated hope in the Polish people by Napoleon's war against Russia was translated into English by Watson Kirkconnell, President of Acadia University.

Henry Sienkewicz (1846–1916)

An outstanding Polish author who was famous for his trilogy depicting the Poland that was. In 1905, he received the Nobel Prize for his famous work, *"Quo Vadis."*

Marie Skladowska-Curie (1867–1934)

She was a physicist who discovered two new radioactive elements: "Polonium" (named for Poland) and Radium. In 1903, she was awarded the Nobel Prize for enabling by her research, the process in which to obtain pure Radium. She received a second Nobel Prize in 1911.

Recent Sons of Poland

Lech Walesa (1943 — ____)

He is an electrician who organized the "solidarity" trade union during riots (1972–1978) in Poland's Baltic Sea ports. A devout Catholic, he was spiritually allied to Pope John Paul II. In 1981, Polish Communist martial law was imposed. All solidarity supporters including Walesa were imprisoned. He was awarded the Nobel Peace Prize in 1983. With the collapse of Communism in 1991, L. Walesa was elected the President of a non-Communist Free Poland.

Pope John Paul II (1920-____)

He is an activist, Priest, Bishop, Cardinal who became the first non Italian Pope.

A Few Polish Contributors to the Development of Canada

Sir Casimir Stanislaus Gzowski (1813-1898)

His genealogical tree reveals that his family lived in the northeastern part of Poland, close to the city of Grodno. Gzowski's father was a military man and a diplomat. He took part in the 1830 rebellion against the Tsarist-Russian occupants. The insurrection failed, and he and several other rebels fled to America. His grasp of English was completed in only a very short time and he gained employment in Erie, Pennsylvania on railway and canal projects.

By 1841, he was supervisor of roads and waterways in London, Ontario. When this work was completed, his firm was deluged with railroad contracts (e.g., connecting Toronto to Guelph). He successfully completed a railroad between Montréal and the eastern townships of Québec, to Portland, U.S.A. and the Atlantic Ocean.

His company also constructed the international bridge between Buffalo and Fort Erie. This bridge was seen as one of the most important engineering projects on the American continent at that time. For these accomplishments, and more, he received a Knighthood, the highest honour available to a Canadian. He acted as interim Lieutenant Governor of Ontario (1896-1897). His career forms a unique link between Canada and Poland.

Maximilien Globenski (1793-1866)

He was an exiled Polish colonel, who led a British Garrison in skirmishes around St. Eustache with rebels of Lower Canada. His son, Carl M. Globenski was the Mayor of St. Eustache and was elected in 1875 as Member of the Federal Parliament in his riding.

Andrew Charles Mynarski (1916–1944)

He was a Canadian Lieutenant of the Royal Canadian Air Force, a Winnipegger of Canadian-Polish extraction, and 23-years-old. He was a gunner on a mission over Germany in a Lancaster on June 12th, 1940 when the plane's engine was shot by the Germans, and the crew ordered to parachute. Andrew stayed behind to assist a crewmember who was stuck, to bailout; he sacrificed his own life for his comrade. Posthumously, his mother accepted the "Victoria Cross," the highest military decoration awarded to a Canadian in World War II.

Chaim Goldberg (1920–____)

He wrote "The Odyssey of a Polish Jew," a biographical sketch of the author's trials when Germans and Soviet Russia invaded Poland. It details his escape to Vilna, then Moscow and onto the trans-Siberian railway to Vladivostok, Japan, and Canada where he joined the Polish army. He describes the war in Europe and his settling in Windsor, Ontario, Canada.

Louis Dudek (1918–2001)

He was a poet, professor, anthologist, editor, and publisher who animated a large multitude of Canadian poets and scholars. He was born in the east end of Montréal, the son of Polish immigrant parents—Victor and Stella Dudek. He was an outstanding Canadian-Polish poet and scholar and a Professor of English at McGill University (1969–1984).

From 1955 to 1966, he published "Delta" magazine associated with "C.I.V." (Civilization is not one man's job), a literary magazine of the 1950s showcasing poems of Irving Layton, Raymond Souster, his own, and countless others.

Louis Dudek was one of Canada's major modernist poets. In 1984, he received Canada's highest decoration, The Order of Canada. He was made Doctor of Law (St. Francis Xavier University–1995) and Doctor of Letters (York University–1983).

Chapter One
The Montréal Era

My father Julian was born in 1879 in the former Polish (then Tsarist-Russian) occupied village of Swislocz, on the banks of the Berezina River. Napoleon and his defeated Grand army crossed upon this river in their retreat from Moscow in the winter of 1812. The Grand army suffered heavy casualties. Prior to 1772, this area was part of the Kingdom of Poland and the Duchy of Lithuania. Hitler's Nazi armies crossed this river in July 1941, in their thwarted attempt to defeat the then Soviet Russia.

My mother, Rosalie Kawecka, was born in 1888 in the Berezynski Reyon, a few kilometres from Swislocz.

My father served as a Russian conscript in the Russo-Japanese war (1904–1905). In February 1904, Japanese torpedo boats launched a sneak attack against the Russian Far Eastern naval base of Port Arthur in Manchuria, two days before Japan's Declaration of War. This war was between two imperialist autocratic monarchies expanding into Korea, and the large Chinese province of Manchuria. My father was sent to Port Arthur by mid-April of 1904. In his contingent, there were a handful of Poles. The Russians did not trust Poles, as their last problems were the Polish insurrections of 1830, 1863, and 1905 in "Russian-Occupied Poland," which the Russian Army subdued with great difficulty. By about May 15th, 1904, my father was transferred to Mukden.

As the Japanese were about to lay siege to it, the Tsarist's Cossacks, Vodka-driven, shouted that with their sabres and nagaiki (tall hats), they would expunge these cretins! However, Japan was victorious. Russia's

Far East fleet, and later its Baltic fleet were both destroyed by the new Western-built and Western-trained Japanese Navy.

When we were children, my father told us that many Russian artillery pieces had not been modernized and shot iron balls and shrapnel. The Japanese artillery (modernized by Germany and England) caused havoc, exploding shells and shrapnel, causing a multitude of casualties to Russian soldiers. While attacking, the Russians would loudly shout *"Hurrah – Hurrah."* When the Japanese infantry attacked, they shouted *"Banzai – Banzai"* ("Long live the Emperor").

The "Portsmouth Treaty" of 1905 ended the war between these two expanding Imperialist Empires. After peace was brought about, my father was demobilized and sent home to the Village of Swislocz on the banks of Berezina. He soon found out through multicultural pamphlets decimated by German and British shipping lines, that he could earn American dollars by working in the coalmines around Scranton, PA and Holyoke, MA. Upon arriving in the U.S.A. in 1907 with his brother Wincenty, via the Hamburg-American Line, they worked solidly for two years, sent about sixty (60%) percent of their earnings back home to their parents in Swislocz, and by 1909 had returned to their homeland.

Russians as a whole distrusted the Tsar after unarmed citizens in 1905 outside his palace were decimated by his Cossacks. The losses of the Japanese war unsettled the majority of the people of Russia, who lost faith in their Tsar, which no doubt contributed to his downfall in 1917.

My father met our mother by chance, during an excursion to Russian Poland, at a town in Mazovia. It was "love at first sight." They were engaged in 1911 and married in Swislocz in 1912. One year later, they boarded an ocean going ship, part of the Hamburg-American Line, and arrived in Canada. My father's first occupation in Canada was that of a carpenter–labourer and my mother's that of a seamstress. On disembarking at Halifax, they proceeded by rail to Montréal, Québec. Upon arrival, my father had a few precious dollars safely tucked away in his pockets. Shortly after landing, he found a job, and on completing his first day's work, he reached into his coat pocket for the few dollars he had left — alas, they had been stolen!

My parents settled in the St. Lawrence area near St. Urbain Street. They told their landlords, a kindly Jewish immigrant couple, of their plight. That night they feasted on kosher stew, beans, potatoes, and bread, and tea — dinner guests of their newfound friends.

Early the next morning, my father was able to walk to work and my mother, being a seamstress, discovered that there were several clothing shops in the area. As she bustled down St. Lawrence Street, an older Jewish gentleman beckoned to her in Russian. He offered her 0.25¢ to wash his veranda and kitchen floor. She agreed, but sobbed as she scrubbed the floors. When she finished, her employer discovered that she was a trained seamstress. He told her to return the next day, as he knew of an owner of a clothing factory where he might secure her employment. Thanks to that Jewish gentleman's support, my mother was engaged as a seamstress based on piecework and a six-day week.

When the First World War broke out, August 1914, my father was anxious to join the Allied-Polish army being organized at Niagara-on-the-Lake under General Haler. My mother, heavy with child, talked him out of joining up. My oldest living sister Eugene was born Christmas Eve, 1914 (This thankfully cooled my father's fervour to join the army!).

Father got a job as a carpenter in 1915 at C.P.R's Angus Shop where he stayed on to work for 50 years. He became a member of a Railway Brotherhood Union. During the depression of 1930, C.P.R. management gave its men a choice to lay off about fifty (50%) percent of the workers in its shop, or every worker could stay on and only work for half a month. The workers agreed to work half time. This went on almost until World War II, when the railway work increased once again.

The Travesty of Joseph

When I was still very young, I kept questioning my parents about a bicycle that I saw in the shed. When I persisted, prodding over a two-week period, one of my sisters told me this in confidence; Joseph, my oldest brother, had been caught skipping school repeatedly, and was finally strapped by my father who had undoubtedly lost his temper with him. The next morning at the break of dawn, Joseph, at 17 years of age, packed a suitcase and ran away, never to be seen again—except for one letter from Arizona. In it, he promised to visit once a month, but never did. Even after extensive Canadian and American police searches, they never found a trace of him.

Since I was born on June 4th, 1925, I never knew Joseph. Joseph's disappearance became a disgrace to our family in our Polish Parish. My mother and sisters on their way to work, church, store, etc., would inevitably be asked by neighbours, *"How is Joe? – Where is he?"*

Mother went on a pilgrimage to St. Anne de Beaupré in Québec, sanctuary of Miracles, praying for the safe and quick return of Joseph. Many of our other family members went to the St. Joseph Oratory in Montréal, a vast and impressive church to which miracles had been ascribed. We all prayed sincerely and incessantly for Joe's expedient return. Finally, in early 1940, Joseph wrote a short letter to Mother and Father informing them that he had joined the Canadian Merchant Navy. He promised to send money, but he never did.

Once again, exhaustive searches were made in the Merchant Navy, but to no avail. However, this new development greatly assisted our family in saving face with the nosy neighbours. To say that Joe was in the "Merchant Navy" was a more palatable explanation to our parishioners and community than the fact that he had been beaten with my father's belt for playing hooky from school and had run away, never to return.

A decade after Joseph's disappearance, my oldest sister Eugene revealed to me that Joseph had never liked school. He had found great pleasure in working part-time with a milkman. He learned some Lithuanian on the milk run, and successfully sold a lot of sweet cream to little old lady Lithuanian customers.

Eugene further related to me how he excelled in helping the "iceman" sell blocks of ice to customers (there were no electric fridges in those years). He would gather the ice chips in a bag and sell the large chips for a penny to the gaggle of children that always gathered around the iceman's wagon. Eugene also related to me that his main goal was to earn money; school was an anathema to him.

Only in and around the mid–1990s did another elder sister of mine, Vera, commence corresponding with the local Montréal police, reopening the search for missing Joseph. By that point, he had been missing for over 70 years. He was never found.

My Early Years

When I reached the age of about three-and-a-half, I recall my parents hiring a lady to look after my brother John and I. Mother brought home empty thread spools from work. John and I had great fun building cities of bridges and skeleton homes, which kept us occupied for hours on end. This lady prepared breakfast and lunch for us. Weather permitting, she would bundle us up and take us for walks up Rue Montgomery to Rue Sherbrooke, to the C.P.R. Bridge and back home.

I seem to remember that this went on for about a year or so. Then, when I was about four-years-old, our "Nanny" suddenly died. It wasn't until about six years later that I found out that she had run away to relatives in Detroit as her husband, apparently intoxicated, had beaten her severely. We were told that she died some time after that.

By the age of six, I was attending St. Anselm Catholic School (a bilingual school), located on the corner of Rouen St. and Bercy St. in Montréal East. The school was run by French-Canadian Nuns. They allowed the teaching of French, Polish, and English in the three lower grades. The 3rd grade up to the 8th grade was in English only. Language or nationality was not an issue in Québec at that time. Poverty bonded everyone.

After school, we all played hockey. No one could afford anything but rolls of newspaper for goalie pads and homemade hockey sticks. The only purchased item was the precious puck. People, especially of ethnic origin, would refer to the area as "Frontenac Place," because Frontenac Street ran then from Sherbrooke Street East, south to Ontario Street with the eastern boundary being accounted for by the railway tracks.

The population at that time was predominantly French-Canadian, intermingled with sizable pockets of Lithuanians, Ukrainians, Poles, and a few Italians. Our family's Roman Catholic Polish Parish of St. Mary's of Czestochowa was located on the west side of Montgomery Street, south of Rouen Street. Father Bernard was the parish priest and Father Blaze was his assistant. Both priests were from the order of Polish-Franciscan Fathers whose motherhouse was in Baltimore, Maryland.

St. Mary of Czestochowa (widely known as the *Black Madonna*) is considered to have miraculously saved the Polish realm in 1654 at a time when the Swedish invasion occupied most of Poland and the Grand Duchy of Lithuania. This invasion was referred to as the "Deluge" in Polish history. It was the only fortress and monastery where the "Madonna" was worshipped by the Pauline Monks. The Monks, in addition to thousands of Knights and soldiers, withstood a 40–day siege, then hurled their forces, routing the Swedes in that area.

This miraculous act was the beginning of the loss of the Swedish grip throughout Poland. Sadly, in the early 1940s, robbers in Montréal stole the numerous gems that decorated the painting in St. Mary's church. These priceless gemstones were never recovered. Both pastor and assistant were model priests to us all. In retrospect, their only fault, on recollection, was that the assistant pastor smoked incessantly, only to die at an early age.

I remember the first funeral that I attended as an altar boy, when Father Bernard intoned the Gregorian chant on entering the home of the deceased; *"Dies irae, dies illa, Solvet saeclum in favilla; teste David cum Sibylla"* [Day of wrath! Oh day of mourning/See fulfilled the prophet's warning/Heaven and earth in ashes burning]. I would pull out my starched white hankie to dry my tears, as that sad intonation would overcome me with remorse.

I still get shivers until this day when I hear that same melody on the radio the odd time. In those days, there were no funeral parlours and apart from the coffin, the embalmer would prepare the corpse of a deceased for viewing in the home of the deceased.

The staff from the funeral parlour on the day of the funeral carried the closed casket to the hearse, and from the hearse to church. When the funeral Mass ended, the casket was driven in a hearse to the "Côte de Neiges" Cemetery (located on Mount Royal) for interment. On some occasions of a funeral, when I acted as an altar boy, I had the job of pulling the long rope to ring the church bell once, and a second time one minute later, until all of the mourners were inside the church.

After the Mass for the dead was complete, I would intone the mournful bell incessantly, until the cortege had left. Before a funeral, some of us would help the Sexton to assemble the funeral bier, on top of which a coffin was placed in front of the altar of the church. We placed three brass candleholders with tall candles on each side of the bier.

I recall with a smile that Father Blaze rescued me this one time in the altar boy's room when some of the altar boys were taunting me with the words, "A broken heart for $7,000.00," "A broken heart for $7,000..." He scolded them until they stopped.

Apparently, my parents were suing a Mr. X in our town at that time for that amount, for breach of promise to marry one of my sisters. However, on a happy note, this dispute was settled within six months and Mr. X became my brother-in-law in 1935, when I was 10-years-old. He proved to be one of my favourite family members.

During most summers, our parish held a Bazaar, which they called "Tombola." It took place outside in the large garden adjoining the church. All of the church elders, including my father, supervised the many entertainment booths. I was proud of that fact.

The church, together with some lay organizations, would hold picnics before the war at a farm in Ville Emard. Liquor was forbidden, but ultimately some was brought in by individuals anyway. There was an orchestra, and dancing on a hardwood platform was provided by the owners of the place. The orchestra played Polkas, Mazurkas, Obereks, and slow pieces, which were danced to by both old and young alike.

At the few picnics our family attended, there was this short stocky man (5'2"), a Mr. John Gajski. When liquored up, he would always start a fistfight with the tallest man nearest to him. It took six committeemen to separate this feisty, puny aggressor from his towering defender. I remember when they fed Mr. Gajski hearty plates of rich Polish food at the farm, to half sober him up before his wife and son would finally attempt to *haul* him home by streetcar.

Apart from the church, my parents were members of "Dom Polski" (Polish White Eagle Society) on Frontenac Street, which was founded at the beginning of the century. In or about 1915–1916, the Russian-Tsarist consulate in Montréal, on several occasions, pressured the Canadian Government to disband "The Polish White Eagle Society" and barricade it, alleging that this club was against the war and trying to tar them as "Communist Revolutionaries." Fortunately, the Canadian Government demurred. It was aware that in Niagara-on-the-Lake, in Southern Ontario, about 40,000 Polish-Americans and Polish-Canadians had joined General Haler's Polish army. This army fought for the Allied cause in the trenches of France against the Boche until Armistice Day.

After 1918, Haler's army was transferred to Poland. It took part in helping the Polish Army of J. Pilsudski in routing the Bolsheviks at the gates of Warsaw (1920). Although Lenin's Trotsky Communist Army outnumbered the Polish defenders five to one, the Soviets lost their campaign to spread the plague of Communism through Poland, to Germany and Western Europe.

Free Poland commemorated this as the miracle of the "Vistula" until August 1939. This commemoration was not renewed until 1990, when Soviet Russia disintegrated and a Free Poland rose from its bondage.

Polish Festivities in Montréal

Every month of May on Corpus Christi Day, our parish held a large religious procession organized by our Franciscan Fathers, in which many members and organizations of the Polish community took part.

The first ranks of the procession consisted of about 70 primary school children, led by their Polish (St. Anselm School) teachers. They threw flower petals en route. Our Pastor, Father Bernard, walked behind them, adorned in golden ecclesiastical vestments, walking under a canopy held by four church elders.

Our Pastor was holding the Monstrance upright (a receptacle in which the Holy Host is held and exhibited to the congregation in a form of a blessing). Behind were about 30 altar boys; four altar boys took turns in swinging incense towards the faithful as the procession moved along. Members of our church choir sang "Agnus Dei" intermittently with "Rex Christe Primogenite," and "Boze cos Polsce" (God protect Poland).

Following behind the choir were about 100 members of the Women's Catholic League, and about 30 members of St. Anthony's League all with their flags held high. Behind this meandering procession were members of the Polish White Eagle Society, about 100 strong, with their emblem the White Eagle Flag, carried in front of them together with a large Union Jack. Following them were about 70 members of the Polish Veteran's Association, some in Polish military uniforms carrying a White Eagle flag. It was rumoured that Marshal J. Pilsudski, the founder of the then Free Poland (1867–1935), presented the flag to their president.

Our parish and the two lay organizations arranged a dinner and dance at "Dom Polski" in May, 1935. After a sumptuous dinner of baked chicken, vegetables, dessert and a speech by Rev. Father Bernard, the dancing commenced.

By about 9:00 p.m., the death of Marshal Pilsudski in Warsaw was reported by radio and some felt that out of respect, the dance should end. Father Bernard and many individuals left. I happened to be a few feet away from Father Blaze. He argued that the ball should proceed, citing as an example, that when a U.S. President dies, the Vice-President takes charge, or when a King dies, a successor replaces him. Father Blaze's opponents won the debate, and the remainder of the 350 guests slowly lined up to leave the hall. Pilsudski, a liberal socialist, did not abolish parliamentary rule in Poland (1926–1935). It was said that partly because of his previous camaraderie with Russian-Tsarist revolutionaries, he respected the large Jewish minority, unlike his neighbour Adolph Hitler in Germany. Marshal Pilsudski's moral statement was—

"To be defeated but not to surrender, that is victory."

In May 1936, the M.S. Pilsudski, a great Polish cruise liner was docked at Montréal's Pier 14 on the St. Lawrence River. Prior to that, as the giant flagship was cruising under Jacques Cartier's Bridge, a large number of Canadian-Polish school children scattered flower petals on the incoming craft from the heights of the Jacques Cartier harbour bridge. Both French and English newspapers of Montréal covered the historic visit. At the pier, the captain of the first Polish ship to anchor in Canada was presented with bread and salt—ancient symbols of hospitality. For days, receptions and tours by native Montréalers were held. My parents even took us for a guided tour of the ship, which made us very proud. In World War II, the M.S. Pilsudski was converted into a troop ship. It transferred allied troops and equipment across the English Channel to France. One night in early 1940, it was sunk by a German magnetic mine. The "Batory" survived World War II; it is now anchored outside of the Polish Port of Gdynia.

Elementary School Days

When I was about 10-years-old, having become an altar boy, I was deeply moved by the singing of the Mass in Latin by the priests, especially the sacred hymns at Christmas, Lent, and Easter. I often used my mother's Singer sewing machine, pretending it was an altar and tried to sing: "Pater Noster," "Tantum Ergo," "Agnus Dei," etc. I did that quite often. Mother began to say to the family that I would most certainly become a priest. Time proved her wrong. However, to this day, in my humble opinion, Pope John XXIII made a grave mistake in not preserving Latin music in the church. Not only was Mass Latin eradicated and replaced with lay words, the rich repertoire of sacred music, which had been preserved and sung for centuries, was lost forever. As a Catholic, I still miss the haunting sounds of the Mass's Latin music.

At Church Vespers, Sundays at 4:00 p.m., we sang "Tantum Ergo," in addition to other Latin and Polish songs. Prior to Vespers, a Polish-speaking Cleric taught us religion. Mostly boys attended. One "John Bednarz" and I whispered to one another. Mr. Stanley Godenski Sr. (Mr. G.) would shush us. One of Mr. G's sons became a doctor some years later. It is said that he experimented with some chemicals that exploded, and he perished in his corner Frontenac and Sherbrooke Street East office. Pope John XXIII discontinued vespers. Now on Sunday afternoons, Mass is celebrated.

One night, a gang of us boys were peeking at a disrobed girl in the lane off Montgomery Street. The window was 6-inches from the bottom of the lane. A standing ethnic girl was surrounded by four or five elderly French-Canadian men, smoking pipes, and sitting on what looked like chairs around her, like an audience. A whole gang of older boys, who were taller than my partner Albert Norkis and I were, obliterated from most of what was going on.

When a tall boy of our gang couldn't suppress a cough, the lights dimmed in the room, the girl scrambled, and two old men came out and chased us all down the lane past the other street; shouting. Luckily, no one was caught by our "fired up" elderly pursuers!

We had a boys' clubhouse in the cellar under our shed at 2557 Montgomery Street. Two old chairs, an old car seat, and candles were our furniture. One day, my brother John found a Mouser Revolver in the main cellar hidden behind a beam. The six club members present passed it around to look at it. When it came to me, I pointed it to the ceiling, fired one shot and a "loud bang" ensued. Everybody scrambled out of the clubhouse. John swiftly put the revolver back where he found it. It was no doubt fathers; to this day, we never told him what happened.

Frank and Eugene Gryszówka

Frank Gryszówka married my sister Eugene, on June 8th, 1935. Frank was born in Poland in the Krakow Province. During the Polish-Bolshevik War (1919–1920) with a re-born Poland, he was a Polish volunteer and saw action in North-Eastern Poland where the routed Soviets were pursued. He arrived in Canada in 1926 and settled in Sherbrooke, Québec. Most days he worked, nights he studied English, French, and Canada's history. After two years of hard day's work and long hours, he mastered English and gained employment at the Kayzer & Co., manufacturers of silk stockings. Thanks to his abilities, he soon was chosen as a superintendent at Kayzer & Co. in Sherbrooke, Québec.

My sister Eugene, a Montréaler, was born December 24th, 1914. She vividly recalled that when baby Jadwiga Wanda died of pneumonia, during the service at our parish "St. Mary's," a white glass carriage was pulled by two white horses, carrying a white glass coffin. The coffin was held in a storeroom of the cemetery. When the coffin was opened for just a moment, everyone there noticed that one of our deceased sister's eyes had sunken. My sister Reggie blurted out, *"Let's take her home and replace it with a glass doll's eye!"*

Eugene was trained in and played the church organ (1929 and 1933–1934). Eugene reminded me that we were always well dressed as our mother was a seamstress and a couturiere, and that our parents loved music and often entertained artists, our father having an elegant voice. On most Sunday mornings at church, he sang solo religious songs, like "Kiedy Ranne Wstaja Zorze" ("When the Morning Dawn Arises").

Because of our parents' love of music, every Staniszewski child was taught piano or violin. During World War II, Frank (my brother-in-law) organized a drive for Polish Airmen training in Canada.

The seven Polish families in Sherbrooke, Québec, with the help of their English-Canadians and French-Canadians, collected a substantial sum of money. Frank and Eugene also organized a concert with renowned pianist *W. Malcuzynski* in Sherbrooke, Québec that was a great success; all the proceeds were donated to the Canadian Red Cross.

After the end of World War II, since many Poles from the Second Corps chose not to return to a Communist-dominated Poland, some settled in Sherbrooke, Québec. Frank and Eugene helped those in need, morally and materially. Frank assisted the numerous Polish girls who arrived as domestics, by pushing for an increase in their amount of remuneration, and speaking out to improve their working conditions. For many new arrivals, he procured a large number of jobs at Kayzer & Co. in Sherbrooke, Québec.

Frank also collected monies for food parcels to help former Polish troops and families in Germany. He intervened for medical help and hospitalization, for demobilized Poles as well as displaced persons. The demobilized Polish soldiers in Germany decorated Frank with a Cross of Honour for his patriotic work in the community (circa 1950). He acted as president of the Polish (Pilsudski) Veterans Association and of the Polish-Canadian Congress (Montréal Branch).

In 1938, he purchased a large plot of land, which bordered onto Lake Massawippi, located next to North Hatley in Québec's Eastern Township; here he built a stylish log cabin with a spectacular fireplace, composed entirely of local coloured stones. This noble man was laid to rest on July 3rd, 1980 at the North Hatley cemetery. He is greatly missed by us all…

My Brother John

My older brother John resented parental, as well as all other authority. When he was about six-years-old, my mother curled his hair into long locks, similar to the hairstyles of Louis XIV of France. His playmates had to smother their laughter; otherwise, he would have beaten them up with his small angry fists. At elementary school, on one occasion, the Principal punished him for a classroom fight he initiated. After the Principal had strapped his open right hand, John pulled his left hand out and stared right at him — no tears, and no remorse.

John was rejected from joining the Canadian Air Force. He had to be content, because of his poor eyesight, to serve in the Canadian Army Service Corps. That's where he began to abuse liquor. Almost every Sunday after Mass, friends would say to me, "Hey, what's with your brother causing a big fight with some guys last night at the dance at the Polish Hall?" This was very embarrassing to our family and me. At the military camp, a few times he and his pals landed in the hospital when their jeeps crashed out of control due to drunk driving.

One summer, soldier John borrowed my brother-in-law's car to drive from Lennoxville (where Frank and his family lived) to Sherbrooke, Québec to visit in-laws. Late that night, the local police escorted him home in their cruiser. They stopped him for tossing beer bottles out of the car while under the influence; it is a small miracle that no charges were laid.

One spring Sunday, my parents, John, and I were returning from visiting friends on the south shore of Montréal. In the middle of the Jacques Cartier Bridge, the police stopped us, and seeing that our driver John was in *uniform* and *drunk*, suggested that if neither father nor I could drive, the car would be impounded and he would phone a cab for us; no charges were laid against John again. I drove home that evening. After the war, and a very happy marriage to a great gal, he became a changed man — much to our delight!

D'Arcy McGee High School

This large building on Pine Avenue, Montréal no longer operates as "D'Arcy McGee High School" thanks to René Levesque's scaring "the white Rhodesians" out of central Montréal. Numerous Canadians, fearing the anti-Anglo and anti-ethnic persecution, left Québec. Many well-established companies in the 1980s landed in Ontario, the West, and the Maritimes; my brother and his family also left for Ontario. The school is now bilingual and is called "Victoria High School." The authorities must have taken into account the predominant Anglo and ethnic population and refrained from naming the school "S. Parizeau," or "René Levesque."

When I attended, it was the beginning of World War II. The very first thing I had my parents consent to drop—were my piano lessons. I received my Grade-1 certificate from the Montréal Conservatory. In any event, I was not too good in music, as I never worked hard enough at it.

D'Arcy McGee high school was divided with girls and Nuns on the left side of the building, and boys, brothers, and lay-teachers on the right side of the structure. These years spent at D'Arcy McGee were perhaps the happiest and most formative years of my life. I believe to this day that all of our teachers there were visionaries; even the teachers that taught us "Religion" taught it in such an innovative and devotional fashion. Some of my fondest memories are from those years. My teachers there shaped the mould for who I was to become in the world.

I particularly chummed around with a "René Talbot" and "Simon Lafleche" (who were more interested in music than studies). René Talbot became a lawyer and later acted in different lawsuits for members of my family (I will touch upon René Talbot later).

One of my very best friends at D'Arcy McGee was *Albert Norkis*. His father was a Lithuanian immigrant who was a barber. They lived on Frontenac Street and whilst at "D'Arcy McGee" we often met at a streetcar corner and travelled to school together. He and I shared a love for books and many days after school, we would hang out and look for books at the many "used book stores" on Bleury Street, below St. Catherine Street. We also joined the Book of the Month Club, and with our meagre allowances, occasionally bought the monthly book. I especially cherished books like "Don Quixote," D. Carnegie's "How to Make Friends and Influence People," books on Chopin, Paderewski, Beethoven, Bach, Sir John A. MacDonald, C.P.R's "Last Spike," Sir Casimir Gzowski, and history books.

Our friendship thrived almost until his death. As I taught Albert Norkis the song of "The First Brigade" in Polish, famous in the war (1920) when J. Pilsudski freed Poland from the Bolsheviks, Albert taught me his famous national slogans "Vilnius nie nurymsym"—Vilno will never be forgotten and "Ne Preklausema Lietuva"—Lithuania shall always be independent.

While at school, I tried out in athletics, rugby, basketball, and failed them all! Finally, I joined our "Glee Club"; that I truly enjoyed. The conductor of the Glee Club was a Christian Brother — Brother Mathias.

He was about 5'5," bald, and on the skinny side. He lectured in different — what I would call — *easy* subjects like English, geometry and so forth. Some time shortly after the commencement of World War II, to my disbelief, he propounded excuses for Germany's starting the war, such as its severe treatment by the Allies in the Treaty of Versailles. Although Brother Mathias was of German descent, in spite of the Nazi atrocities, holocaust, etc., he never again spoke on that subject.

As a Canadian of Polish ancestry, I was angered that a teacher was allowed to fuel his propaganda onto a bunch of impressionable 14-year-old kids; I never forgave him for that arrogance. Now, about 50 years later, I must agree that after the armistice of 1918, the victorious Allies punished the vanquished much too severely and laid open the ground to an obsessed, populist, anti-Semite Hitler to lead the German people to its worst calamity ever.

About the same time as Brother Mathias spewed his "pro-Germanicus" line, we also had a lay-teacher, a Mr. O'Neil; I forget what subject he taught us. What does stand out in my mind is that he played the part of a modern war strategist. He admired the swiftness of Nazi Germany's attack on Poland; how their armies (Wermacht) bypassed Polish strong points. What he neglected to say was that both the British Empire and the French Empire were under treaty, obligated to come to Poland's aid. Nor did he mention that by treaty with Hitler, Soviet Russia gave Poland the "coup de grace" by occupying large areas of Eastern Poland.

The holocaust was assured by Stalin's invasion and enslavement of half of Eastern Poland, whilst the Nazi's blitz enslaved the other part of Poland, including about three million Polish Jews, destined to die in gas chambers and ovens. The barbarity of slaughtering unarmed civilians surpassed that of Genghis Khan in his horrific Mongol cruelty.

· Brother Ambrose was our chemistry teacher inter alia, around about the years 1941–1943. In the fall of 1968, after I became a Judge, Brother Ambrose suddenly telephoned after all those years. I invited him for dinner at Edgehill Road, Toronto, as I had not yet moved to my post in Windsor. He informed me that D'Arcy McGee was no longer in existence, because many "White Rhodesian" institutions in Montréal disappeared under René Levesque, and the subtle manoeuvres of the P.Q. regime.

What stunned me more was when Brother Ambrose asked me whether I had lost my faith. I said I had not, but when he drove off in a very old car, I wondered whether he had been shattered by the excesses of P.Q.'s — their nationalism and atheism — or whether he was depressed at being turfed out from Montréal, his students, and the Québec that he loved so much. Now a displaced person, I wondered if he, like Socrates, a re-born Québecer, was craving for a poisonous cup of hemlock, as his service to God and his students were swept away by the so-called "New Order" of the P.Q. government of the time. I never found out...

Canadian Polish Organizations

The first Polish General I met, along with about 75 Boy Scouts and Girl Guides, was General Jozef Haler on April 13th, 1940 at the Montréal-Windsor railroad station. In 1915, he organized 40,000 (at Niagara-on-the-Lake), Polish-American, and Polish-Canadian volunteers to fight the Germans on the Western front. He returned in 1940 to organize Americans and Canadians of Polish ancestry.

I recall that in the fall of 1939, at a banquet at Dom Polski, Consul General Potocki was present as well as the local Consul. The guest speaker was the then famous Polish tenor — *Jan Kiepura*. After praising the allied war preparations in Europe, he advised the audience to leave the war problems to General Gamelin. "We are not war strategists," he added, "Let us leave the war to Gamelin and his Generals." Most guests applauded in agreement and cheered for a Free Poland.

In the early 1960s when I practised law, he was a client of mine (purchasing apartment buildings). I was bold enough to remind him of his 1939 advice at a 1964 Toronto Business Men's banquet. He tersely replied, "One occasionally hits a wrong note." He passed away at the age of 62.

Our Montréal Youth Club had a banquet (circa 1942) at the Polish Veteran's Hall, 63 Prince Arthur Street East, Montréal, and one of our guests was Camilien Houde, Mayor of Montréal. When I escorted him out of the dining room, he confessed that he was told by the authorities in "Ottawa," not to get involved in political matters, nor criticize Canada's part in the war. This was after he was freed from detention. Later on, he was re-elected as Mayor of Montréal. We were told that he kept to himself the admiration he held of parts of the authoritative system of the Mediterranean ally of Nazi Germany.

Sometime around 1947, whilst I was Secretary-General of the National Canadian Polish Congress in Toronto, Stanislaus Mikolajczyk and his Peasant party took part in Communist-occupied Poland's election. Mikolajczyk lost, as the Communists had rigged the elections, and he subsequently had to run for his life. At a Toronto meeting where thousands attended, he did not blame Churchill for pressing him to take part in the election—he blamed his naivety in not heeding "Sosnkowski" in his London Polish-Government-in-Exile, who had warned him about not trusting Communists. He described how some of his Peasant party members and workers had been persecuted, and some maimed or killed by Polish Communists. He related to us that after the "Phoney Election" he fled, and was rescued in the dead of the night by a British destroyer, off Poland's Baltic coast. He died in the U.S.A. some decades later.

At some point, I became treasurer of the Polish Student's Club, 1944. I mistakenly reported *Zbigniew Brzezinski* (best known as U.S. Secretary of State under President Carter) as being delinquent in our club membership fees! I also became president of the Central Committee of Youth Clubs in Montréal (1944–1946), secretary of the Polish Welfare Association, and director of the Committee of Allied Countries (Montréal), with a patriotic French-Canadian as its president.

In or about the late spring of 1944, I attended at the founding of the Canadian Polish Congress (CPC) in Toronto. All of the churches and lay organizations—excluding the minor Communist groups—sent delegates. Organizations and churches from Montréal to Vancouver rallied together for the allied cause and a Constitution was drafted, democratically voted on, and passed. An executive was elected with several standing committees.

What helped was the "The Federation of Poles in Canada," a body constituted in Winnipeg in 1933 and again reconstituted in 1938, under the strong leadership of men like B. B. Dubienski, Q.C. (who was of Jewish descent and a strong Polish patriot) and Joseph Grocholski; both were from Winnipeg, Manitoba. The latter was elected president.

On October 28th, 1944, the Polish-Canadian community of Montréal held a protest march at Plateau Hall (located at Park LaFontaine), protesting the feeble Allied military and air aid to the struggling (40,000 strong) Polish army, fighting the Nazis inside Warsaw. The Polish home army was encircled by Nazis on the west side and by a dormant Communist army on the east side of Warsaw. The insurrectionist Poles were being bled to death by the Nazis; their remnants were sent to Siberian Gulags by the Communist army.

The president of the Canadian Polish Congress "thundered our objections"; so did I, on behalf of the Youth Central Committee, but when the beloved Polish Consul General Dr. Tadeusz Brzezinski spoke, he touched all of our hearts and awoke fears of the dark shadow of a Russian-Communist enslavement that was falling upon Poland. As a diplomat, he was a patriot and a realist.

When the "Warsaw Concerto" was played by a Polish Flight Lieutenant, the haunting melody brought us back to Warsaw's, 27 days' stand against the bombers and artillery poundings of the Nazis in 1939.

During the fall of 1945, a youth convention was organized by others and myself in Montréal and Toronto; 34 Polish-Canadian Youth Clubs were invited and about 23 clubs sent delegates to form the Canadian Youth Congress. The congress went on for several days at the Polish Alliance Hall on Barton Street in Hamilton, Ontario. I spoke to the delegates often (perhaps more than I should have). Debates were rational. Some delegates spoke in Polish, others in English. The Constitution committee drafted a workable Constitution, which was, with a few minor amendments, passed by a large majority. We had a Canadian affairs committee, a finance committee, and an audit committee, etc., all of which were elected democratically.

Some months prior to the convention, we transferred the first Polish youth publication, "The Dawn" (Jutrzenka) to a committee in Toronto (of which my future wife was a member).

I was elected president, Felix Matusiewicz—vice-president, and Ms. Sophie Maslowska—secretary. Our headquarters were in Montréal, which on reflection was a great mistake as the greater majority of our youth clubs were located in Ontario. This led to a slow, but in time inevitable disintegration of the Canadian-Polish Youth Congress. "The Dawn" located now at 700 Queen Street West, Toronto, was published until about mid–1947-1948.

I cite lack of money as the root cause of this misfortune. Some of our members were concluding schools of higher learning, some married, some moved on and some just lost interest. In the 1950s, a Montréal club began to print another monthly "Unity," in which I was not involved.

From Sea to Shining Sea...

In the spring of 1946, my father, who was employed with the C.P.R., arranged for a free return railway ticket for me from Montréal to Vancouver including southern and northern Ontario. In early June (after receiving about $150.00 from my father and a few relatives), I boarded the Montréal train to contact our youth clubs in Ontario and across to Vancouver. It was about 2:00 p.m.; the sun was bright yellow with tinges of orange. It gave one an uplifting feeling. One got used to the staccato noise of the wheels hitting the rails as the train rolled ahead. My first stop was Oshawa, Ontario.

I was met by the Chairman of the Polish Alliance Youth Club, and ushered to his home, where a pleasant dinner was served by his mother. We spoke about the Congress and the publication "The Dawn." I slept at his home and had a rushed breakfast as I had an early train to Toronto. I visited "The Dawn" administrative committee inside the Polish Alliance Press; I took Wanda Boguslawska (my future wife) and a few others out to lunch. That evening, as I ate dinner at Wanda's home, a few of her girlfriends arrived. Wanda played the piano exceptionally well. We sang "Fatal Tango," "Ostatnia Niedziela" (Our Last Sunday Together), "White Cliffs of Dover," "Jealousy," and many other popular songs. I found myself very attracted to Wanda. Before leaving, I promised to write to her after my trip.

I visited club leaders in New Toronto, Hamilton, Brantford, Kitchener, St. Catharine's, Chatham, and Windsor. My next stop was Sudbury (the city was surrounded by ugly slag from the copper mines). From there, I travelled up north to Timmins and Kirkland Lake, catching the northern train, then on to Fort William (now Thunder Bay). From there, the longest stretches of the journey began; in Winnipeg, Manitoba, I met a former Montréal neighbour, active in the youth club. Some of its members, along with me, lunched with B. B. Dubienski, Q.C.

The train made many stops before it crossed the prairies, which because of its endless flatness, appealed to me in a hauntingly familiar way. We finally reached Edmonton, Alberta. I received no sign of animosity of West against East—possibly, because most people I met were of the same background.

The train went on to Vancouver, B.C., and the Pacific Ocean. The Rockies on the left side of the train towered above us like massive centurions guarding our Pacific province; we had a fruitful meeting.

Most youths spoke only English. No matter—after all, it was Canada's official language except for Québec and New Brunswick. I recall that I had to write home twice for money from my father—once from Winnipeg, Manitoba and another time from Vancouver, B.C.

I disembarked from the train at Coleman, Alberta where I met with two directors of the local Polish Youth Club; we held a fruitful business meeting. After arriving back home in Montreal, I took a much-needed rest; a few days later, I gave our Congress executive a report.

That memorable trip opened my eyes and heart to the varied beautiful landscapes of which Canada the mosaic is made up. The Great Lakes of southern Ontario, the mines of Ontario's north, the grandeur of wheat fields, the granary of the world, and the awesome and uplifting Rockies and Lakes of the west, with almost 10 million square kilometres, framed by three oceans. It was only through the generosity of the CPR and the kindness of my father that such a trip could happen to me. It was said by an explorer in the 16th century: *"It is the land God gave to Cain. Let us be on guard and not allow Canada to slip out of our hands!"*

The Canadian Polish Congress

In 1946, at a Canadian-Polish Congress convention held in Montréal, I was chosen Secretary-General, the youngest to hold this post. At the convention, I almost got into hot water when I was misunderstood and was thought to denigrate the handful of former Polish officers!

In or about mid-September, there arrived at Kingston, thousands of demobilized young Polish soldiers. A few Polish-Toronto community leaders and I drove in my father's car to meet these heroes. Most of them had fought in Italy and some in France. The soldiers were in their uniforms, friendly and happy that they had not been forced to return to Communist-occupied Poland.

All we could do was to distribute hundreds of copies of the two local Polish newspapers. The Canadian army fed them and housed them. The Canadian authorities had each one of them sign a two-year contract to work on a farm. The farms were chosen by a Canadian colonel and they were transported to their assigned farms within days of their arrival in Kingston.

In Toronto, there was a Canadian office with a small staff headed by a Canadian Army colonel, who was appointed Acting Administrator. They had a Polish translator, Mrs. Irené Ungar, a volunteer. Mrs. Irené Ungar was active in the Polish community of Toronto for many years; her husband was formerly in the Polish Air Force.

They dealt with complaints about a few farmers who had these veterans sleep in barns (something the Nazis practised on European young boys, doing forced farm labour for the Third Reich). There were various petty complaints—lack of food, long hours of work, no days off, and meagre remuneration. Sometimes, not often, I would be asked to go out to pacify a farmer whose daughter had gotten pregnant by his Polish farmhand, both swearing that they were *in love*.

The best solution, I said, was to have them get married. Other times I was called out for complaints about long hours, low pay, and lack of a day off on Sunday.

These veterans were fighting for a Free Poland and the Allied cause, and Canada was an ally. Most Polish Vets were brought up in cities and towns; now they had to work their guts out for two years on farms. Who knows if their contracts were only in English and complied with our Canadian contract law? If one who does not write, nor read English, signs a contract, that contract could be null and void and unenforceable if such facts could be established.

Now in the 1947 Immigration Practice of Political Asylum, these same Polish soldiers could have faced persecution from a Communist Poland, and as a result been granted political asylum in Canada, with no requirement of signing contracts of farm labour for two years. Ironically, Canadian Immigration at the end of World War II let former German Nazis and some of their collaborators slip into Canada as refugees, some allege in droves.

Canadian veterans, on the other hand, deservedly were showered not only with honours, but also with commensurate rewards. For example, monies paid in various amounts on demobilization, free higher education (medical, dental, law, accountancy, et al.), many positions in police cadres, R.C.M.P. employment, government jobs, etc. No two-year contracts to work on farms faced our Canadian Veterans. The Polish veterans *had* to be grateful not to go back to their relatives in Communist Poland. The Eastern Europeans can't forgive or forget Yalta, where Roosevelt and Churchill succumbed to Stalin and let the Iron Curtain fall, enslaving Eastern Europe.

It took until 1989–1991 for Communism to fall apart, in not only Eastern Europe but also the Soviet Empire from St. Petersburg to

Vladivostok. However, will Russian democracy last? Will expansionism die out?

The first President of Russia—erratic at best; the second—a sober, secret police Colonel. Only time will tell whether President Putin will follow the example of Peter the Great, who from a regional power moulded a European invincible autocracy, or be the cause of Russia's collapse similar to the chaos of 1917. The position I had with the Canadian Polish Congress required monthly meetings of the executive. There were always two factions arguing: the extreme right and the progressive left. This was complicated, as I did my best to push for a centrist position, not always succeeding.

Correspondence was heavier than ever. I would forward the letters from the Polish veterans to Mrs. Irené Ungar at her office. Lunches with Wanda continued, dinners at her place were more frequent, and Wanda's piano playing was inspiring to all who listened to her—her playing and her beauty deeply moved my soul and captured my heart.

After becoming Secretary, I took night courses to complete my studies at the University of Toronto. In mid-September of 1947, I received great help from my old friend Gisele in Montréal. I saw that the Congress wouldn't open any new doors for me. At the fall convention, I decided to resign; although pressed by some to stay on, I had made up my mind.

A Woman Called Wanda

I first met Wanda at the Canadian Youth Congress; I recall being struck by her flawless beauty and impressed by both her intelligence and her musical talent. Shortly after meeting, we began to correspond weekly; on the inside of all of her letters, she imprinted a kiss, with lipstick on her lips. To this, she added the letters "S.W.A.K." — "Sealed with a Kiss." I had saved those precious letters for many years, which totalled into the hundreds. Sadly, when moving to Windsor, they were forever lost.

Shortly after our initial meeting, I took up the position of Secretary of the Congress in Toronto. We began to date often—movies, dinners, and I attended all of the classical piano recitals she gave at her parent's home. When she played Chopin's Polonaises, Etudes, and Mazurkas, the rendition was so potent and played with such deep feeling that shivers ran up and down my spine.

During the summers, Wanda and I, along with some of her girlfriends, would take the short ferry ride across to Toronto Island. It was a good place to swim (and to steal a kiss) when we could sneak off and luxuriate in a few precious moments alone.

On several August nights, Wanda and I, again with her friends, would watch the magical sight of falling stars in the darkened midnight sky, as we all sat together by the western shore of Lake Ontario. This sight filled one with a certain sacred tranquillity and peace of mind. Strangers no more, an intense desire evolved between Wanda and I (like Eros' in ancient mythology), and an overwhelming affection for one another unfolded.

That summer, Wanda and I went fishing on Lake Simcoe on several occasions. One particular time, I caught a small perch and Wanda caught a large pike. Wanda's friends, who owned the cottage, cooked up an amazing fresh fish dinner to celebrate. Before dark, they drove us both back to our respective homes in west Toronto. While in the semi-privacy of the darkened back seat, Wanda and I held hands throughout the trip, kissing and hugging incessantly.

Another summer, we spent a weekend at my sister's cottage at North-Hatley, located in the eastern townships of Québec. The cottage had a huge lake frontage on Lake Massawippi. Wanda and I crossed the lake by motorboat and landed on a sandy beach, which was at the foot of a huge mountain. This uninhabited mountain was located two-miles across from my sister's cottage.

We had located a perfect love nest! Unfortunately, for us, it started to rain almost immediately, and we had to scramble to get back to the cottage. Ten years later, married, we returned to our "Massawippi Love Nest," and consummated what we had only contemplated ten years earlier...

Chapter Two

The Toronto Era

Wanda and I fell deeply in love and soon became inseparable. I continued my studies full-time at University College. I took three histories, plus Spanish and French in the mornings. Most afternoons I had part-time jobs as a butler at the Coulson's, Bongards', Eaton's, and worked Friday afternoons and Saturdays at the Maple Leaf Co., packing trucks. A lady named Mrs. Mary Coulson lent me money twice towards my school fees and I paid her back with work like painting small rooms. I am forever indebted to her kindness.

It was not long before we began planning our marriage. Wanda started attending lectures to become a Catholic, as she was a Baptist. There was only one fly in the ointment. A young aviator friend came a-calling from England. However, Wanda and I were so deeply in love by this point that even this little inconvenience could not keep us apart. We married in June 1948, at Toronto's St. Stanislaus Church. Many of my family members, along with my parents, attended the ceremony and reception. With Wanda's family and a large number of their friends present, we made our vows "till death do us part!" The reception wasn't celebrated in a traditional Polish style. Donations in envelopes were given to Wanda and I before we sat down to eat our meal. The guests and both parents proved to be more than generous. They donated, what for us was a large sum of money, which we promptly gave to Wanda's father to help defray the cost of the wedding. The song wishing us one hundred years of happiness was sung to us repeatedly at the reception: *"Sto lat, Sto lat, Sto lat"* echoed repeatedly. The huge wedding cake was cut up by Wanda with the help of the waitresses, and I proudly served portions to everyone.

We had decided before the wedding to go to Mexico on our honeymoon. Thanks to my father loaning us his Dodge automobile, it became possible with the money that I had saved.

The Mexico Trip

Our first stop was Chicago, Illinois. From our hotel, I contacted Mr. Charles Rozmarek, the President of the American Polish Congress, whom I had met several times before as Secretary-General of the CPC. Mr. Rozmarek invited my new bride and I for lunch at a first-class restaurant located inside a hotel in downtown Chicago. After a very pleasant lunch, Mrs. Rozmarek gave us the name, address, and phone number of the former Polish Military attaché in Mexico City. He apparently operated a *pensionat*. He and his family were very gracious to us once we arrived in Mexico City.

On our departure from Chicago, we drove through St. Louis, Little Rock, Shreveport, and Dallas. Whilst filling up for gas in a small town in Texas, the owner had to call his lawyer to okay our Canadian bill. He said that the bill had a "picture of some man on the face of it," (George VI, our King)! Finally, we crossed the Mexican border at Nuevo Laredo, with nary a problem.

At dusk, we drove on to Monterey. Then, after we had driven for about 50-odd miles, it became dark quite suddenly. Through the blackness, I could barely discern that we were being flagged down about 10:00 p.m. or so, by what appeared to be a dozen Mexican soldiers in full uniform regalia, attired with rifles and open bayonets.

The Mexican in charge could hardly speak English and asked for our passports. I kept saying *"nos turistas"* (we are tourists). That same menacing looking soldier took our passports over to an army van, and after five minutes (which seemed to us like an hour) gave us back our passports and said *"Turistas, Bien!"* The remaining soldiers that surrounded our car moved aside and we were waved on. I drove off in a trail of gravel. We were both quite shaken. Only 10-miles down the road, we saw a sign "Air-Conditioned Motel." Being exhausted by our ordeal, we drove up, paid and registered, and promptly fell deep asleep.

Wanda and I both woke up around midnight to discover that the hotel room was as hot as "Hades." The cooling system had apparently been turned off after we had checked in, which was our first encounter with the sometimes notorious Mexican duplicity.

The next morning upon arising, we drove on to Mexico City. The surrounding landscape with the mountainous peaks of the Sierra Madres reminded me of our majestic Canadian Rocky Mountains. We located our former Polish attaché immediately, and fortunately, for us he had a vacant room in his pensionat… Our gracious host kindly outlined the history of ancient Mexico the next day over lunch. The city was founded in 1325 by Aztecs. The Spaniards arrived in the early 16th century. Our Polish host showed us many interesting places such as an Aztec pyramid at Teocali, not far from Mexico City. We climbed to the top, and saw the lovely Popocatepel Mountain Volcano covered in white snow.

Sadly, but not surprisingly, I also saw the inside of many *"banos"* as I sorely came down with "Montezuma's Revenge." However, my Polish ex-Military attaché friend quickly cured me with potent drinks created from local medicinal herbs he had mixed up himself.

After long goodbyes to our kind hosts and their two grown-up children, we started to motor our way home. Just before Monterey, a sudden fog made driving almost impossible, as we could only see a few feet in front of us. Miraculously, two red backlights of a local truck appeared in front of us. They guided us for about 40-miles or so until the fog had lifted.

At that point, we could now see the 1,000-foot precipices to our right side and sighed how easily we could have plummeted to our doom, had it not been for that truck. To this day, I feel that the Almighty's hand placed that truck in front of us and saved our lives.

We retraced our route to Nuevo Laredo and then over to Laredo, U.S.A. It was dark, around 10:30 p.m., and the U.S. Customs (probably because my passport revealed I was born in Montréal, Québec!) searched me personally, the car, the trunk, the valises, and even looked with a flashlight at the underside of the car. This lasted a good hour or so with no apologies at the end of the ordeal.

When we arrived home, we were cautionary to tell Wanda's family only about the highlights of our honeymoon, and not the difficult situations that we had encountered.

Articling Days as a Law Student

Not long after arriving back from our honeymoon, I was admitted to the prestigious Osgoode Hall Law School. It was not easy. In the midst of my schooling, Wanda's father died of a brain tumour. My dearest Wanda was heartbroken.

At law school, I had my friends, several of which became Federal and Provincial Judges. As law students at Osgoode Hall, we had the opportunities to observe trials and motions that were being conducted in Courtrooms located at Osgoode Hall.

I recall a divorce trial conducted by Mr. Justice Chevrier. A few colleagues and I heard the submissions of Counsel. The judgment of the learned Trial Judge emphasized that the most important thing in this case is, *"not to kill the goose that lays the golden eggs."* That is, not to make the husband's payments to the wife so high that the husband in all honesty would not be able to pay!

On another occasion, I listened to a motion being argued before the Chief Justice of Ontario who was over 92-years of age. In prior years, Judges were nominated for life. This Chief Justice was deaf and had an old-fashioned hearing aid inserted into his left ear. We all noticed that every time the respondent made his representations, the Chief Justice, with his right hand, made a gesture that looked to me like he was shutting off his hearing aid. Sure enough, in a short judgment of the Chief Justice, the motion was lost by the respondent.

There were two notorious gangsters in Toronto at that time that robbed area banks. These two shot a detective Sergeant in cold blood in west Toronto. Justice McRuer presided over their trial (they had previously managed to escape twice from the Don Jail). The Crown-Attorney made a devastating opening speech to the jury.

No defence could undo the evidence against the two accused. I heard Justice McRuer pronounce the death sentence and I found it hard to listen to—almost as hard as it was for Justice McRuer to make the pronouncement of death, even though his peers knew him as "Hanging Jim." The two mobsters were hung back-to-back in the Don Jail; I was a third-year law student articling.

The day after the hanging, I had an errand to make at the Sheriff's office. When I entered his office, the Sheriff sat there motionless, staring into space; you could see that he had been crying. I completed my errand within one minute. The Sheriff muttered to me in a very soft voice, "I hope they stop this killing." Only later did I realize that as Sheriff, he was required by law to be present at all executions of prisoners. That was to be one of the last hangings ever held in Canada.

As a third-year student articling with a law firm, I was on payroll, however small it seemed at the time, about $15.00 a week. I graduated in early spring of 1954 and I was called to the Bar in 1954.

Getting Down to the Practice of Law

My first job out in the real world was with the firm of Bagwell, Stevens, McFarlane at 372 Bay Street, Toronto, Ontario. A year or so later I became a partner and I had a night office located at 220 Roncesvalles Avenue where I worked several nights a week. The location was in a heavily ethnic community. Wanda and I bought a home on Edgehill Road, and together with our first baby Gayle, we moved to the home in Etobicoke, a suburb of Toronto.

At the start, I handled Wills, mostly small estates, contracts, real estate purchases and sales, Magistrate Court infractions, etc. For the few rape or manslaughter cases that I acquired in those early days, I would get our senior partner George Bagwell, Q.C. to handle them.

My first practising certificate from the Law Society of Upper Canada acknowledged that my solicitor and bar fee totalled $50.00 and my compensation fund levy was $10.00. As of 1997, I am told the compensation fund levy was $10,000.00.

On September 19th, 1958, the Toronto Telegram newspaper splashed this headline on the first page: **Drinking Party Raid Uncovers Woman's Nude Battered Body**. Underneath appeared three large photos; one of the husband of the murdered woman, one of two handcuffed murder suspects being led to a police wagon, and one of an earlier photo of Valerie Riley, the victim. The three photos combined covered one-third of the first page of the newspaper.

The article went on at length describing that 12 hours after a routine liquor raid on the Augusta Avenue house, police found the naked body of Mrs. Riley in a box, covered with a tarpaulin and some blankets. The autopsy revealed death caused by multiple brain haemorrhages caused by many blows. The police found a trail of blood with hand smears, which helped them to discover the naked body of Mrs. Riley. In this two-story home, in every corner of every room, lay empty beer, wine, and whisky bottles, confirming a neighbour's statement that all-night parties commonly went on at the Augusta house. Bereznitsky and Gwizd were arrested that day and charged with murder, and the other eight people at that party were charged as material witnesses.

Shortly after, I was retained by the mother of the accused Bernard Gwizd. Hugh Locke (now Mr. Justice Hugh R. Locke) defended the co-accused Sam Bereznitsky. We both attended a preliminary hearing that lasted three full days, with Mr. Arthur Klein (known as a hard-as-steel prosecutor) as the Crown Prosecutor.

After nine Crown witnesses were heard in Chief, and cross-examined, and 450 pages of transcript compiled, on October 21st, 1958, the presiding magistrate committed the two accused on the charge as laid. The trial was set to commence on February 1st. My client pleaded guilty, I filed a full "Presentence Report" Justice wilson sentenced my client to four years. 1959 in front of The Honourable Mr. Justice Joseph B. Wilson of the Ontario Supreme Court. He was the only Justice in the County of York who insisted that lawyers all wear "new linen" every day. Justice Wilson was selected some time later to go to Cyprus to instil our "Common-Law" into Cyprian law. I never heard if Justice Joseph B. Wilson succeeded, although it seems that the Greeks and Turks seem more tranquil now!

There are other memorable events over the course of one's career, amongst one's daily drudgery, that bears witness.

My memory is roused by Mr. Justice Hugh R. Locke who recalled that Mr. Justice Joseph B. Wilson was the one who said to the lawyer who walked into his Courtroom wearing grey flannel pants instead of dark striped pants, "Mr. Smith, I can't see you." When the "Mr. Smith, I can't see you" was repeated about three times, Mr. Smith replied, "That's kind of funny, my Lord, because I can see you." It finally dawned on Smith that the Judge did not like his pants. The story goes that Smith, walking out of the Courtroom muttered, *"the higher the monkey climbs the pole, the more you can see of his bare ass!"*

A friend who later became a good client — Adam Eckhardt, a Polish air force veteran, started a ladies shop, "Ruth Frocks." Within a few years, he had purchased the whole building located at Queen and King Streets in Toronto West.

I acted for "Ruth Frocks" as their lawyer for incorporation and real estate, including the collection of unpaid accounts. This one delinquent account (a former Polish veteran) misinterpreted my letter of demand, which advised him that if he did not pay the monies owed, that he could be sued, and furthermore, if judgment was procured, he could be subject to the sheriff's seizure of assets and/or legal *execution* of the judgment. The veteran angrily replied that he had survived Stalin's Siberia, only to be *executed* in Canada over a $200.00 debt! I could not calm him. When my client was informed of this exasperating incident, he just took the loss and ended the matter.

When business started to slip around 1965 Adam was with his accountant, a Mr. A. Golden, in a hotel room sequestered for two days. He agreed to purchase a downtown Toronto department store; this turned out to be "Northway" located north of the old Eaton Department Store on Yonge Street.

One of my duties, apart from acting on the purchase of "Northway," was also to raise monies by way of mortgages on "Ruth Frocks" their home, and their relatives' homes, etc. This proved to be Adam's *"Waterloo."* I even loaned him monies in the late 1970s.

He died in late 1992; his wife Phyllis was stricken with Alzheimer's disease and passed away almost at the same time that Adam did. He died penniless, and he was buried by the Canadian Veterans in their cemetery. Only two of his three children attended the burial. Sadly, his oldest son, a *guru* of sorts of some obscure American sect, was barred from attending.

I became a member of the County of York Law Association shortly after graduating, the Civil Liberties Committee, and the Legal Aid Committee. The latter met consistently. Members of that committee were asked about once a month to defend a manslaughter case or an attempted rape, etc. It was not a compulsory requirement but a voluntary duty; one received no fee for this. I also did my share of Legal Aid cases. Each May, I was invited to attend a Legal Aid dinner. I was always too busy in Court, at my office, and at home, to ever find the time to attend. My secretary (the best I ever had) Mrs. Connie Hubbard, would ultimately phone in my regrets.

I recall that near the middle of 1967, Legal Aid assigned to me a "Badger case" in County Court, in front of Judge J. Kelly. A Badger case, in simple language, was to bait a person like a badger. The criminal offence incurred (in this case) when a decoy girl induced the male victim to enter her home, presumably for sex. On entering, the victim was struck down by a male accomplice, robbed of valuables and money, and ejected out of the house. I lost the case, as did the other lawyer acting for the decoy woman. At the end of the trial, Judge Joseph Kelly asked both lawyers to join him in his chambers. He congratulated me on my address to the jury (Wow!). Other Judges or Justices usually just stared me down when I lost.

Sometime during the late 1960s, I was called in to see an inmate at the Don Jail. This Toronto Jail is well known to all judicial and non-judicial persons alike.

I interviewed a Jon Kanju, a short Russian immigrant, single, about 50-years-old, sentenced to four years for hitting a friend with a baseball bat on the head. Both of them had been drunk at the time. He asked me to file an appeal. I did so, and it came up several months later with the Court of Appeal. I spent almost a full day in the great library at Osgoode Hall reading pertinent law. My appeal was to be heard at 10:00 a.m.

I brought with me about 40 heavy, hardcover law books with case law to sustain the appeal. At 10:00 a.m. Hon. Justices Roach, Schroeder, and I believe Wells arrived. We all bowed to each other and sat down. Before I could even say a word, one of the Justices said, "We all agreed that the sentence should be reduced to two years from four years. Still quite green, I proudly thought that I had scared them off with the 40-odd legal books I had brought with me! It was only later that I realized I that I was number one on their list of 10 appeals to be heard that day, and that they needed the additional time to deal with appeals that were of a more serious nature.

Polish Tenor Jan Kiepura

A world-renowned Polish tenor — Jan Kiepura — was a client of mine from the early 1960s onwards. Apart from purchasing several apartment buildings in Toronto, his biggest problem was finding honest staff and an accountant. I contacted an accountant I knew who also worked for a Credit Union.

I arranged a meeting in my office for both to meet and discuss Kiepura's problems. Within an hour, they arrived at an arrangement. Prior to my meeting Jan Kiepura for a second time (the first you will recall was in Montréal in the late fall of 1939), was in Toronto, May 1964 at a Toronto Polish Businessmen's Club. Months passed and all seemed well.

Our family and friends rented adjoining cottages in the month of August 1966 in Wasaga Beach. One evening it was dark out and the children were already in bed.

About 11:00 p.m., a car drove up our driveway and the accountant jumped out, white, trembling, and begging for a coffee. My wife Wanda prepared a cup of coffee for him. He gulped it down, and then ran to the bathroom. We could hear him throwing up through the wooden door. He appeared to rinse his mouth out with water, and returned to the kitchen where all of the adults were sitting. Before I could say, "what's the matter?" the accountant blurted out, *"Jan Kiepura is dead."* We were all startled, and never got around to asking him who had given out our cottage address, which was about 90-miles from Toronto.

The next day by telephone, I paid my respects to his widow and family. As to legal matters (meaning probate, etc.) she informed me that she had engaged an American law firm, as he was an American citizen. Some time later, she accompanied his remains to Warsaw for burial in his beloved Poland.

She was quoted as saying in the interment in Poland, *"I give you Jan Kiepura, a son of Poland."* I never did find out the cause of the strange behaviour of his accountant the night of Jan Kiepura's death.

Judge Frank Denton

County Court Judge Frank Denton in Toronto was probably the most colourful Judge that I ever had the pleasure of meeting. I recall that one day I had a Landlord and Tenant case. My opponent was the late Mr. K. The hearing took place in the Judge's Chambers with a long desk running almost the whole length of the room. Judge Denton sat at the end of the long table. We faced each other. In the middle of my argument, the Judge went to the bathroom to urinate, and yelled "Go on, I can hear you!"

The same Judge was very fond of painting country scenes. Stories circulated that he would stop his car, forget his pressing destination to some rural Small Claims Court, take out the palette and brushes, which he always carried with him, and wile away the rest of the day painting, while others were anxiously waiting on him to deliver Judgement! He was known to decorate his office with his ever-changing precious "Rembrandts."

Political Encounters of the Liberal Kind

In the late 1950s, I was approached by The Hon. Paul Hellyer (Associate Minister of Defence) to run federally as the Liberal candidate in the riding of "Trinity" (in the Bathurst Street, Toronto area). My wife and I were wined and dined by the Minister, together with his charming wife. One reason for approaching me was my previous association with the Canadian-Polish Congress and Youth Associations, both locally and nationally. Reluctantly I declined. I had a growing family, a Toronto practice, and I said that if I were to run, I'd rather run as a Liberal provincially.

Dr. Stanley Hajdasz, however, readily agreed to run. He had clipped a "J" out of his surname, with the help of Provincial Minister John Yaremko. He attended elocution lessons, which helped him, gain the nomination in the riding of Trinity, and he developed a speaking style reminiscent of an evangelist! After Prime Minister Louis St. Laurent lost the National Election to Diefenbaker, Stan Haidasz was the only Liberal M.P. elected in Toronto. He developed an enormous following, he occupied ministries, and finally he was appointed to the Senate of Canada, until his term expired in 1998, upon reaching the age of 75.

Later, when I had decided to run in High Park as Provincial Liberal Candidate, some urged me to contest the nomination of Jim Trotter in the adjoining riding of Parkdale. Among them were the late Casimir Bielski and John Stroz. They said that in politics "everything is fair game." They underlined that Parkdale had more Polish-Canadian voters than High Park. They forecasted that I would have a better chance there of securing the seat. As I was in partnership with G. Bagwell, "Stevens and Senator A. Roebuck, Q.C." shared office space with our law firm. Shortly after being told of "the so-called fair game politics," I asked the Senator out to lunch.

Being a novice in politics, I sought the Senator's advice on the proposed "bumping off" of my good friend Jim Trotter in the riding of Parkdale. He told me in summary, not to go that way, as good Liberals never do such things. Neither do individuals of integrity in their private life or their professional life.

Senator Roebuck was a true friend of the underdog in his long political life. He spoke for portable pensions and against early Senatorial retirement. Roebuck conducted a committee study of legislation— subsequently passed into law that outlawed racist propaganda. His working hours in his Parliament Hill office were from 10:00 a.m. until closing time at 10:00 p.m.

Although he wore a Liberal label in the Ontario Legislature, the House of Commons, and the Senate, he often was at odds with his

Party's leadership, including Ontario Liberal Premier, Mitchell Hepburn. In 1937, a strike of a General Motors plant in Oshawa occurred; the Premier, insisting that the Union was foreign dominated (by Americans), marshalled the entire police of the whole province, and subdued the strikers. A. Roebuck and the Ontario Labour Minister, David Croll (from Windsor) as they opposed Hepburn, were both dismissed. The Senator always sympathized with the less privileged. An example goes back to 1928; criticizing the Monarchy at that time was a criminal offence. In December 1928, the editor of a Finnish paper, one Aaro Varra was charged with seditious libel against the Monarchy. His defence Counsel was Arthur Roebuck, then a rookie Toronto lawyer.

The trial took place in Sudbury, Ontario. The Crown also tarred the Finn with Communism and the charge of seditious libel. Roebuck, after what was said to be a great defence, lost. His client was sentenced to six months. In 1932, Aaro Varra was deported to Finland without a trial— (unheard of today).

Roebuck, at 16 years of age operated an elevator for $1.00 a week; at 20 years of age, he earned $5.00 a week as a reporter with The Toronto Daily Star. By 1947, he was called to the Bar to practice law. He ran four times; he was elected with the Liberal sweep in 1934 because of the Tory Hydro mismanagement. As Attorney General, he saved Ontarians seven million dollars; he streamlined the Provincial Courts. His recipe for longevity was simple: *"Never waste time or vitality."* He died at the ripe old age of 93 in a Cobourg nursing home. His funeral was held at St. Paul's Anglican Cathedral (Toronto), November 18th, 1971.

The 1959 Election

Pat Cameron, Q.C., was the Federal Liberal member of the riding of High Park in Toronto West. When I joined the association in 1958, the Treasurer reported that $14.20 was all the cash there was on hand. When I left the Association in 1967, the amount had climbed to well over $450.00. Mrs. Peter Wright, Pat and Mrs. Cameron, Mr. DeBatisse, Mr. Savona, Mr. Keith Russell, and countless others assisted me to gain the nomination as Liberal Provincial candidate in February 1959. The election was called for June 11th, 1959.

The sitting member was Alf Cowling (William Temple of the CCF) whose highlight in his political career was defeating George Drew in 1948. Then there was John Weir, of the Labour Progressive Party

(Communist), and myself as Liberal candidate. Our headquarters were located on Dundas Street West. We had a good part-time campaign manager and two capable secretaries. The other 200 persons were volunteers, mostly canvassers. I had tremendous support from the Polish press especially "the Alliancer" and Ukrainian and Maltese publications.

I was pleased during the 1959 election that my oldest sister had come from Montréal to help. In hindsight, one big mistake our headquarters made was sending out canvassers who had pronounced "non-English accents," which proved counter-productive. We had a proverbial melting pot of volunteers of Lithuanian descent, Yugoslav, Polish-Ukrainian, Maltese, Greek, Italian, English, and Canadians, most of them fluent in English.

Pat Cameron, Q.C., was a great help to me; he took me around and introduced me to at least 150 to 200 voting families in the riding, generally after suppertime. We had some good press, especially in the Telegram of May 25th, 1959. The headline of a huge picture of five women with Wintermeyer was, *"Paul Martin Swings at Wintermeyer Foes."* This was the father of the present Minister of Finance. I was lucky if I slept five hours a night during the campaign. One of my most active volunteers and friends was engineer Joseph Kicinski. His home became my secondary campaign office.

Diefenbaker's destruction of the Arrow Aeroplane project and the loss of several thousands of skilled workers gave our campaign some much-needed support. The loss to Canada of its great test pilot, Janusz Zurakowski did not help our Tory opponents. However, it was very difficult to overthrow the Frost machine and their accomplishments were in tune with what many Ontarians wanted. They did not attempt any so-called ultra-right-wing "common sense revolutions."

Although our headquarters installed scrutineers into ninety (90%) percent of the polling booths, many were inexperienced and on that crucial voting day, they were ineffective at best. Made cognizant of losing the election by 504 votes, I went to Cowling's committee room with my campaign manager and congratulated him.

The Tories lost 12 seats in Ontario; the Liberals doubled their seats to 22 from 11. The CCF got five seats, an addition of two from three in 1955.

In Windsor, Bernard Newman (Nowosielski) was elected, the first Canadian of Polish descent to be elected (as a Liberal) in the Ontario legislature. After the election, I returned to the practice of law (*and* the unpaid campaign bills). I got a warm and encouraging telegram from John Wintermeyer, directed to myself, and my volunteer workers to stand fast. At the end of the evening at our committee room packed with disappointed volunteers, I got up on a desk and attempted to lift their spirits. "After all," I said at the end of my speech, "We *only* lost by 504 votes."

The Polish Alliancer (a weekly), in a two-page analysis of the 1959 election dated June 17th, 1959 wrote that to them, I was by far the most devoted candidate, and that I had lost High Park by only a handful of votes.

The Canadian Polish Congress—Toronto Chapter

On February 29th, 1959, I was elected President of the Toronto Branch of the Canadian Polish Congress, thanks to Mrs. Irené Ungar and other members of a few associations (the Polish Engineers Association, Polish Alliance, and several other centrist clubs). Knowing the endless technical quarrels that some of the delegates constantly engaged in, I nominated my dear friend engineer Joseph Kicinski to be my vice-president and preside over all the executive meetings. I must say he conducted them excellently, like an experienced arbitrator.

On November 8th, 1959, the Toronto Congress celebrated Poland's Independence Day. All organizations took an active role at the Toronto Cenotaph. Polish, Canadian flags, and the Union Jack were abundantly displayed. I gave the speech as President, reiterating how Poles fought in 1939 against the Nazis and Communist Russia in France in 1940 at Narvik, Norway at Monte Casino and so forth, spilling blood for freedom and at the collapse of Nazi Germany.

On Citizenship Day, September 8th, two new Canadians were honoured: one Sir Sanford Fleming from Scotland, and the other the late Sir Casimir Gzowski from Poland. They were both active in building railroads and bridges and giving a boost to industry and commerce in the provinces of Ontario and Québec.

Prior to this campaign, at the nomination meeting, my opponent plastered numerous, *huge* pictures of himself throughout the walls of the hall. Some of my supporters begged me to allow them to tear these pictures down. The President and I said, *"No, let him hang."* Hang he did as he got less than 70 votes out of the 428 that I received.

I always considered myself fortunate that my partners on Bay Street willingly looked after my clients when I took the leave to campaign. I did what work I could at my night office. My wife Wanda, who stood by me for all three elections, was my real Campaign Manager. She corralled countless friends to work as volunteers; when things looked rough, she inspired me to plough ahead. She also cared for our children, their needs, and assisted them with their homework and schooling. She was my rock.

Essentially, 1963 was a replay of the 1959 campaign. Our past volunteers returned, some new ones joined the ranks, and a few school friends from University and Law School came on board as well. John Munro, an M.P. from Hamilton, arrived at our headquarters and made a rousing speech, which was a "call to arms." It was very well received.

I was offered, by my dear friend J. Kicinski and former vice-president of the Congress, the possibility of working and sleeping at his home on Evelyn Avenue during the crunch of campaign time. As it was centrally located in the riding, I happily agreed. J. Kudlak, a local Ukrainian businessman, created a sign out of plywood that was 35-feet long and stretched all the way from the edge of his home, out to the sidewalk. It said, *"Vote Paul Staniszewski – Liberal."* The lettering was in bold red, on a white background. It could be read from both sides of the sidewalk.

That's how much *"esprit de couer"* many of our supporters had. Although we did everything by the book, and the campaign started off with a bang, sadly I lost by about 780 votes to the Conservative incumbent.

In the end, I was left with a stack of campaign bills. I even had to negotiate a settlement from a large claim my campaign manager made, surprising me by the hefty sum he demanded for part-time work, but it all worked out, somehow.

Due in part to the publicity of my campaigns, from about 1964–1966, my law practice expanded. I was swamped with requests, acting on behalf of a mortgage institution, which helped me pay off the bank loan I took out for the campaign. Both newly arrived ethnic and Canadian clients began to seek out my legal services in increasing numbers.

Somewhere around that time, I happened to have lunch with J. Trotter at the "Savarin" on Bay Street. As we were leaving, we ran into NDP organizer Mr. Stephen Lewis. We exchanged pleasantries and between his words, he wished me luck, suppressing a grin.

Later I found out that Stephen Lewis had launched a formidable opponent in the 1967 election—a Dr. Shulman; he was a former coroner, a multimillionaire, a former active Conservative, now re-born New Democrat candidate for the NDP.

He was widely known as the Chief Coroner of Metro Toronto thanks to his Tory connections. His supporters (NDP now) claimed him as the *"guardian of public interest."* His literature also claimed his vigilance, getting our hospitals to practice higher operating standards than before. The NDP downplayed the fact or denied entirely that he was a Tory, or a multimillionaire.

My nomination went smoothly some months before the election of 1967. We had several politicians as speakers at our meetings; the most noteworthy was the Hon. Walter Gordon, who addressed us at one of our rallies. He spoke to us vehemently on how "foreign capital" was taking over much of our Canadian industries, manufacturing, technology, fisheries, and so forth. He included in his speech some detailed examples of this. He concluded with this simple analogy, *"that if the rich get richer and the poor get poorer throughout the world, expect a violent shaking up."* When he finished, he was given a standing ovation by the crowd.

Walter Gordon was the greatest Canadian Nationalist of all times. As Chairman of the Royal Commission on Canada's Economic Prospects, his report divulged the threat to Canada from foreign and especially U.S. encroachments if not regulated. In politics, his central theme was— Canadian interests first. I recall the Americans, on one of their Time Magazine's outside covers displayed a cartoon of Walter Gordon, lampooning him draped in a Canadian Flag.

He was in Lester Pearson's cabinet, as well as Trudeau's, forever-steering Canada away from the menacing elephant to our south. He founded the Committee for an Independent Canada. Since he passed away in 1987, I have not seen many Canadians willing to carry his torch.

Today, about 16 years after his death, the American potentate does not have much further to go to reduce the whole of Canada to a "satellite status"; this looming disaster is sadly well underway—beneath a smoke screen of economics, the Trade Agreement, NAFTA, with a final strangulation awaiting from the snares of Global Capitalism. Our cultural institutions, all of our vast natural resources, manufacturing, newspapers, agriculture, etc., all face being plundered by globalization, propelled by monetary greed, by a potent few to the detriment of those outside their wealth; that amount estimated to be ninety-eight (98%) percent of the population.

Mr. Eric Kierans, outstanding economist, member of provincial and national ministries in the last chapter of his book, "Remembering" published in 2001, wrote, *"We are not born to live in a Corporate Globe, yet this is the world we are moving towards. Moreover, we have created a society in which so much of the world's riches are accumulated in so few hands. When people have nothing to lose… plunged into poverty for the enrichment of others, they must either subside or rebel, and there is an end to community, responsibility, and society"…* He dedicated the "Massey Lectures" to Walter Gordon, who foresaw most of this long before the rest of us.

The Election of 1967

I recall when Keith Davey ("The Rainmaker") later to become a Senator called me and asked what I thought of Shulman running. I replied, *"I was now running against two wealthy Conservatives…"* We cranked our machine as usual—I secured a committee room on Dundas Street West; we had to find a (less-expensive) campaign manager! We brought on board (once again) our previous dedicated and hard working office staff. The first incursion was when multimillionaire Dr. Shulman flew to Malta, and after a private audience with Maltese politicians, returned to publicize his meetings widely with the local Maltese community. This sadly reduced a large number of Liberal Maltese followers.

I only was made aware of this" Maltese incursion" (as it became known) after my wife, four children, and myself returned from visiting Expo '67 in Montréal—the most magnificent World's Fair I had ever attended. The French General—Charles DeGaulle, was an Anglophobe since World War II (Canadian internal files confirmed that under the General's direction, France's "Agents Provocateurs," since 1965 had been stirring Québecers to separate).

At the Expo 1967 in Montréal with his infamous cry—*"Vive le Québec Libre"*—he turned Canadian citizen against Canadian citizen: those who had lived side by side as brothers and sisters for several centuries in peace. His open foreign policy is clandestinely continued by the French authorities today—attempting to plant a French-speaking "vassal state" in America to replace the loss of French colonies in Africa, Viet Nam, Haiti, Algiers, Lebanon, Syria, Tunisia, and Morocco among others.

General De Gaulle first laid the seeds of discontent and of secession in Québec, which still divides our nation, endangers the existence of Canada, and threatens the very stability of the North American Continent.

In 1999, President Chirac became the last Gaullist in France. He was a more diplomatic man—although surreptitious and more injurious than Charles DeGaulle's encroachment. The "Franco-phonie" inspired by France and the (then) Canadian Ambassador to Paris, Mr. Bouchard (Mulroney's appointment) does not dare expel the tyrannical and murderous rulers of the once French-African states and the former Belgian Congo in Africa. Perhaps its true name should be..."Franco-Emperiale."

When we arrived back in Toronto the next morning, I immediately went over to our campaign office but some "ardent Democratic" NDP's had conveniently tied up all of our phone lines for three whole hours. They kept this up doggedly until the following week, when we changed all of our telephone numbers and made two unlisted telephone numbers a secret, thus avoiding Shulman's Democratic subversions.

Some of our ardent followers turned in plastic records full of ethnic music handed out by the NDP's, workers, and some unionists. "Was that against the Election Act?" We were too busy canvassing and putting up our signs to check and see if an election law was breached or not. We received several reports that some of our signs had been torn down or replaced with NDP signs.

However, we were determined to fight on! Our canvassers, both telephonic and pedestrian were urged on by Pat Cameron, Q.C., who was a Federal Liberal Member. Ten other campaign veterans from Parkdale came on board to work for us. Wanda and I spent our fair share of time canvassing ourselves, and in the end, we had more signs up than all of our opponents put together. Altogether, we had about 200 volunteers helping.

Two weeks before election time, learning from past-experience, we had assigned seasoned scrutineers for all the polls in the whole riding.

We also had an emergency meeting to deal with the "tricks" being dealt our honest campaign from multimillionaire Shulman's workers. We turned the heat up, and I organized extensive canvassing in areas where we had won in 1963. I also began telephone canvassing of these same areas. The Tory provincial government that spring had changed the provincial electoral boundaries of High Park, from south of Bloor to King (roughly), and east of High Park to Sorauren.

It was all new territory for us. As early as April 1997, my close friend James Trotter MPP of Parkdale sent out a letter of endorsement of myself. This covered the new area that had been added on to High Park.

While canvassing, and whenever I got a request for help from a voter, I kept a daily record in the newly added areas of High Park. One of our secretaries would type out a letter of a voter's request to the president of the Privy Counsel, The Honourable Walter Gordon in Ottawa. The replies to the voters from Ottawa were swift and to the point, and copies of Gordon's letters were always sent back to me. I still have copies of the numerous letters of Walter Gordon in my files. This was of great help to my campaign.

On election night, very few of our workers felt we were going down the chute. The scrutineers reported by telephone the results in each poll. After 65 polls, I realized that we had lost another election. Once again, I had to cheer up our numerous volunteers including my oldest sister who had come all the way from Montréal to cheer me on.

In the rain that day, my wife drove me to the NDP election headquarters. I congratulated Shulman. He looked startled upon seeing me, but managed to shake my hand limply. Perhaps he was startled to find out that I could be such a gentleman. I lost by several thousand votes to Shulman in that election, but I received more votes than the Tory incumbent did.

After the election of 1967, I began to have periods of mental stress, and my doctor, Dr. W. S. Metzler treated me for that problem. The unpaid bills were eventually paid. November was creeping in on us, and I kept busy at work and at home.

There were times when Wanda and I felt as though we had neglected our children, because of our many political involvements. To make up for these long absences, we tried to spend most Augusts with them at Wasaga Beach, my parent's cottage in Val David, Québec, or at my sister Eugene and Frank's North Hatley cottage on Lake Massawippi.

Some of their summer weeks were spent at a Polish Girl Guide Camp near Wilno, Ontario. *"Why did our daughters have to be outfitted with Polish Girl Guide Uniforms?"* a neighbour asked me one day. I replied — maybe the refugees who organized the Girl Guides and Scouts felt that there was no Free Poland after 1945 and wished to keep their traditional uniforms in honour of Poland (The *then* Polish Communist government made Scouts and Girl Guides illegal).

Windsor Judgeship

After the elections, I returned to my work as a Prosecutor for the Attorney-General of Canada twice a week. I was kept busy in my legal practice with sales and purchases of realty, arranging mortgages, Wills, defending driving offenders, ability impaired cases, assault, robberies, and sexual offences, etc. Christmas 1967 came round and we invited friends, family, and relatives for Christmas. The girls and Wanda decorated the Christmas tree.

On December 19th, 1967, I was busy with a client at my office when my secretary, Mrs. Connie Hubbard buzzed me and said; *"The Honourable Minister of Justice, Pierre Trudeau"* was on the line. I picked up, and the Minister asked me whether I would accept a County Court Judgeship in Windsor? He added, "If you wish to, talk it over with your wife, and call me back." This was the best news ever! Suddenly I realized why Mr. P. Martin Sr. (then Minister of Foreign Affairs) had interviewed me outside of the Royal York Hotel and "tested" my French in mid-November 1967.

When I arrived home from work that day, I couldn't wait to tell my wife Wanda. She was one-hundred (100%) percent for it. The children however were not so enthusiastic. They complained that they would have to leave their school and lose their close friends. After talking it over with the family, it was decided that I would accept. The next day I called the Minister and accepted the judicial post.

When the news was announced to the public, I was showered with congratulatory letters and phone calls from many old and new friends— Pat Cameron, Q.C., Senator A. Roebuck, Senator C. Croll, Jim Trotter, MPP, the editors of the two Polish-Toronto presses, numerous lawyers, and Toronto Judges. The only mildly sour note for me was when Dr. Shulman, in a brief article in the Toronto Star, sarcastically criticized Federal appointments, including mine.

When my sister and brother-in-law arrived from Montréal, about December 22nd, 1967, we played games with them like Monopoly, sang Polish folk songs, World War I Polish Army songs, and Christmas carols. Cocktails and food were plentiful. Frank was my fondest relative. Our family visited him and my sister Eugene many summers at their cottage located on Lake Massawippi.

On Christmas Eve, our family along with Frank and Eugene drove to St. Casimir's Parish Church on Roncesvalles Avenue (West Toronto) for Midnight Mass. The Mass, although in Polish, intoned the music of the former Latin Mass I so missed. It was uplifting to the adults but tedious for our girls, as their Polish was rusty to say the least. Back at home the girls opened one Christmas gift and after kisses and hugs, climbed into their beds.

On Christmas morning, around 9:30 a.m., everyone gathered round the tree to unwrap gifts. The children attacked the wrapping paper with zest and high-pitched screams of joy to get to their presents. When all of the gifts had been opened, the living room floor was completely piled with multicoloured wrapping papers, cardboard boxes, and ribbons; it appeared as if a cyclone hit the room!

By 1:00 p.m., relatives and guests arrived. English and Polish Christmas songs were sung and Christmas wishes were exchanged by breaking the host (Oplatek) a long-standing Polish Christmas tradition. I said Grace that night with special prayers for God's blessing on all of us.

In keeping with Polish Christmas dinner tradition we had our cook serve twelve dishes, commencing with "Barsch," turkey and vegetables, ending with honey cake. We always kept one seat unoccupied, for a poor person that might come and join us. It was a magical Christmas, full of love and laughter, that I shall never forget. *Little did I know then what tragedy was soon to befall my daughters and I...*

After the year-end (as we now had a permanent babysitter), Wanda and I attended several parties, where we always enjoyed good dancing — especially tangos and light jazz. I was winding up my practice, closing files, and I transferred unfinished files to reputable lawyers (with the consent of my clients). The Wills I left with my former partner.

I was nervous about my new undertaking and read any book, pamphlet, or digest about the judiciary. In my time, there were no preparatory courses for new judicial "recruits" as have been established in the last ten years. These new courses I understand, teach novitiates in several weeks, the basics of the function of a Judge, his behaviour in and out of Courtroom, approach to lawyers, witnesses, application of law and statutes, etc. Many of these things I learned in my first months as a County Court Judge, very often through deliberations with my judicial colleagues.

In early February, I took my secretary Connie Hubbard out for lunch, as she had been my right-hand for so very many years. She took my leaving harder than I ever thought she would. A decade earlier, I had been asked by my senior partner to interview four applicants for the position of legal secretary. I picked Connie. My senior partner warned me that if she were not as good as required, the partners would blame me. Within months, she proved to be the best legal secretary we ever had.

After the end of 1971, we lost contact. About a year or two later, my former law partner informed me that Connie and her husband had moved out to British Columbia and that she had died shortly after. I am very grateful for all the dedicated years of service Connie gave to us. *May God grant her eternal peace...*

Here Comes the Judge!

The Senior Judge Sydney Clunis and I agreed to have my "swearing in" (as a County Court Judge) to take place at the large Windsor Courtroom on February 23rd, 1968 in the Windsor County Court House. My four girls, Wanda and I and our respective mothers, sisters, legal, and lay-friends attended the ceremony.

Before the swearing in ceremony, many Judges, Crown-Attorneys, and Provincial Judges like Chief Judge Stewart, ministers and priests mingled in an anteroom to the Courtroom. Rev. L. A. Wnuk, parish priest of the Polish Windsor Parish ebulliently congratulated my wife and I. The Windsor and O.P.P. constabulary were present; also adding some colour, pomp, and circumstance were two uniformed Mounted Policemen.

The swearing in ceremony, immaculately prepared in all details by Senior Judge Sydney Clunis, commenced on time and the ceremony went off faultlessly. The Registrar assisted the Chief Judge, A. R. Willmot, who administered the oath of office. Senior Judge Sydney Clunis administered the oath of a Surrogate Judge, and District Judge Lang administered the oath of allegiance. Then His Honour Senior District Court Judge Harold Lang of Stratford proceeded rather swiftly to assist me to take my lawyer's black robe off and assisted me to put my judicial robe on.

Seeing this, my youngest daughter became agitated and later said that she was slightly alarmed for my well-being. Then the orations followed, Chief Judge Arthur R. Willmot from Toronto spoke eloquently on a Judge's impartiality. Judge Harold Lang, our Senior Judge of District

One, thoughtfully articulated that a Judge must be diligent and proper at all times. Judge Lang wished me and my family, health, and much happiness.

Next came my turn.

Senior Judge Sydney Clunis graciously introduced me, setting out a skeletal dissertation, commencing with my birth in Montréal, my activity in both senior and junior Canadian-Polish Congresses, my studies at University of Toronto—Osgoode Hall, my marriage to Wanda, and our family of four lovely girls; he added that I had practised law in Toronto for over a decade.

I was so nervous that I remember very little of my speech. I remember thanking Wanda, my children, my mother, father, and the rest of the family who really had been instrumental in helping me to enter into my chosen profession.

I thanked the preceding speakers for their genuine kindness and whilst I trembled slightly, I promised to do my utmost in the daunting responsibility and capacity as a County Court Judge in the lovely City of Windsor (I *believe* I also promised to be a good Judge!).

At my swearing in, also in attendance were—Judges Bram Beardall from Chatham, Judge Bruce MacDonald, "roving" (travelling) Judge in Windsor, and Dr. Frank DeMarco, member of a prominent family of Canadian-Italian Windsorites. A reception followed, sponsored by the Essex Law Association at the Windsor County Court House.

After the reception of February 23rd, 1968, Senior Judge Sydney Clunis and his charming wife Freddie held another small reception for Wanda and I at their stately home in South Windsor. Wanda and her girlfriends brought some Polish delicacies, appetizers, petit fours (ala Polonaise) Ponczkis, honey, and poppy seed cakes, which were consumed with great relish by all! Several Judges were in attendance and quite a number of Windsor and Toronto lawyers. Wanda and I thanked our hosts, the Judges, and friends and took leave by 11:00 p.m.

A former classmate of mine complained that there were so few "ethnic" Judges in our province. I disagreed with him; I cited S. Roberts (Ukrainian) Kurisko, Stortini, W. Luchak (deceased), E. Loukedelis, Borins, and Grossberg, naming but a few. However, in the early 1970s it is true that Anglophone Judges were in *majority* in all the levels of Courts.

Judge Bruce MacDonald shared an interesting and highly dramatic war experience that he had in World War II. As the Lieutenant-Colonel

Commander of the Essex Scottish Regiment, he was appointed to the Allied inquiry on War Crimes against Canadian soldiers in 1944. He presided over the sensational trial of Major General Kurt Meyer, accused of murdering a minimum of 48 Canadian prisoners of war.

The German General was the commander of the savage 12th S.S. Panzer Division—"Hitler Youth." After a lengthy trial, the General was found guilty on several counts and ordered executed. The Commander of Canadian occupation forces commuted the sentence to life imprisonment. Kurt Meyer was transferred to the New Brunswick's Dorchester Penitentiary. After almost five years of incarceration, he was transferred to a British zone prison and he was pardoned in 1954.

Canadians were shocked and a coast-to-coast outcry ensued; the fact that at least 48 Canadian war prisoners were shot, run over by S.S. tanks, and the General that gave the command was allowed to go free. It was explained that the Western allies and the U.S.A. were now courting Germany to re-arm, and prepare for a probable Communist attack to enslave Western Europe; an atomic Russian attack was highly possible. The late Judge B. MacDonald published a book in 1954 entitled "The Trial of Kurt Meyer."

The late Bruce J. S. MacDonald, prior to being elevated to a Judgeship, had been the Senior Crown Prosecutor in Windsor. I have been told that in those days he was a very tough prosecutor. His stout endurance put him in the same category as the then two Senior Crown-Attorneys we had in Toronto (1954–1968): Henry Bull, Q.C., and Arthur Klein, Q.C.

It is sad for me to note that our Senior Judge Sydney Clunis, Chief Provincial Judge Stewart, Chief Judge Arthur R. Willmot, Judge Harold Lang—Senior Judge of District One, Judge Beardall, and Judge B. MacDonald, who were all in attendance at my February 1968 swearing in ceremony, by 1989 had all been taken by the grim reaper.

Sunday, following my swearing in, our family attended a Mass at Our Lady of Guadalupe Church on Wyandotte Street East. A friend of my mother suggested we go to Joe Muir's in Detroit for lunch. We agreed and he and his wife drove their car and we followed. We found it to be a delectable eating-place. The children had small steaks, as fish was not their forte.

Our mother's friends were the "Kwiecinski's." Our parents befriended them in the 1930s in Montréal. Mr. K. was a pianist "par excellence." In the 1917 Russian revolution, Kwiecinski was a lieutenant in the Tsarist cavalry who had fought the Germans and Austro-Hungarians, although he was Polish. Later, he volunteered to the "White Army" to fight the Bolsheviks.

His unit was mangled in late autumn 1918, in the outskirts of the Port of Odessa on the Black Sea. He and a comrade somehow managed to change out of their uniforms, as they bartered with some gypsies for old civilian clothes. With difficulty, they reached Romania, and eventually through Bulgaria — Istanbul, Turkey.

Eventually Mr. K. procured work as a Russian pianist in an exiled White Russian cabaret in Istanbul. In Canada, my parents and neighbours assisted him and his wife. That day, our host and Wanda played a medley of classical works. At the end, Wanda intoned Chopin's "Polonaise Militaire" and all present were moved by her stirring rendition. I was very proud of her and loved her deeply.

Later, Wanda and the children left for Toronto in her Camaro. My sister and mother taxied to the railway station for their train to Montréal. I left shortly thereafter to drive to my hotel, the Holiday Inn by the Detroit River. I became lost and had to ask a policeman for directions. He saw my Judge's license plates and courteously said, "Sir, Judge, follow me." It felt great! When we reached the hotel, I thanked the police officer profusely; I slept extremely well that night.

My first morning at the Judge's chambers at the Court House, I arrived at 9:30 a.m. A dozen or more lawyers swarmed my office. They asked me to sign their ex-parte orders. An ex-parte order is an application in a judicial proceeding, usually by one party in the absence of the other party, often referred to as an "uncontested order." As Court was scheduled to be in session at 10:00 a.m., it was impossible for me to read and sanction all these orders. I warned these lawyers that if any one of them misleads me, it would be their first and last time to have me execute their orders.

As time went by, I began to come to work earlier at the Court House to examine these applications carefully. I discovered that one or two lawyers erred in the wording of their ex-parte orders. I would have our secretary call these "sluggish lawyers" to see me. Confronted with their mistakes, they would apologize. I would tell them that was their last chance. These irregularities were not numerous but repetitive; however they did last until the time of my retirement in 1991.

After Court hours, I was kept busy looking for a home to purchase, with the assistance of a realtor. It was no easy task.

During the first weeks of March 1968, I was assigned to the Small Claims Court. I sat an entire week in Windsor deciding non-appealable and appealable cases and judgment summons hearings.

The plaintiffs varied from contract cases, to promissory notes, damages for assaults — the whole rostrum of legal issues. The following week I attended Small Claims Court trials all over the County. I had to drive from Windsor to Amherstburg, Belle River, Leamington, Kingsville, and Essex — several towns located in the County of Essex. In all of my twenty-three years of sitting as a Small Claims Court Judge, I never shouted, "shut up" to litigants, or called them "stupid" as some American Small Claim Judges dramatically do on "television shows." Unlike the American televised "Small Claims Courts," our Court judgments are subject to appeal.

It was announced recently on FOX TV, that a former American family court Judge signed a 10-year contract with FOX for 100 million US dollars! No lawyers are allowed in the TV courtrooms; the Judges assume the roles of lawyers and gallop through the cases, dispensing entertainment, not justice. There is no appeal process set up for the cases which are "tried" on air; however, litigants are remunerated for their "once in a lifetime" appearance on national television. In my long and vast experience — *Canadian Courts dispense justice, not theatricals.*

Chapter Three

The Windsor Era

"They Brought Me Bitter News to Hear and Bitter Tears to Shed..."

(Heraclitus)

L ate every Friday afternoon I drove from Windsor, home to Toronto, and spent the weekend with Wanda and the children. I shared with Wanda some of the more interesting, and at times funny cases I presided over in my new position as a Windsor Federal Judge. On weekends, Wanda played the piano, very moving selections, varying from Bach, Sibelius, Chopin, Beethoven, and others. We shared photos with the children of the swearing-in ceremony. The children were still not happy at the thought of moving.

One Friday in late March 1968, I arrived home to find Wanda ill. She could not walk, and had a stabbing pain in her abdomen. I called a doctor friend, who arranged for admission to our local hospital. On admission, the doctor examining her cited that it was probably diverticulitis. Within days, she was operated on. The operation lasted three hours, which seemed like days. This woman was my sweet angel.

The chief surgeon called me in. In a nervous voice, I asked him, "Serious? Grave? Not Serious?" The surgeon looked straight into my eyes and in a trembling voice said, "It is cancer, of the mesenteric wall. She has several, maybe six months to live." He said, "Sorry, there is nothing we can do," and he left the room. I was stunned, unbelieving; I felt like an arrow had pierced my heart and my brain; my darling Wanda that I loved so deeply, the mother of our four children, to slip away from us all so soon. It was too much to bear. I sat and cried alone in the hospital room and lost track of time, of everything. Finally, I made my way home by cab, said nothing to my children, locked myself in our bedroom, and sobbed all night long in the lonely darkness as my Angel of Love lay mortally wounded in a hospital bed.

The Windsor Judges and the Chief Ontario Judge Willmot granted me an exemption from judicial duties when informed of Wanda's fatal illness. However, in an attempt to keep occupied, I sat as a replacement in Sarnia and Chatham. Shortly after, Chief Judge Willmot agreed that I should spend time now with my children and especially with my dying wife.

In July 1968, all of the family spent weekends at Wasaga Beach located on the shore of Nottawasaga Bay, at a friend's cottage. Sometime in mid-July, I drove home via Highway 400 with the children jammed in the back seat. As we approached Etobicoke, Wanda rolled the window down and threw up several times. She used a handful of Kleenex to wipe up, and then began sobbing uncontrollably.

When we arrived home, I put the children to bed. I helped Wanda into the shower, assisted her to slip into her nightgown, and settled her into bed. She lightly groaned during the night twice, but seemed to sleep comfortably. The next morning she said that the builder who renovated our bedroom did a great job (The renovation was a long time ago). She spoke incoherently, at times, other times foolishly.

In my sequestered library, I telephoned her doctor and told him what happened the night before, and in the morning. He instructed me to drive her to Princess Margaret Hospital right away. I arranged for the girls' maternal grandmother to take charge of them. I drove Wanda in her new red Camaro and delivered her to the nurses at Princess Margaret Hospital.

Wanda looked very pale and was extremely weak, unable to walk. The hospital staff placed her in a comfortable room. As her stomach (I found out after the fact) was now cancerous, she could not eat solids. She went through a round of chemotherapy. A staff doctor each day asked if she had pain in her "tummy" or threw up. Each time she said no. She and I thought that it was a good sign. Subsequently, I found out the opposite was true.

For the last four weeks, I spent the whole day at the bedside of my beloved Wanda. I brought her many long Popsicles day after day. She enjoyed them immensely, as she could take no solids. Then one day, she turned to me and asked to see the children. I drove them to the hospital. By this time, they knew about their mother's fatal illness. I had to be brave and fight back tears as she hugged them, one at a time, saying in her own way goodbye to each of them. As the cancer spread, Wanda became weaker every day. I spent the entire day with her on August 17th and 18th, 1968. On August 18th, 1968 in the early afternoon, she gave me a gentle whisper of a kiss.

She was very sleepy as I said, "See you tomorrow darling." She limply waved her right hand. That was to be the last time that I saw her alive. Around 10:00 p.m. that night, I was called by a hospital official to come quickly. I drove with her mother. She was laid in a large room, and the Chaplain stood next to Wanda and a nurse. The nurse told us gently she was dead.

Thus, my beloved Wanda expired in the hands of angels…

At Wanda's funeral parlour, the people were extremely numerous, ranging from a Federal-Minister, M.P.'s, law partners, to down-to-earth friends. Friends like the friend of a family who, seeing my depression, said to me in Polish, *"Nic niema zlego – co na dobrego nie wyjdzie."* Translated this means, "There is nothing bad which cannot turn to good."

At the Funeral Mass, a Polish-Canadian priest and an Irish-Canadian priest celebrated Mass together. Numerous people attended, including the Chief Judge of Ontario.

Wanda was buried next to her father, who was buried in 1950. I was able to show little external emotion throughout this trying time, as my physician had prescribed some tranquillizing pills.

One of our dear friends, Aleck Cowe, arranged the traditional luncheon after the funeral. I was driven to the restaurant where it was being held, and upon entering, I retreated at the sight of revelry and had to be driven home.

Senior Judge Arthur Willmot of Ontario invited me to lunch about a week after the funeral. He proposed to me that if I wanted to, I could stay on as a County Court Judge in Toronto. I thanked him and said I'd sleep on it. The next morning I called Judge Willmot with sincere thanks – I declined. In early September, I drove back to the Windsor Court House, and whilst driving on the 401 I hummed the song, *"Those were the days my friend, you thought they'd never end..."* repeatedly, fighting back tears in my eyes.

My sister Reggie and I, a week after Wanda's funeral, visited her grave and noticed that parts of it had shoddy sod. We drove to a nursery nearby, bought some fresh vivid green sod, a large bag of black earth, and replaced it. I shovelled out the old sod and watered the new sod.

When we were about to leave, Robert my nephew (Reggie's son) arrived on his motorcycle all the way from Montréal. Reggie scolded him for not telling her before. I warned him how dangerous it was to make such a long trip on a mere motorcycle. That evening, Reggie, at our Edgehill home, prepared a steak dinner with vegetables and dessert for all of us. My daughters helped with the dishes.

The next morning after breakfast, Robert drove back on his motorcycle back to Montréal (a month and a day later after Wanda's tragic demise). In the late evening of October 19th, 1968, my sister Eugene called. She informed me that Reggie's son Robert, my nephew (in his first year at Sir William's College) was killed in a motorcycle accident. She promised that she would fill me in about funeral arrangements the next day.

I was so shaken up that I don't remember which of my daughters, if any, flew with me to Montréal for Robert's funeral. At the D'Allaire Funeral Parlour, I ran into Reggie's former husband, crippled and shuffling as he walked. I recall how father and mother pleaded with my sister Reggie not to marry him. Even our Pastor, Father Bernard, tried to put some sense into her. However, they went ahead and married anyway and the marriage ended after two years.

The funeral was held at St. Mary's Church. The new Polish Priest, Father Francis, celebrated the Funeral Mass and attended at the open grave. When he finished singing the last prayer for the dead and reciting the "Pater Noster," he grabbed a shovel imbedded in the pile of dirt and hurled three shovels full of earth on top of Robert's coffin that lay at the bottom of the grave.

The only time I had seen such a gesture as this, was when I was about seven-years-old, in the Laurentian village of Val David, Québec, which was effected by a French-Canadian Priest. Before leaving for Windsor, I contacted René Talbot, a French-Canadian lawyer who was a classmate at

D'Arcy McGee High School in the early 1940s. He told me that he would take care of Reggie's claim.

I left for home assured that René would do his best. My sister and I were constantly in contact about Robert's case; I also spoke with René by phone often. One witness saw the defendant in his automobile, which failed to stop at a sign and struck Robert on his motorcycle.

This crash propelled Robert, bike and all, underneath a parked car. He was pronounced dead on arrival at the hospital. Reggie worked as a stenographer for the Notaries "Solomon and Malus." They were a Godsend to her during these difficult times and cared for her as their own daughter.

René Talbot sued the defendant and his insurance company. This dragged on for about three years. At the end of all this stress, poor Reggie, for the loss of her beloved Robert, received a niggardly sum of $1,400.00. It seems that Québec car insurance law is very different from our Common-Law system.

Mr. René Talbot handled Reggie's affairs when she died on October 19th, 1979, eleven years after Robert; strangely, it was on the same day and the same month, October 19th, 1968. She had left behind a holograph Will and all of the surviving three sisters and two brothers (including myself) agreed to have the Staniszewski cottage and Montréal home sold, the net proceeds to be divided between the five siblings. The agreement was in writing, signed by all, witnessed by lawyer René Talbot.

However, it was not to be that easy. One of our sister's husbands chose litigation. The case dragged on and on and finalized with the Staniszewski $50,000.00 home being awarded to a "niece" and the $10,000.00 cottage divided between three siblings.

Some say Reggie was tricked into writing the holograph Will and naming the beneficiary that she did, because she was afraid to reside alone and the promise to live with them was broken, which frightened her to death. Who knows the true story? Her wishes went to the grave with her...

Return to Judicial Duties

After completing my judicial duties for the day, some late afternoons I continued my search for a home for the girls and myself. At first, the children had one of my sisters looking after them. At Christmas time, when we all greatly needed to have at least the semblance of Christmas, church, Christmas tree, presents, and family dinner, we had none of this. The girls and I did the best we could, but I found it grim. I still could not acquiesce with the loss of my Angel of Love.

That sister seemed at the time to have been the best choice to care for my daughters. As time progressed, I wondered; in retrospect I feel like my daughters may have felt that, she replaced their mother too soon, which was to cause me great pain down the road. When my sister had to leave, my elderly mother filled the gap until about January 1969. Several months later, I chose a large home abutting the Detroit River on Riverside Drive East. We moved into it in mid-April 1969. During the daytime hours, when I sat as a Judge fulfilling my duties, they were fulfilling times for me. Back at home in the evenings, alone with the girls, I was still shell-shocked at our sudden cruel loss of Wanda.

Minor tasks like shopping for food at the A&P, clothing stores, etc., felt as if I was struggling in ten-feet of muddy water—depressed, disinterested, half-alive, and barely cognizant of my responsibilities to my four young daughters. Every Sunday, in an effort to connect with a higher good, we attended Mass at Our Lady of Guadalupe as a family.

The Senior Judge Sydney Clunis once mentioned that a nice lady could be just what the girls and I needed. She was introduced to me. The only manner in which she was helpful was doing the grocery shopping occasionally. She helped me find a cook—Mrs. Huggard—who also acted as a nanny. Judge Sydney Clunis' kind idea didn't lead to anything more than that. My sister Reggie visited often and by the end of 1969, I had begun the long climb out of my shell.

Another matchmaker was a priest. He had a Polish widow invite me over for tea one day. I reckoned she must have been some years older than I was. She was very articulate in Polish and English, good looking, neat, and pleasant but she did not light a spark in me. There was another well-intentioned matchmaker, a Toronto friend of Wanda's, who visited me several times, with her widowed niece; that did not work out either.

In the spring of 1970, Andrea, our youngest, was in an automobile accident and suffered a fractured femur. At Hôtel-Dieu Hospital, a cast was put on. We were sent home and told to come back in about six weeks for the removal of the cast.

The children were busy at school and with homework. On weekends, we would shop at the A&P and/or N&D grocery stores. Sometimes we visited the Detroit Zoo. Other times we drove to "Jack Miners Migratory Bird Sanctuary" or spent a few hours at Colasanti's nursery. The children slowly acquired friends their age. I began to come alive once more, and befriended some neighbours in our immediate neighbourhood.

With the onset of the summer holidays of 1970, Gayle, Camille, and Michelle were anxious to leave for Val David, Québec, to spend their holidays with their grandmother and Aunt Reggie. Reggie picked them up and drove them to the Laurentian cottage. When Andrea's cast was removed, I decided to drive with her to Val David, Québec. As her leg still pained her, I laid her on the back seat of my car for her to be comfortable. We stopped several times along the way for refreshments. After about a seven-hour drive, we arrived at my mother's cottage.

Mother took care of the light cooking and Reggie and I prepared most dinners. The girls helped with the washing of dishes and the clean up. On an average of twice a week, we would go out for dinner, at St. Agathe and its surrounding area. There was no restaurant in the village of Val David, Québec unless you were a paying guest residing at the hotel "La Sapinaire." Reggie came over every Friday around 6:00 p.m., and brought a variety of roasted chicken, cooked vegetables, cakes, and biscuits from a restaurant about a quarter of a mile from us. With Reggie around, everyone had fun. She told our girls repeatedly, *"Do not fear, Reggie's here."*

The highlight of our holiday in the Laurentians ended when all of the adults and some close friends attended a huge buffet on Saturday evening at the St. Marguerite Hotel—a grand table lavishly spread with whatever your pallet craved, arranged in Victorian plates, silver goblets, and cutlery. This was a buffet worthy of a Tsar of Imperial Russia, or an Emperor of Austria-Hungary. We had to control our appetites not to overeat. This was and still is the crowning jewel of "eateries" in Québec's Laurentians!

The night before we left to go back home to Windsor, we celebrated with an evening of fireworks, thanking mother and Reggie for their hospitality and all the fun that we had. This festive salute lasted well over an hour. The next day after breakfast, hugs, goodbyes, and thanks were exchanged by all. With all five of us aboard, I honked the horn and started our seven-hour drive back home.

Once we were back in Windsor, school-time commenced for the girls. The two older ones walked to Riverside High School; the younger two walked to local elementary schools. The children were well fed by our cook; one morning I saw her fry eggs up with toast and jam, which they loved! My work that fall consisted of performing marriages, conducting mechanic lien trials, criminal trials, Lower Court Appeals, civil jury and non-jury trials, bail hearings, adoptions, motions, family law, divorces, and other matters. In about 1974, our Senior Judge made me a "Master" of our Court, adding even more stress to my judicial workload.

"...True Love hath no bounds... but is immortal in its wing-ed flight..."
(T. P.)

We began to attend Holy Trinity Polish Church as a family. It was a little further than the Guadalupe Church was, but here we were exposed to the Polish language and our heritage. We made new friends, the Monsignor Lawrence Wnuk, P.A., the Polish Ursuline Nuns, and befriended many Polish families. I enrolled my youngest daughter in the Polish language classes that the Nuns taught two evenings a week. On several Saturdays before Easter Sunday, some of the Nuns even came to our home and helped the girls to decorate Easter eggs, cut out angels, whilst reading Lenten and Easter stories to them.

In the late spring of 1970, I was invited by the Longs (who lived right across the street from us) to a party. Betty Long, who was a teacher, introduced me to her several guests who turned out to all be teachers, consultants, or principals.

This party is where I met Tevis Bagnell, the beautiful lady who was to become my present wife.

Tevis stood out from the other guests. She was petite, had beautifully coiffed hair and gorgeous lips, eyes, and face; in short, I saw in her a version of the Greek Goddess "Athena." As this was a party of teachers, consultants, and principals, I did not have much occasion to converse with Tevis that first time. I left the party early but could not get Tevis out of my mind that night. I had become fascinated by her charm and beauty. The next morning, our housekeeper fed the children as usual and off to school they went. After toast and coffee, I began my drive to the Courthouse.

It wasn't long before the 1970 summer holidays had commenced. Our neighbour from across the street, Mrs. Betty Long, helped me out by shopping for the girls — summer blouses, swimming trunks, shoes, etc. on Ouellette Avenue and Ottawa Street. Before heading out on our annual summer holiday, I arranged to have our housekeeper stay on at our house and provided her with ample money for wages and food while we were gone.

With my girls in tow, I drove westerly on the 401, by way of Manning Road, made the usual necessary stops, and about seven-and-a-half hours later arrived at the Laurentian cottage, which my sister Reggie idealistically called "Shangri-La." It was always good to land there — like a breath of fresh air.

After breaking bread with mother, Reggie, and the children, I laid down for a nap, exhausted after the long drive. I had not been able to get the goddess "Athena" out of my mind since that party. Here at the cottage, away from all the stresses and mental pressures of my work, there was ample time to daydream about Tevis and a possible future together...

The children made new friends. I engaged a French-Canadian lady painter in Val David, Québec to create a painting of our Riverside Drive, Windsor home from large coloured photos. She produced a marvellous piece of art, which still hangs in our present home in Tecumseh. We engaged in the same ritual as our last visit.

The night before our departure, we built a large bonfire and celebrated a lovely summer with colourful fireworks; including a glittering, awe inspiring Québec "Fleur-de-lis." That was our goodbye to Val David and Québec that summer. All the way back to Windsor, my heart was filled with longing to see "Athena" once more.

By the fall 1970 opening of the Courts, I had summoned up enough courage to telephone, and ask Tevis out for lunch with me downtown. She acted surprised to hear from me on the phone, but readily accepted.

That lunch was the beginning of our romance (September 1970); I began to lunch with Tevis several times a week after that second meeting. I regularly visited her apartment in South Windsor where her parents and her son by a previous marriage resided. I recall that in those "early days," six or seven girlfriends of Tev used to drop in casually (as they lived in the same apartment building) to diplomatically look over Tevis' judicial beau.

Several times that fall, whilst driving home no later than 10:30 p.m., I found myself starting to fall asleep at the wheel. It was some time later before I found out that it was a common side effect. This was of a medication I was taking at that time, prescribed to me by a doctor. Had it not been for my determination to fight off a dreadful and persistent desire to sleep, willing my eyes to stay wide open, I might have left my four daughters orphans that fall.

The 1970 October Crisis

When the 1970 Québec October crisis erupted, I was particularly disturbed by the news, as I had lived for twenty years in East Montréal. I also had blood relatives still residing in the province. The bombings and kidnappings worried me greatly. When our Prime Minister sent in the army, under the "War Measures Act" into Québec, I sighed with some degree of relief and wrote to him personally about my worries, congratulating him on his bold step.

In due time, he acknowledged my letter. As you may recall, Québec refused to free about seventeen fiery F.L.Q. members, nor to negotiate with the F.L.Q. capture of James Cross, nor Pierre LaPorte (Québec's Labour Minister). One of the members of the F.L.Q. arrested was J. Lanctot, whose father was a henchman of Québec's Fascist-Nazi party during World War II.

Although Québec's Pierre LaPorte was brutally murdered, it is ironic that Cross' life was exchanged for half-a-million dollars and that a number of terrorists, along with their spouses were all flown as part of a deal to Fidel Castro's Communist Cuba. At the end of this mess, the Prime Minister was to have said — *"If a few want to throw bombs and kidnap important individuals, and if that is allowed to happen, then it is the end of freedom in this country."*

With that, the seeds of an anti-Canada movement were sown. They were nurtured to this day by ex-Liberal René Levesque (now deceased), calling Anglo-Québecers "Rhodesians," Parizeau (famous for his lament "We lost because of money and ethnics..."), Lucien Bouchard, formerly an NDP, later Liberal, and then Mulroney's Ambassador to France and Conservative Minister. In recent years, he became the standard-bearer, not for "Separatists" but for "Sovereigntists," a more devious word in my opinion...

Bouchard quit, just as Separatism seemed to be shrivelling out of existence. The Québec problem has distracted me repeatedly over the years, because of my great love and affection for "la Belle Province." I came to realize how "narrow nationalism," nurtured by a small group of desperate individuals, both in France and Québec was attempting to revive a "Nouvelle France" lost in 1759.

One tenet of the Separatists was always the protection of the French language, from a North-American English sea. No Federal or Provincial governments of Canada to my knowledge have ever legislated laws against the development of the French language. The Francophone enclaves spread across Canada have flourishing French schools, in all probability thanks to their municipal Anglo Councils.

The Engagement of Tevis and I

Falling in love with Tevis, I began to feel magnificently reincarnated, like "Lazarus risen from the dead." Apart from lunching regularly, we often crossed over to Detroit to the Fisher Theatre, to see "Mazowsze," a Polish dance ensemble, or to hear Nana Mouskouri, the famous Greek songstress in Windsor. We attended a concert of Ivan Rebroff singing Gypsy songs, and because of the preposterous cost of the tickets, he was aptly nicknamed locally as "Rebroff the rip off." Although my working life continued to be as stressful as my very first trial, two days after having been sworn in, I began to feel a little more at ease at work, better able to cope with the never-ending demands put on me by both family and judicial duties.

In December that year, lawyers continuously adjourned most of their cases on my December calendar. This gave me a much-needed chance to do some special Christmas shopping for my girls, for Tevis and her family. Unable to bring myself to do so since 1968, I went out on my own and I bought Christmas cards and stamps.

I bought a beautiful diamond engagement ring for my bride-to-be at Birk's that Christmas. Her father immediately gave his blessing to us with a fiat of "be good to her." After I had formally asked him for her hand in marriage, Tevis and I agreed to hold our engagement on New Year's Day. I recall that Tevis called her sister Lally and told her the good news. When informed that I had *four* daughters, there was stark silence on the other end of the line…cautious admonitions to Tevis from her adoring sister.

Tevis had a great artistic talent—she painted on twelve hollow lacquered eggs, "The Twelve Gifts" from the carol "The Twelve Days of Christmas," starting with a "partridge in a pear tree" and ending with the "twelve drummers drumming." These became ornaments on our Christmas tree that year.

I selected a tree once again, and we all decorated it as a family. It was good to be in the Christmas spirit again, and I thanked God for sending me Tevis. Tevis' family spent Christmas dinner at our home that year, bringing with them a turkey, the trimmings, and all kinds of delicious savouries and sweets.

The adults toasted Christmas with bubbly wine. Everyone thanked Tevis' mother for the savoury dinner and desserts. The children rushed to open the gifts after dessert and tea. Following the excitement of opening gifts, we all joined in to sing Christmas carols. The Windsor Star supplied its readers with sheets of about 30 favourite Christmas carols. It was the best Christmas my daughters and I had celebrated together since 1968.

Then on New Year's Day 1971 at our home—Tevis, her parents, son, and our family congregated in the large library. After having wished each other a happy 1971, we chatted for a while. I said a few words, toasted Tevis, and her family with bubbly wine. Tevis' dad toasted both of us back.

I solemnly placed the engagement ring on Tevis' finger and a burst of applause resounded at our table as I kissed Tev, celebrating our love in front of the whole family. We feasted on tasty roast beef that night, followed by chocolate cake, ice cream, and tea. Tevis and I embraced, staring lovingly into each other's eyes. Expressions of joy and congratulations once again filled the room. My daughters, in keeping with the spirit of the evening, showered us with good will.

I had my doubts later on, as to whether or not they were completely accepting of our engagement, but I loved Tevis and I strongly believed that with the passage of time we would become family.

After my engagement to Tevis, I felt spiritually uplifted, and blessed that Tevis had agreed to be my wife. With only a few days of holidays left, we decided to drive to a small ski lodge east of Detroit. It was fun— our dollar was worth $1.05 to the American dollar at that time!

We stopped at a snack bar and Andrea was the only girl to drink hot chocolate. Driving back that night, Andrea cuddled up to Tevis on the car seat. After crossing the border, Andrea threw-up all over Tevis' fur coat. Tev had truly become part of the family...

Wedding Bells!

After our engagement, Tevis and I saw a lot more of each other. Sometimes after school, Tevis would come over to our home, help Gayle and Michelle with their painting, and assist the other two girls with their school assignments. We would all eat dinner (prepared by our indispensable Mrs. Huggard), and then sit and chat on the couch downstairs after the girls had been put to bed. There was lots of hugging and kissing on the couch in those days! It was a very respectable courtship.

Tev and I both aspired our wedding to be simple, with a modest reception at home. Her parents organized the reception. Tev, although Anglican, was divorced and it would take a long time for a church dispensation. I had a meeting with our Parish Priest who dispelled all worries and he urged me to marry with his blessing. When I married my now deceased Wanda, who was a Baptist, she had to adopt the Roman Catholic faith in order to marry me. How a few decades had changed Christian outlook as to marriage.

As a result, we settled on being married in a United Church. The date chosen was July 3rd, 1971. It seemed to me, in the winter of 1971, that July 3rd, 1971 was as far away as July 1983. In an effort to look more dapper for the wedding, I embarked on the "Scarsdale Diet" and lost about 20-pounds. I had a new suit made to order, bought some summer suits, shorts, shirts, shoes, and sandals etc. as we had chosen Bermuda as our honeymoon destination.

A few days before our wedding set for July 3rd, 1971, Tev's sister and her husband arrived with their children, as did my mother and my sister Reggie.

Tevis was resplendent in her white gown and jewellery. Her face was radiant—I truly thought of her as the Goddess Athena. The girls wore white; Kurt (reluctantly) wore a dark jacket.

We were married at the Riverside United Church. The bridal song was played, the ceremony took place, and with the exchange of rings, we heard the Minister pronounce, *"In sickness and in health, till death do you part."* I shuddered inside when "death" was spoken.

We kissed tenderly in front of the small gathering, two people happily engulfed in love. We held the reception at home; about 30 people attended — Windsor Judges, lawyers, a doctor, an architect and his wife, and a few neighbours and their wives. Two of my very dear friends, along with their wives came from Toronto. In keeping with our wishes, it was small, private, and family orientated.

Tev's mother chose a fabulous caterer. By late afternoon, we received a grand send-off, after the traditional throwing of Tev's bouquet and we left by cab to our first stop—Detroit's Ponchartrain Hotel—where we indulged in Mum's champagne and savoured petit fours. The next morning, after enjoying a light breakfast served in our room, we dressed and tried to pack between kisses. We ordered a taxi to the Detroit airport and we were off on our Bermuda honeymoon!

A Love Poem to Tevis

<u>*My Dearest Tev*</u>

A passing glance from you and my will is dissolved.
A quiver of your lovely lips and I am enthralled.
A glow on your angelic cheeks and I am embalmed,
By your spell, that has encompassed my soul.
Never, never shall this end, is my feverish prayer
Yet I know that at the river Styx we shall part forever.

November 26th, 1970.

"Television—Final Conflict"

Having arrived in Windsor, the girls seemed to settle quickly back into their school routines. Tevis and I returned to our mutual professions. The girls gradually seemed to accept Tevis as "a mother" rather than a "stepmother." I could see that our cook/housekeeper was delighted. Both Tevis and I were rather distressed at some low marks that the children scored in some subjects, so I took the hard-nosed stance of cancelling their privileges to watch TV. They disobeyed (of course) and persisted in being seduced by the magic box, to the detriment of their school assignments.

One afternoon when I came home from work, I finally disconnected the TV set. It was brought to my attention by our housekeeper that the children had reconnected the TV and were watching it, disconnecting it whenever they heard one of their parent's cars pull into the driveway. When I caught on to their "slick intrigue," I removed several television tubes in their absence, successfully "neutering" the set. Camille, a few days later, found the tubes and reinstalled them, much to my amazement, and the girls resumed "watching the box" to my chagrin.

One day I decided to come home early and caught them red-handed! I felt I had no recourse but to lock it away in a closet, until a time when their grades had improved. The housekeeper was the guardian of the key. Thus, by sheer will, mine against theirs, we ended the battle of the television and their grades soon improved...

Death in the Witness Box

I attended at Belle River Small Claims Court. The list of cases was lengthy. After disposing of a number of smaller cases, the clerk called out a case concerning a certain dispute over the title of land. The plaintiff was an elderly gentleman—the defendant a Roman Catholic Priest. Both parties were represented by able Counsel.

The plaintiff was called to the witness box, sworn, and then abruptly proceeded to collapse on the floor. A medic who happened to be in the audience, subpoenaed for another case, rushed to the prostrate plaintiff, and on finding no pulse, attempted CPR, but to no avail. After about 20 tense minutes, the medic announced to the court that the plaintiff was dead.

The defendant Priest automatically approached the body to minister the Last Rites to the deceased when the deceased's nephew yelled at the Priest, "Don't you dare... you @#$%^$#@." The Priest stepped back. An ambulance arrived, and the attendants removed the body. I never did find out how that land dispute was resolved.

Christmas 1971

By late November 1971, the commercialism of Christmas had us shopping early for gifts. My sister Reggie arrived from Montréal to spend the Christmas season with us. We had to keep Reggie busy, as she had lost her son a short time before. She helped in the preparation of our Christmas turkey. Tevis prepared the English Pudding and our housekeeper did the rest. After Midnight Mass, each one of us opened one Christmas present. On Christmas morning, the remaining presents were opened, and hugs and kisses exchanged. The telephone rang all morning long—Tev's sister and family from Vancouver, my oldest sister, and my mother from Montréal.

Tevis' parents arrived by mid-day. I served champagne. We sang Christmas carols. Our girls started with "Holy Night" followed by "Little Drummer Boy" and "Minuit Chrétien's." Then we sang "Oh Christmas Tree, Oh Christmas Tree," ensemble and other popular songs right up until dinner.

Tev's dad said Grace. I broke a piece of wafer (Oplatek) and individually wished everyone present a Merry Christmas, starting with Tevis. In the spirit of an old Polish tradition, the wafer is broken with the closest family member; salutations for health, wealth, and prosperity are spoken, then the wafer is broken jointly with the remaining members of the family and good wishes are spread all around for the coming year.

Later that evening, I didn't seem to feel very well. I sat down for a few moments, hoping that it would pass and when I tried to stand up, I fainted. I half-awoke in a hospital bed the next morning. I went through a ream of blood tests, x-rays, etc. Nothing definitive showed up through the tests at that point. A doctor finally came over to my bed and stated that what I needed was a good long rest…

My darling Tevis visited me faithfully every evening, thank God, as her visits ameliorated my spirits greatly. After several days, I was discharged, given a script for medication, and told to remain at home and rest for some weeks. After the ordered rest, I was told that I could resume my work as usual at the Court House.

I returned to my Court duties a few weeks after Christmas in February 1972. My calendar of cases was extremely full; however, I kept my pace at work slower than it had been before my rest. Within two weeks, I had returned to my normal workload. I began to have lunch with Tevis again almost regularly. The odd time I lunched with the late Bernie Newman, MPP, or several of our Judges. Tevis and I went often to dine at, "Joe Muir's Restaurant," located in Detroit with neighbours and friends. "Joe Muir's" used to serve the best seafood in the U.S.A. and Windsor. In mid–1972, Tevis and I invited several Judges and their wives, together with the whole Court staff, to a cocktail party we held at our home on Riverside Drive. It turned out to be a great success.

Most Court cases generally slipped by quite agreeably, but were always peppered with some unpleasant and nasty ones. I had a Judgment Week in May. I caught up on my sparse reserve judgments. Easter was celebrated in our usual manner with all of the family. My sister Reggie was unable to come, as Mother was ill in Montréal. Reggie was fortunate in working for "Solomon and Malus" — Montréal Jewish Notaries who treated her like family. The Friday before 1972 Victoria Day, we had a "Judge's Meeting," which was very productive.

When school and Court closed, my sister Reggie arrived and drove all our daughters to Mother's cottage in Val David in the Québec Laurentians. Tevis and I booked a flight to Mexico City and arranged "Luxury Hotels" for ten days. The trip was short lived — the hotels were second class, the food mediocre at best, and I came down with "Montezuma's Revenge" on the second day of the trip. We headed back home.

With September on our backs, our children returned to their respective schools, Tevis and I back to work. The first day, Judge Bruce MacDonald burst into my office and informed me that I was upheld by the Court of Appeal in a motor vehicle case I had recently adjudicated. He was jovial and sincere. I thanked him profoundly. A good way to start my fall sittings I thought. How wrong it proved to be. I held a meeting with some members of the Essex Bar Association concerning handling of Civil Court Lists. There was concern that Civil Lists were too swiftly forced on by the Senior Judge. We arranged to have our Master handle the Civil Lists, which he did, and this proved to be more satisfactory.

On November 4th, 1972, Tevis' father, Mr. Daniel MacLean died suddenly of a heart attack. He was 72-years-old. We were all shocked, but especially my dear Tevis, her mother, and her family. The family of Tevis arrived. They arranged for funeral services and the burial. It was a sad day and a big blow to this closely-knit family. We had a family wake of sorts at our home. I could not deal with family funerals too well because of my past grief, but I found myself uplifted by the deep, yet noble sorrow displayed by Tevis' family. I tried my hardest to accept that we are all ephemeral and all destined to meet our God eventually...

The school advised us that our eldest, Gayle, had been skipping school full days at a time. Before we could confront her, she ran away from home. She turned 18 and I surmise that gave her, the right to freedom that seems to be some of modern day youth's hazardous, perilous touchstone of today. We found out later that she ran off with a co-student who was a native Indian.

For weeks, we did not hear a thing, although we reported her missing. Some week's later information came in dribbles that she married this student in eastern Ontario, a Rob Smith. Whether by tribal ritual, or church, or none, I do not know to this day. They crept in some months later while we were out, to carry away furniture that did not belong to her. We decided to make no fuss; even though we were unhappy with her decision; she was still our daughter and we loved her.

Some time later, Gayle was struck with a cancer similar to her mothers. Tevis spent days with her before and after the operation. Gayle was much luckier than her deceased mother was. Tevis and I were frequently at her hospital bedside, so was her Rob. Fortunately, the operation eradicated all of the cancer, and after six months or so of recuperation, she beat the odds. The only sad part for her now is that she cannot bear a child.

When the holidays came round again, two dear persons were no longer with us. However, we had to make the best of it. We shopped for presents, bought a Christmas tree, but did this all with sorrow in our hearts and at a slowed down pace. Midnight Mass, sung in Polish with the old Latin chant always stirred me, and gave me the peace of mind and comfort that I so longed for that year.

At Christmas day dinner, I opened the toasts by breaking a blessed wafer (Oplatek) with everyone beginning with Tevis once again. I said a short prayer, especially about the sad loss of my beloved Tevis' father and husband of Mrs. Mary Roy MacLean, and for Gayle's well-being, safety, and happiness. After dinner, I had invited a few neighbours and their children over for dessert. The children added some much-needed joy to our downcast home, singing Christmas carols, and playing games. We celebrated New Year's Day at a colleague Judge's home. Our three remaining daughters played games with the other children.

The adults made small talk sipping Mum's champagne and snacking from a cornucopia of dips, nuts, and snacks.

Summer Solstice 1974

That summer (1974) our three daughters were driven to their Grandma's cottage located in Québec's scenic Laurentians, in the village of Val David. The North River flows gently by the cottage. It was encircled with many ethnic cottagers, with an abundance of children of our girl's ages to play with.

In the spring of 1974, Tevis and I had read up on the Caribbean Islands, hoping to select one for our summer holiday. We read that the first visitors to Barbados were the Portuguese, who named it "Los Barbados" because of the plentiful bearded fig trees on the island. Then, by 1627, the British settled an Earl and followers to colonize the island. The island prospered mainly on sugar and fish exports. About seventy-five (75%) percent of its 250,000 population are descendants of African slaves. They won their independence in 1966, after almost 300 years of British occupancy. We chose the island as it appeared to be steeped in a wealth of magic, history, and tradition.

Therefore, that summer of 1974 we made all necessary airline reservations, packed, and flew to Barbados. The airport was some distance from our seashore hotel. We noticed that after being taxied a short while, that one of our important pieces of impedimenta (luggage) was missing. No problem! The native taxi driver screeched the tires, turned around, and drove us back to the airport at high speed. Within only minutes, our luggage was safely retrieved and we were driven to our beach hotel.

After checking in at our hotel, we enjoyed a long swim. Dinner that night, to our surprise, was "Haute-Cuisine." Several times during our stay, we went to Bridgetown by taxi (the capital of Barbados), which was divided between areas of well-to-do people and the poor.

Sports abounded from sailing, deep-sea fishing, golf, tennis, snorkelling, and horseback riding to name a few. Our hotel advertised the pirate ship "Jolly Roger," which cruised daily. One day we decided to sail on this pirate ship. The price of the ticket included free rum and a life jacket. After every paid passenger was inebriated to various degrees, the "Jolly Roger" laid anchor on the Atlantic side of the island.

Many individuals jumped overboard. In spite of Tevis' pleading and protestations, I jumped overboard as well; the cool, refreshing Atlantic was invigorating.

Shortly after our return home, we drove to Val David, Québec to see our girls, and to visit mother, and my sister Reggie. The children were in great spirits and so was mother. Reggie arrived Friday night to the cottage she called "Shangri-La." We decided after telephoning my sister Eugene, to drive down to their chalet at Lake Massawippi. When I was 12-years-old, I had named it "Gdynia," Free Poland's port on the Baltic (built circa 1936-37).

Tevis, the children, Frank, and I drove to the nearest border town in Vermont, where the girls bought some small souvenirs and Frank purchased imported beverages. We stopped for dinner at a French-Canadian restaurant and arrived back at the cottage late. As time always seems to pass at a gallop while on holidays, it wasn't long before the last night before our departure faced us once again; we all assembled and held our ritual farewell bonfire resplendent with fireworks, already dreaming of next year...

County Court Judge

I started back at the Court House deluged by sittings in Small Claims Court in Windsor for a whole week. Then I heard cases out in the assigned county towns for another week. Back in Windsor, I tried Family Law hearings; some lasted days, mainly because of the acrimony of the parties. In Bail Review hearings, I was designated as "a hanging Judge" as I seldom granted bail to applicants who were accused of first or second-degree murder, manslaughter, robbery with a weapon or with violence, rape, and heinous sexual crimes. In the case of lesser offences, I was more lenient.

In any event, our criminal bar of that time (the odd one intemperate, but all asserting to be steeped in the wisdom of King Solomon) did their utmost not to let me hear bail reviews. The Crown on the other hand, did their utmost so that bail reviews were heard by me.

Our Judges met informally with "the Task Force on Legal Aid" chaired by Hon. Justice Osler, with Ian Scott, Q.C. as Counsel, at the Holiday Inn in Windsor. Gone were the days when Legal Aid in Toronto asked volunteers like me to represent an accused in all manner of criminal offences.

Our fee for these services consisted of a formal dinner at Osgoode Hall. In the mid–1970s, lawyers had the option to take part in the plan, and which (if I can recollect) depending on the nature of the case, were entitled to about seventy-five (75%) percent of the Law Society's set tariff fee.

The Winter of 1975

Tevis and I planned our 1975 winter getaway. We perused countless pamphlets from different travel agencies, looking for the perfect Caribbean sanctuary. At the tip of Venezuela's peninsula, we were enamoured by the Dutch island of Aruba, which had among other amenities, a rich history of Dutch Naval forays against the English in the

18th century, and Dutch skirmishes with natives. Its capital, Oranjestad, took its name from the Netherlands's "House of Orange."

Tevis and I flew south that winter, out of Detroit airport, landing only hours later at Aruba's airport. The customs forms we completed in transit made our entry perfunctory. Cabs were plentiful and we arrived swiftly at our hotel.

About 100-yards from our inn lay a white sandy beach that meandered for miles, destitute of neither any edifices nor any populace. I marvelled whether this erratic rarity was the portal to paradise! During the day, we swam in the Caribbean Sea. The island offered a multitude of sports, deep-sea fishing, snorkelling, and sailing, in addition to tennis and golf. Car rentals were easily attainable.

We made some new friends, mostly Americans; one Polish couple that we met were musicians with the Venezuelan Symphony Orchestra. They confided to us that since leaving Poland with 25 other musicians in 1972, they were virtual prisoners of Venezuela. They were allowed to vacation in Aruba, but had to leave their two children in Venezuela. Before they left, we exchanged our business cards with each other.

Aruba we found out was the "A" in the three Dutch islands commonly referred to as "A, B, C" — "B" for the nearby island of Bonaire, and "C" for the island of Curacao. We decided to fly and visit Caracas, the capital of nearby Venezuela. An inoculation was required.

We visited a Dutch doctor's office in Oranjestad, where we were approached by a nurse with a rather grotesque looking face — she did not speak, but beckoned to us by hand gestures to the doctor's small infirmary. We were attended to quickly, paid, and left.

The plane we embarked for Caracas was medium-sized and pleasant. On arrival at the airport, I exchanged some U.S. dollars into Bolivars. At the hotel, we had a light fish dinner, and once back in our room, I rang up the number, and in my rudimentary college Spanish, asked to speak to the Polish musicians. The reply I got was a furious indignant shout, "One nadie Polaco aqui," (There are no Polish people here). Over 25 years have lapsed since. On our arrival home, I wrote twice to the Polish musicians in Venezuela; my letters were never returned and I never once got a reply.

One day in Aruba, we decided to walk on the meandering beach. After a few miles, we came upon a large hotel and casino. Our hotel management informed us that there were several more such hotel-casinos all on the Dutch island and more are being built. Apparently, gamblers flew in from all parts of North America, South America, Europe, Asia, Saudi Arabia, and most other parts of the world.

Casinos were said to be an octopus with their tentacles grasping their prey's money. (An Arubian hotel owner told me that in twenty odd years later we will be "enriched"), by these huge gambling dens which are operated by *"Diabolos"* and *"Momus"* (the *Devil* and the ancient Greek God of Ridicule). In the province of Ontario, thanks to the Tory "common sense revolution," in the other Canadian province thanks to greed and deceit, casinos a lá Nevada are now cropping up in abundance.

The national language of Aruba is Papiamento, although English is spoken by most. Balashi, its capital, and many towns we visited abounded in architecturally Dutch style buildings. The restaurants flourish with French, Italian, Dutch, American, and local foods. After an enthralling visit, our plane took off once again for home...

Apart from the usual Small Claims and Judgment Summons' hearings, I was swamped that winter and spring with Estate Applications for Directions, Passing of Accounts, Bail Reviews, and Audits, in addition to many civil jury and non-jury trials and criminal trials, hearing Chamber Motions, Divorces, Landlord-Tenant Applications, Custodies, and Appeals from Provincial Court. The load seemed *endless* sometimes. If I did not have Tevis in my life, the burden of my extensive workload and joint family responsibilities would probably have made me collapse from the strain and stress of it all.

I was the only bilingual Judge in Windsor, and the French population was extensive, with only about ninety (90%) percent Anglicized. A continuous French settlement, antedating the British conquest thrived in the Windsor area on the (now) Canadian side of the Detroit River. After the American revolutionary war, this frontier region became a haven for the United Empire Loyalists.

The descendants of these two pioneer groups, one French, the other mostly English, constitute a large proportion of the citizens of Essex County. In order to hear a French trial the Court clerk had to engage a French Court Reporter (mostly from Ottawa), which was negotiated with great difficulty.

In any event, I heard only three, maybe four at most, 1/2-day trials in the French language, in the 23 years that I was on the Bench. However, it is my hope that with French schools starting to be established widely in a serious fashion, that the French language will regain its original status in our area.

Our Fourth Year of Wedlock

Having had our winter holiday in Aruba, during the summer of 1975, our three daughters, Tevis, and I intended to drive to my mother's home in Montréal. We were to celebrate my mother's birthday. The neighbours on Montgomery Street and some members of the Polish Parish nicknamed her the "Iron Lady." This name stuck because she was always busy, active, walked briskly, and was full of life. We were subsequently told that my sister Reggie had prepared a huge birthday cake. She invited a few of mother's adult friends and some children who sang an old Polish birthday song, wishing mother "a hundred years." Reggie told us the entire cake was eaten within the hour!

Several hours before reaching Montréal, the weather slowed us down. It was cool with intermittent rain showers. As I drove leisurely on the Highway 401, just past the city of Kingston, my car sputtered and I directed my car to a safe right shoulder, when its motor quit. Here we were, some miles north of Kingston with not much traffic. Luckily, I thumbed a ride to a gas station where through their phone book, I located Justice William Henderson's telephone number and luckily, he was home.

After I explained our predicament, he assured me that he would send his garage friend to tow and repair the car and send me over a rental car. Within less than one hour, we were back on the road to Montréal in a Chevrolet Impala rental — all thanks to having met this Judge a few years back in Windsor, and his kindly assistance to our vehicular plight. Just hours later, we arrived at Val David, Québec at mother's cottage and settled in. We wished her a happy birthday as we had unhappily missed her party in Montréal.

The next day, mother and I went shopping in Latulipe's Meat Market. This family also owned the Hotel "La Sapiniere" and the only hardware store in the village. I heard mother in her broken French order a three to four pound cut of sirloin steak; she asked the butcher to trim it, slice it, and put it through the grinder. That evening we had delicious hamburger cutlets and a variety of vegetables for dinner. Reggie surprised us with a home-baked carrot cake, lavished with vanilla ice cream.

About six days later, we were advised that the car was ready. The next morning after loading our luggage, we said our long goodbyes and pressed on with the Chevy Impala to the car repair shop near Kingston. I paid their bill, received a 60-day warranty, and we drove on to our capital, Ottawa. When we arrived at the Château Laurier, we found out that a Commonwealth Conference was in progress. Since we were five in number, the only thing the manager could arrange for us was to convert a display room, usually employed by clothing salesmen on the road, with male and female wardrobes! Not having much of a choice in the matter, we agreed and went in. Our girls loved the adventure and giggled the whole night.

The next morning Tevis called her son Kurt who was studying at Dalhousie and who had a summer job as a gardener in the Governor-General's Gardens. He and his girlfriend Heather (wife-to-be) agreed to have lunch with us. Before lunch, we were to drive to a bookstore but my car (newly repaired) would not start. An Ottawa garage had the car towed again to repair it.

Since only two days had passed since I paid the Kingston repair shop by cheque, I telephoned my bank in Windsor and had a stop payment placed on that cheque. Later I picked up my car from the Ottawa garage and paid my account there. We all had lunch, surprisingly at the Château, as the Commonwealth had almost taken over much of the place. We drove to the Rideau Canal and embarked on an Ottawa tour boat.

We saw many Canadian Government edifices and that of some foreign embassies as well. On the recommendation of a Senator (who had best be nameless), one evening the five of us purchased tickets to a concert; after paying non-refundable "big bucks" for these tickets, we discovered to our shock that it was a "rock and roll concert" of sorts. The screeching clamour and staccato shrieks were so sneeringly loud, that after being exposed to this tormenting, loud eerie noise, within only minutes we escaped to the peace and quiet outside the building.

The morning after the aborted concert, we admired the uplifting architectural structure of the Supreme Court of Canada. We spent our final day in the capital sightseeing some government buildings and Canada's formidable and memorable War Memorial. After a light dinner, we packed our bags. The next morning we drove to the west shore of the clear blue waters of Georgian Bay. We arrived at the cottage of our daughters' doctor where our car ran out of power and promptly stalled in the middle of their steep driveway.

Dr. Vera Solowski was a perfect hostess. An unpleasant event occurred that day at the white sandy beach; our (youngest) Andrea's eyes had some sand blown into them. She got panicky and ran into the house, shrieking in pain and fearfulness.

Dr. Solowski quietly calmed her and immediately applied water which flushed her eyes. We were on our way the next morning and somehow (miraculously) the car started. We eventually reached Windsor and home, after our many side trips.

The manufacturers of my car had their main shop in Windsor give my car a once over from "tip-to-toe" and kept it in the garage for a whole week at no charge. In good conscience, I sent the Kingston repair shop a new cheque, realizing the problem was with the car. Not surprisingly, shortly thereafter I purchased a brand new car.

The fall of 1975 commenced like the previous one; school for the girls and back to work for Tevis and I. Sometime in 1973, I assumed the position of "Local Master of the Supreme Court of Ontario at Windsor," over and above my onerous duties as County and District Court Judge.

The foreclosure, bankruptcy, mortgage, and trust matters, among others, exposed me to numerous short trials that I had to keep notes on (as no Court Reporter was made available). I had to arrive at decisions, which required a typed format with my signature attached to have effect. I began to find my Master's task quite the encumbrance. In October 1975, my old Toronto friend James B. Trotter was sworn in as County and District Court Judge for the County of York (Toronto).

On November 7th, 1975, when I was about to attend to adjudicate on a reference, the Court Secretary, visibly upset and in tears, rushed into my office and asked me to go immediately to Chief Judge Sydney Clunis' office. When I arrived there, I found him slumped over his chair. A guard present helped me to lay him out on the floor, flat on his back.

I yelled to the secretary to call 911 for an ambulance. I leaned over Judge Sydney Clunis, pinched his nose, and started mouth-to-mouth resuscitation. When I took a break, a Court guard pressed down on his chest — we both did for some time. About 10 members of the staff began to assemble around us and I ordered them out. I was just about to repeat the resuscitation when the ambulance men arrived and took the Judge to the hospital, where he was pronounced dead. Everybody that knew him was in a state of shock—no one more than his wife and children. He was buried a few days later in Kingsville, Ontario. He was a good Judge, a family man, and a friend to be remembered.

Journey to Communist Poland...

In the summer of 1976, Tevis, Reggie, and I made our way to Poland. We all applied for the necessary documentation and photos for Canadian passports as well as Polish Visas. I made airline reservations for the three of us on the state-owned Polish Airline "Lot."

I digress for a moment to correct the repeated error in the Western press treating Poland as a Communist dominated country from the time when the Russian Communist revolutionaries injected Communism into Russia (1917). After 1918, Poland was resurrected following 123 years of enslavement at the hands of her three expansionist Empires: German, Austrian, and Tsarist-Russia.

During the 21 years as a Free Poland, it was a relatively tolerant, free market society. With the 1939 Nazi and Russia Communist rape of Poland (in spite of the fact that the Western Allies guaranteed a Free Poland), Polish troops were fourth in number in fighting the Nazis; their pilots and seamen made a great contribution to win World War II.

Through the Yalta Agreement, most of Central and Eastern Europe, after "soviet-style" elections, forced Communism on Poland, the Baltic States, Czechoslovakia, East Germany, Hungary, Romania, Bulgaria, and Yugoslavia. "The Iron Curtain fell on Europe" by 1946, as Sir Winston Churchill so aptly remarked at the Westminster College in Fulton, Missouri U.S.A. He added words to this effect, *"This is not the liberated Europe we fought to build up!"*[1]

From the London Polish-Government-in-Exile, the leader of the Polish Peasant Party, Stanislaus Mikolajczyk, travelled to Poland in 1944. He tried to assemble and organize his party for the Allied guaranteed "free" democratic vote. After the sabotage of his party by Moscow and the pre-arranged Soviet vote that announced ninety-eight-and-a-half (98.5%) percent for Communism, Stanislaus Mikolajczyk fled for his life. That's how, by 1946, Communism was forcibly imposed on Poland and its people. "Allied Guaranteed Democratic Elections" were brutally brushed aside.

---

[1] Europe A History, Norman Davies, 1996, UP, p. 1065.

I arranged for my daughters to be cared for by relatives in our absence. We flew out of Detroit, direct to Warsaw. Having arrived at Warsaw's airport, "Okecie," which was built in 1934, we made our way through customs; there was quite a bit of pandemonium, as passengers struggled to locate their luggage. There were numerous baggage handlers on the floor. I nodded to one of them and he courteously manoeuvred a small wagon, picked our luggage, and helped insert the luggage into the trunk of our cab.

We arrived at Warsaw's newest hotel at that time, called "Forum," built by a Swedish company (circa 1973-74); a 25-floor brand new structure with all the amenities of any recently built Canadian or American hotel. We arranged for adjoining rooms with Reggie.

Reggie had a pen pal outside of Warsaw that she had never met; she arranged that we would all have dinner with her pen pal at our hotel's dining room the next day. However, Reggie was sadly disappointed. Her pen pal was almost 20 years older, poorly dressed, and lived on a pension, which would be equivalent to about $17.00 a month, Canadian. This did not impress Reggie in the least, and any possible future relations evaporated.

We stayed at the Hotel Forum for a few days. Whenever we left our hotel, a dozen or so moneychangers would accost us, offering from 80 to 120 Zloty's for one Canadian dollar. Our tour guide informed us that there were 11 palaces in the Warsaw area. We saw part of the famous Palace of Belweder, built in 1659. We were required to put special soft socks over top our shoes, to not to mark the highly polished floors. The last King of Poland had lived there. Today it is used as a government house. Our guide informed us there are 36 churches in Warsaw and its suburbs.

We visited the Church of St. Joseph Oblubienca (The Betrothed). Built in 1654, it is one of the most treasured churches in Warsaw. We were taken to the sacristy and shown how all of the long wooden tables and the altar were painted white to camouflage the golden decor to save it from the Nazis, who were adept at plundering precious things throughout Europe (circa 1938–1945). This camouflaging was put into place before the Nazis overpowered Warsaw on September 27th, 1939.

We visited L. Zamenhofa Street in Warsaw and were able to see the long and tall monument dedicated to the heroic uprising of the Jewish people in the Jewish Ghetto in 1943, against the Nazi oppressors and mass murderers. Our guide shared with us in detail how the Nazis had herded Jewish men, women, and children into this Warsaw Ghetto and shipped thousands at a time to their deaths in camps. He relayed the story of how a small Jewish underground surprised their captors by their courageous insurrection against the Nazi hordes.

Sadly, this only slowed down the onslaught and delayed the tragedy somewhat of the barbaric extermination of six million defenceless, God-fearing Jewish families in the infamous holocaust.

The next day upon waking, our same guide escorted us to the old city "Stare Miasto." Eighty (80%) percent of Warsaw had been destroyed by German dynamite and artillery shells (Hitler's punishment for the uprising of the Polish underground in Warsaw in the fall of 1944). After the war had ended, Polish citizens banded together in unity, to begin the long task of rebuilding it — brick-by-brick.

All of the medieval buildings were rebuilt at that time, including the President's palace. We also visited the district of "Praga" in east Warsaw, where the Polish underground of 1944 fought the Nazis. We were driven to the home of Chopin known as "Zelazowa Wola" (Iron Will) located some miles outside of Warsaw.

We were guided through the home, which was not large by any means and possessed a wooden floor and wooden ceiling. It was adorned with fresh flowers, curtains, and furnishings for the tours. Outside of the entrance to Chopin's home, there were multiple rows of benches set up.

We were asked to sit down on one of them and as we did, a lady concert pianist commenced to play some of Chopin's compositions: Mazurkas, Etudes, Polonaise, and the haunting "Polonaise Militaire" — the surprise concert lasted well over two hours. The whole group of us sat hushed, captivated by Chopin's music. This was one of our most unforgettable moments in Poland.

Later, we drove to another palace — the Palace of Willanow, located south of Warsaw, built in 1677. It was the residence of the famous Polish King Jan Sobieski, who routed the Turks from the siege of Vienna of 1683, only to have Catholic Austria help Prussia and Russia wipe Poland off Europe's map by 1795.

Surrounded by beautifully long, groomed multiple gardens, this palace was spared by the swiftly retreating Nazis in 1944–1945 as the dreaded Russians were crushing their front. We also visited parts of Malbork castle dating back to the Middle Ages, constructed with red brick. The Nazi used it as a fortress in 1944; parts of it were destroyed. In the 1960s, the Poles restored it and it serves as a museum today.

At Gdansk (formerly Danzig), we attended Mass at the Gothic church of the Blessed Mary. There was no open talk of solidarity or any anti-Communist activity of "solidarity" yet. We were bussed to the town of Torun, where we toured through the home turned museum of Copernicus (M. Kopernik).It was he who discovered and proved the heliocentric system. He upset the medieval notion that the earth was the centre of the universe.

Back at Hotel Forum, after a lovely dinner, there was small talk with others who were in our tour. The three of us retired, feeling satiated from all the magnificent sights and sounds we had encountered the past few days.

After breakfast the following morning, our tour guide scolded us that "one of us" had two pieces of toast, instead of the allotted quota of one piece (an example of the disciplined Communism of that time!). Upon leaving, we were driven to the town of Czestochowa, where monks and soldiers stopped the Swedish-attempted subjugation of Poland in 1655.

Reggie and I would have liked to spend more time sightseeing Czestochowa, as when we lived in East Montréal in the "Frontenac District," our family Parish was named "Our Lady of Czestochowa." The interior of our church in Montreal had inscribed by the altar "Polonia Semper Fidelis" (Poland Always Faithful). We stopped shortly at Wieliczka, the ancient salt quarry that runs several miles deep.

We passed Nowa Huta, a vast metallurgical combine with dozens of chimneys belching black smoke (unintentionally, I pray), poisoning citizens; Communism had no environmental laws. Finally, we reached Cracow, the ancient capital of the Kingdom of Poland.

Our guide told us that the Polish National prize was said to be Wawel—the Royal Castle and Cathedral where Polish kings were crowned. In the 16th century, Florentine architects and masters transformed the castle that few equal in the world, north of the Alps.

We visited the crypt of Polish kings; we viewed the crypt of Marshall J. Pilsudski, who liberated Poland from 123 years of slavery to a free and independent country (It was gossiped that the Polish Communists had dumped his remains and replaced them with someone else's old corpse). There was a sort of a "museum of a home." This is where *Lenin* lived for a short while before 1914; no one in our sightseeing group opted to tour that dictator's hideaway.

The following day, we arrived at Zakopane, which lies at the foot of the Tatra Mountains. This area plays host to thousands of mountaineers, skiers, tourists, and holidaymakers. The atmosphere here is clear and bright and it boasts peace and quiet. The inn we stayed at was very comfortable and the meals were excellent.

We walked to see the famous "Morskie Oko," "Eye of the Sea," a dead volcano of sorts, whose opening was full of what, appeared to be seawater. There were a handful of mountaineers standing on the side of the street selling trinkets. I witnessed them being asked to move on by a policeman; I took him aside and asked him why he was so rough on poor people just trying to earn a few extra zlotys. His reply was—"I let them go further down the street, where there are *more* tourists." True or not, I never found out.

There was no mention at all by any of our Polish Communist guides of Wadowice—birthplace of Cardinal Karol Wojtyla, widely known Catholic activist, located within a stone's throw from Zakopane (who was elected Pope John Paul II two years later, on October 16th, 1978).

After our return to Warsaw, Joseph Kicinski's cousin John Gassoski met with us. He was a medical doctor, but doctors in the "Red Paradise" as it was called, were not allowed to be addressed as, nor use the title "Dr." on their letterhead, office entrances, etc. The doctor drove us to his home at Sadlo, a small agricultural village not far from Warsaw. His wife, a paediatrician, prepared lunch for us.

They were awaiting the completion of a new home, near Lodz, a large cloth-manufacturing city (west of Warsaw). He drove us to Poznan where Dr. Andrzej Kicinski and his wife, both medical doctors, entertained us in their comfortable home. At my suggestion, we ate out. A luxurious French restaurant that our hosts suggested turned out to be excellent and not in the least expensive. I tipped the waiter in Canadian dollars, which seemed to make him very happy!

The next morning, right after breakfast, we left for Gdynia, the Baltic Sea port Free Poland built before 1939. This is the most modern port on the Baltic today. It was Free Poland's pre-war most notable and praiseworthy achievement. Kosciuszko Square in Gdynia, surrounded by trees, bushes, and flowers, stunned us with its symmetrical beauty.

We all decided spontaneously that we wanted to go to Sweden by an available ferry. Although Dr. John Gassoski had his passport with him, he told us he couldn't go without permission of the Central Warsaw office (I called it the Polish K.G.B. secret police). We looked out into the sea (called Bay of Gdansk) and saw retired World War II destroyers and submarines laid anchored in somewhat of a square design. Most of these naval units had fought with the Western allies.

Before we left, I borrowed a few hundred dollars from Tevis and Reggie, added a few hundred of my own U.S. dollars, and presented the money to Dr. John Gassoski towards his new home in Lodz. He was shy, and declined to accept it at first, but finally we persuaded him to accept. That made us all feel good. We could contribute what for us, was a relatively small amount, but it would help him greatly towards realizing his dream.

We arrived late at Warsaw and flew home the next morning. My only regret was my inability to visit Swislocz on the Berezina prior to 1795; that former Polish land had been gobbled up during Poland's partitions by the Russian (Tsars) and since 1920 it had became part of Soviet Russia.

I had kept to the last, our visit to Auschwitz, the Nazi killing camp of six million Jews and one million Poles, anti-Nazis, Gypsies, gays, etc; falsely accused by the Nazi leader that they had caused Germany to lose World War I. The victims—men, women, and children—were stripped naked and commanded to enter a shower chamber (in reality a gas chamber), and their corpses burnt in special ovens. In Germanic thoroughness, their ashes were boxed and sent to the Third Reich for use as fertilizer. Several millions met the same fate—Poles, Russians, anti-Nazis, Gypsies, Jehovah Witnesses, and countless others.

As one entered the front gate, an iron plaque cynically read, "Work Makes One Free," "Arbeit Macht Frei" (in German). There were exhibits displayed that were frightful; thousands of eyeglasses jammed together, like in a department store window, and thousands of shoes crammed in another display window. There was another display of thousands of-pounds of cut human hair, and yet another thousands of different size suitcases. We could not go on, as it was so disturbing…

We were shown where multitudes of victims had been executed by firing squads. The victims were made to stand up in front of a huge, square, thick board, about 50-feet long and 40-feet high.

When we touched the wood where the executions had taken place, there was no smooth spot anywhere; it was jaggedly chipped away by the countless thousands of bullets imbedded into the wood. The sight of the merciless slaughter of six million Jews, known world over as the holocaust, shook every nerve in the very fibre of one's soul. This crime of all crimes is impossible to forget.

Our girls were thrilled to see Aunty Reggie and us on our return. They adored the scarves we brought back for them from Poland, and the small dolls we had hand picked from different Polish regions, dressed in different peasant attire. September slid by and we all went back to school and work...

The Royal Tribunals of Poland

I was invited to a seminar in Poland of lawyers and Judges of Polish origin from abroad, August 11th, 1978 to August 17th, 1978. This was to commemorate the 400th anniversary of the implementation of tribunals held by the "Kings of Poland" in 1578. Our Communist hosts reluctantly called it, "The Royal Tribunals of Poland." As I received my invitation several months before and received clearance from our Chief Judge, I procured a Polish Visa. I had written a paper on "A Unified Family Court" and had the 20 pages translated into Polish.

I left for Warsaw on August 10th, 1978 to be fresh for the seminar commencing on August 11th, 1978 in Warsaw at the "Europejski Hotel." I had reservations at the "Victoria Hotel," a modern hotel close by the "Europejski Hotel." This is where the first meeting was to take place on August 11th, 1978.

Promptly at 10:00 a.m., the meeting was called to order and the chairman announced that he was very pleased with the large number of participants in attendance from countries like France, Holland, Switzerland, Germany, Great Britain, the United States, Canada, and Ethiopia, to which he expressed the gratitude of the association of lawyers and the Society of Poles abroad.

The chairman asked the president Professor Dr. Adam Lapatka to address us. After very sincere expressions of welcome, the president very eloquently, in essence, said that this seminar is a dedication and commemoration of the 400th year anniversary of the establishment of the Royal Tribunals (Courts) in Poland, after the union with the Grand Duchy of Lithuania (1569). The population of both was 7.5 million at that time. It was the largest Joint Monarchy in Central and Eastern Europe. However, Polish lands were distinguished from the Lithuanian territories, as was the legal system of the time. As a result, Polish law was known as "the law of the Crown"; feudalism reigned in the land. After the death of the Jagelonian Kings, the elective system of kings was introduced and this weakened the country. King Stefan Batory agreed in 1577 to form special Crown tribunals. The location of this tribunal was at "Piotrkow Trybunalski," which was one of the oldest cities in Poland.

The professor went on to share with us how the first famous law statutes evolved there, and how the codification of Polish law commenced. The tribunal of the Crown heard appeals from verdicts of municipal Courts, county, and higher Courts in matters concerning civil and criminal matters. Fortunately, we all were given a copy of his deliberation entitled: "400 years of the Tribunal of the Crown in Poland." The ending of the professor's speech was taken by me "tongue in cheek."

Poland's (i.e., Communist) People's Court, whose "highest Court" is the Supreme Court of Poland, has superintendence over all lower Courts. A government Council appoints and dismisses members (Judges) of the Supreme Court. The People's Supreme Court follows the spirit of the tribunal of the Crown, applying it to a certain degree, because of the changed times and freedom. *All citizens are equal in the face of the law.* For me it was very hard to swallow—this being uttered by a so-called intellectual, Communist.

After a long lunch, whilst mingling with other members of this seminar, I entered into a friendly chat with a few Americans, one from Utica, N.Y., one from Florida, and one from Chicago. I also spoke with a French barrister and an English barrister. I found it curious that not one of these non-Polish citizens uttered a word about the countless killings of the shipyard workers and others that had taken place in 1970 and 1971 by the Polish police.

At the afternoon meeting, our delegates were joined by several Polish Judges from the Warsaw region. Personnel of the "Polish Ministry of Justice," including the Deputy Minister of Justice joined us. I wondered at that time whether I should make enquiries about Tadeusz Koyera, the Canadian citizen arrested in Poland in 1960 for alleged partisan murders. My sixth sense told me I could get into trouble if I did so, as the Polish Secret Police are known to be as swift, treacherous, and trained by the K.G.B. (Soviet Secret Police) in methods of "neutralizing" snooping anti-Communists.

On the completion of speeches by the executive who organized this seminar, the last speaker that afternoon was the chairman of the Society of Poles abroad called "Polonia." I remember that before the war, this society was in existence (with my father's participation) at Dom Polski in Montréal. We heard a speaker from Poland propagate about how Polish people living abroad should "keep in contact with mother Poland." The Communist regime took over "Polonia" around about 1947, and did its best to carry on what was started by the Free Poland from 1932 and ended abruptly with the fall of Poland in 1939. At 5:00 p.m., the meeting promptly broke up.

We were given two huge legal textbooks: one entitled "Regulations Regarding Lawyers," and the other entitled "Civil Law System," which included property law and substantive law. Both books numbered over 500 pages. The "Civil Law" book, printed in 1977, is filled with assertions that whereas in the capitalist system, possessions, real and personal, are in private hands or corporations, in People's Poland, all possessions are totally national. The book is filled with legal decrees with their dates of proclamation and sections that apply, and more often than not—Latin phrases are employed to reinforce a legal position.

The book presumes to analyse, compare, and sometimes apply the civil codes of Austria, Czechoslovakia, France, The Napoleonic Code, German, and the Soviet Union's Codes. It is a very complexly written book, but wholly outdated since the collapse of Communism in 1990, and the election that year of "Solidarity's" Noble Peace Prize winner (1983) Lech Walesa, as president of a free and democratic Republic of Poland.

The book entitled, "The Relation of Lawyers" I found quite abhorrent. No democratic country could tolerate such a complete domination of the legal profession and the judiciary by a Central Anti-Democratic Committee of Commissars. It decreed that as a Polish lawyer or Judge fulfils his duties, he must not abuse the freedom ascribed to him by the State. If he is accused of a malfeasance, he faces Court charges, severe disciplinary action, loss of practice or office, and incarceration may ensue.

On the second day of the seminar, the foreign speakers were called upon to deliver the papers that they had prepared for the assembly. The first speaker was Magistrate J. Houtappel from Holland. His subject was entitled, "The Assessment of Justice in the Common-Law Countries and the European Continental Countries." We were handed a copy of the Dutchman's speech, in Polish. It was a brilliant expose of the very deep differences between the two very different systems. As an example, unlike Common-Law jurisdiction in continental Courts, the onus of proving innocence lies with the accused, faced with the multitude of all of the prosecutorial, police, and the magnanimous forces of the State. In Common-Law countries, the onus of proving guilt, "without a reasonable doubt," lies with the "State" prosecution.

Under our system, the accused is not obliged to give evidence that is to take the stand in the witness box. In the continental countries, the accused is forced to do so, often, as I have seen, whilst in a huge prisoner's cage whilst attempting to prove his innocence.

The next speaker was Ms. Celing Weiner from the National Research Centre of Paris, France. Her treatise was, "Basic Trends in the Structural and Procedural Reforms in Administration."

Her subject matter was lengthy and most complex with a disguised, clandestine censorship of despotic rule. She spoke of the technoratization of sophistic management, pursued stringently in some jurisdictions that should be balanced by measures to preserve or restitution to administration its humanitarian character. Furthermore, she related in effect that social aspirations are getting more numerous in all fields... reform constitutes at any time a search for balance. She cited how some governments created new ministries to handle new problems. She stated how in 1972, Great Britain instituted the secretariat for Northern Ireland affairs. France later created a secretariat for women's affairs.

She spoke at length on coordination being essential to all the big ministries; also, control in administration praising the popularity of the ombudsman in Britain. She touched upon the drastic reduction of communes (sort of counties) in the 1970s, by Sweden, Belgium, and the Federal Republic of Germany. Under codification, she notes that Sweden's code had only 20 sections, while Yugoslavia had 500 sections in its code. She ended her submission as follows, "is not the best of reforms that which one is able to reform itself."

On August 13th, 1978, I delivered my prepared text on "The Unification of Family Courts." I read it in Polish and had copies distributed. I did not realize that this subject was so popular with the Polish lawyers. They asked how 800 Court rules were replaced with 74 new rules without changing the basic law and about custody, maintenance, and other matters in our unified family Court. In fact, the then Deputy Minister of Justice, Dr. Maria Rolechowicz approached me at the end of my session.

She was interested in finding out more about our Unification of Family Law Courts. In September of that year, after receiving materials from Judge D. M. Steinberg who presided over the Unified Family Law Courts in Ontario, I sent them on to the Polish Deputy Minister of Justice in Warsaw, Poland.

The speaker that followed me was Dr. S. Lammich from Köln, Germany. His work was entitled, "Studies in West Germany of the Legal Problems of Socialist Countries," essentially outlining the joint co-operation of West Germany and Polish law schools. There was a short adjournment, and when we returned to our seats there was a six-page, anonymous pamphlet placed on all of our seats. The committee mobilized to remove them promptly. I managed to peruse the first page quickly, before it was whisked away from right under my nose.

It recalled how in 1926 Marshall Pilsudski had launched a coup d'état to rid Communism as—free men must have a free homeland. That's all that I was able to read. This clearly was an underground Polish Anti-Communist declaration that was smartly planted (a side job, as we would say!). Neither the executive of our Seminar nor their members made any mention of this incident after the "clean up."

On the morning of August 13th, 1978 we reached (in several buses) the town of "Piotrkow, Trybunalski" located southwest of Warsaw, and south of Lodz. A dozen or so participants, along with myself, were dropped off at a small but recently built hotel. I was surprised to find out that several prosecutors were in our group. They were all young ladies who were able to tell us about the Tribunal of the Polish Crown (our hosts always avoided that title, instead saying Royal Tribunals of Poland), which was established in this town four centuries ago. Time passed quickly and it was not long before dinner was announced.

A lawyer from Holland and I agreed to order wine for the ten others present at our table. The roast chicken, vegetables, poppy-seed cake, and coffee were excellent. Most of us adjourned in the main sitting room. The ladies started singing a well-known "Góral" (mountaineer) song, and continued with other folk songs. Eventually, after a few glasses of wine, I sang an old soldier's song, "Jak szlo wojsko raz ulica" (Our soldiers once marched). The ending of this song was simple, "Wgóre chlopcy na Moskala" (Forward boys—let's attack the Moscovites!) All hell broke loose; the prosecutor ladies lunged at me saying you can't sing that! What if a Party member reports this gathering! The singing ended. *Now I really knew I was "behind the Iron Curtain."*

The next day we arrived at the site of the Royal Polish Tribunal. There seemed to be two separate ruins. Fortunately, we were greeted by a Priest who conducted a tour and explained how one large structure preceded the second one. It appears that the Sejm (Parliament) controlled all matters including the purse of the ruling king in the Kingdom of Poland, whereas all other monarchies evolved into absolute monarchies.

In Poland, the nobility was very powerful and consisted of ten (10%) percent of the Polish population. This democracy of the nobility evolved many good emoluments; a larger number of individuals had political rights, which also gave rise to development of the realm, trade, agriculture, culture, and education. That era of time was aptly named the "Polish Golden Era."

The Crown (or Royal) Tribunal with its inception, evolved into Poland's Supreme Court (ludicium ordinarium generale Tribunitas Regni). In 1581, a separate Tribunal was founded in Wilno under the Grand Duchy of Lithuania. The Crown Tribunal also sat in Lublin located at "Mala Polska," a region known as Little Poland. The Royal Tribunal had 33 Judges. To be a Judge it sometimes required the support of the nobles.

In 1791 parliament, on the initiative of King S. Poniatowski, the liberal Constitution of the 3rd of May was passed. The three tyrannical neighbours completely partitioned Poland by 1795. The Royal Tribunal was thereby liquidated, along with all other Polish institutions. However, it left a lasting memento of the inception of instituted Polish laws.

What surprised me greatly was how the organizers of this seminar, commemorating the 400th anniversary of the founding of the Royal Polish Tribunals, covertly slipped in the 60th anniversary of (Communist) Poland's independence! The seminar's executive laid a wreath at the tomb of the Unknown Soldier's cenotaph located near the Hotel Europejski. In the daily "Kurier Polski" of August 14th, 1978, hidden on page four in small print, there was a heading concerning our seminar. *In addition to that, it stated that our delegates were celebrating the Polish Communist anniversary!*

The Governor of Piotrkow Trybunalski marshalled our delegation from the market place to a large old marble tablet affixed to one of the oldest tenements pronouncing that, *"In this town, the Prussians paid homage to Poland's king. Here five kings were elected, countless "Sejms" (Parliaments) and multiple times Knights convened. For 249 years, the Royal Polish Tribunals thrived."* The Tsarist-Russian appointed Governor had the building where the Tribunals met after the insurrection of 1831 blown up, and systematically had all other legal papers, minutes of Parliament and the like burnt, continuing the *repression of all matters Polish.*

We left Piotrków Trybunalski on August 16th, 1978, and had lunch that day at Warsaw's Hotel Europski. I took a cab with a local lawyer to sit in on a criminal rape case in a nearby Warsaw Court. The accused sat in a caged cell (which is part of the Courtroom) and a Lady Judge did the cross-examination of the accused. His defence seemed an alibi. The accused had to confer in whispers with his gowned lawyer.

On each side of the Judge there sat two civilian men acting as assessors. We did not have time to stay and hear the outcome of the trial but I was not impressed when the accused had put the onus to prove his innocence on himself. That's onerous, if not downright impossible!

The reverse is true in our Common-Law, where the Crown-Attorney must prove his case, through a jury, that the accused is guilty beyond a reasonable doubt, and our accused does not have to give evidence; in this Polish system, all accused persons are *obliged* to give evidence.

The organizers held a farewell dinner on our behalf the final day of the seminar at the Grand hall of the Hotel Europejski (European). All of the delegates and some members from the Ministry of Justice, including the lady Deputy Minister of Justice were present.

After the dinner, I was approached by a member of an institute of law. He asked me if I could get some specific information on recent improvements in agricultural matters from the Canadian Agricultural Ministry. I undertook to do so upon my arrival home. I contacted Mr. Eugene Whelan, our Federal Minister of Agriculture to kindly honour the request, which he did.

I was greatly impressed by a Polish law professor who hailed from Ethiopia. I asked how it came about that he teaches law in such a far off country. He cited to me his flight after Poland's debacle, through Hungary and Italy to France where he served in the army of Sikorski; in June 1940, he was evacuated to England. He served in the Normandy Landings and eventually pushed to Holland and armistice. He elected not to return to his fatherland under the Soviet Bayonets. He worked in

France, and he was accepted to the Ethiopian Law School at Adis Ababa, not only because of law school but also because of the fact that he was also fluent in French, English, Italian, and German.

The beginnings and organizing of the law school were difficult until now. Today the school is vibrantly successful and has about 400 students enrolled. I noticed that he never mentioned the violent deposition of Emperor Haile Selassie in 1974 and the ardent socialist dictatorship that took over, helped by the Soviets and Cubans. I have always found it interesting in life, what people do *not* speak.

The last evening, after packaging my luggage, I sent a telegram to my dear Tevis telling her just how much I missed her. She managed to answer my telegram, which relayed to me to get home fast, so that she can kiss me instead of merely missing me!

After about two weeks passed since my return to Canada, I received a short letter from the attorney from Utica, N.Y., who also attended the Polish seminar. He advised me how he had just been decorated with the Medal of Merit by the Consulate of Poland (he didn't mention in his letter that it was from the Polish People's Republic-Communist dominated Poland).

The attorney helped the regime uncover heirs in Poland, probate and finalize such estates, and after deducting attorney's fees, sent the balance of monies to the Polish People's representatives and not directly to the beneficiaries. Whilst I was a lawyer in Toronto, Canada, I fought this intrusion by Communist "apparatchiks," exposing their confiscating of estates of Polish citizens who had died in Canada. I am grateful that eventually this practice was barred in Canada by the time of my appointment as a County Court Judge in Windsor in 1968.

"Habemus Papum..."

On October 16th, 1978, the Vatican Conclave of Cardinals, "Habemus Papum" (in Latin) announced that a Pope had been chosen — Cardinal Karol Wojtyla. The choice stunned many Roman Catholics worldwide. The Italians were not only surprised but some were also appalled at Vatican's Cardinals choosing a Polish Pope, Pope John Paul II. Over a 2,000-year history of the Papacy, in the final 500 years all the Popes were Italian. However, there was astonishment, pride, and great happiness in the streets of Communist-occupied Poland, which professed Catholicism since the early 9th century.

The same was true of Roman Catholic Poles abroad. Thus, this was the 264th Bishop of Rome, successor of St. Peter, the first Pontiff, and head of the Roman Catholic Church on earth, considered by Roman Catholics to be, by apostolic succession from St. Peter, the Vicar of Christ on earth. Messages of congratulations were showered on His Holiness from the whole Catholic, Christian, and non-Christian world as well. Perhaps the most surprising note came from the Communist Leaders of Poland. Their felicitations ended with reassurances that the Polish Peoples' Republic would continue to evolve good relations with the apostolic head...

The Pope was born in 1920 in the small Polish town of Wadowice, where he had many playmates including both Polish and Jewish children. His mother died when he was very young.

When the Nazis overran Poland with Soviet Communist Russia in 1939, all schooling was interrupted. As a young adult, he was active as a writer and actor in underground plays. When his whole family died, he attended a clandestine Theological Seminary; he was anointed a priest in 1946. By 1949, he was posted as a Parish priest in some small rural Polish town. He progressed swiftly, becoming Archbishop of the Diocese of Cracow in 1961 and was later elevated to the position of Cardinal.

As a Cardinal, he was a fervent theologian who subtly preached, throughout the four corners of Poland, that Communist Marxism was the Anti-Christ. The Cardinal's messages inspired L. Walesa and the Solidarity Movement among others; they were a much-needed boost in extinguishing Communism from Eastern Europe by 1989. These few words written down here do not begin to touch upon this great man, this Polish Pope. He was shot at and miraculously lived.

He is the only Pope (so far) who visited and solemnized Mass with millions of Catholics in several dozens of countries. It is said of him, with his bold and stirring sermons in Poland starting in the 1970s and the 1980s, that he inspired Poland's Solidarity Movement and the insurrection in Gdansk and the rest of Poland against Communism.

This insurrection was harshly put down in 1982, by the brutal force of the government — only by 1989, without a shot, Polish Communism crumbled. Some historians say, *"History must give the Poles the principal credit for bringing the Soviet Block to its knees."*[2] However, in October 1990,

---

[2] Europe A History, Norman Davies, 1996, UP, p. 1108.

some leaders claimed that having abetted in the breach of the Berlin Wall in 1989 was the cause of the collapse of Communism. Among the assertors were former U.S. President George Bush Sr., former President Kohl of Germany, and former Committee Chairman of the USSR Gorbachev. These men played a part no doubt, but in due time, history itself will assert its final verdict. This Pope has devoted much effort to reconciliation with all Christian denominations, including the Orthodox Christian, Judaic, Islamic, and all other religions around the globe.

In 1970, a Polish Catholic publication described how Bishop Gerald Emmett Carter, together with the (then) Cardinal Wojtyla and the primate of Poland, led a religious procession on the main streets of Cracow, followed by thousands of faithful Poles. The timing of the procession was no coincidence since the Communist militia had about forty-four solidarity shipyard workers shot, and over 1,000 wounded, after the end of an "illegal strike" at the Port of Gdynia in 1970.

The Cracow religious parade took place as a protest to the slaughter of unarmed workers, wounding 1,165, and arresting thousands. This began the struggle of Polish workers, which by the early 1980s had its government recognize a non-Communist union.

An upheaval occurred, and a controlled revolution spread throughout the Polish land. On October 8th, 1982, all previous concessions were revoked by the Polish Communist regime and martial law was imposed. At that time, solidarity had twelve million members signed-up. The Pope had bestowed Sainthood on an Auschwitz martyr two days previously and verbally attacked this Communist persecution, whilst the Polish primate Glemb seemed to side with the government repressions. In the elections of 1989, after the Communists acquiesced to a coalition government with solidarity and non-Communists—in a Democratic election, these Marxists were wiped out and solidarity's L. Walesa became the first president of Free Poland.

The Pope had in November 1989, created a rallying point for freedom in Czechoslovakia, by canonizing the first Czechoslovakian Saint in 300 years. That was Agnes of Bohemia, who gave up her riches to live with the poor. The underground church, Charter 77 Movement, and Vaclav Ravel freed this East European country from its imposed Marxism.

In 1986, the Pope had organized a multi-faith religious event at Assisi, (home of St. Francis), consisting of 150 religious leaders (for the first time in history), to come to discuss and pray for peace. This event included

Rabbis, Mullahs, Sikhs, African Animists, Buddhists (including Dalai Lama), Protestant Evangelicals, Shintoists, other Protestant Sects, and the Archbishop of Canterbury. The theme of this conclave was, *"There is no peace without passionate love for peace."*[3]

Pope John Paul II visited and performed an open mass to millions of faithful in over 100 different countries during his first 25 years as Pontiff. He has written 13 encyclicals since 1979 (Encyclicals are authoritative Papal statements and deal with the most important teachings of the pontiff, directed at Catholic Bishops Hierarchy and Catholics worldwide). Jonathan Kwitny's book on the Pope entitled "Man of the Century" was published in 1997. The author examines in detail the relationship between John Paul II as a Pole and his church. "He exposes his doubts about American and global Capitalism, which perfects the work rather than the worker and overvalues corporate leaders and neglects the trampling of the poor."[4]

In October 2000 AD, a stunning monument of Pope John Paul II was erected in front of the Holy Ghost RC Church in Windsor, Ontario — thanks to its Parish Priest Rev. Canon Sanczenko and his generous parishioners.

The Death of Mother and Sister Reggie...

In 1979, I suffered two additional family losses. I received an urgent call from my sister Reggie that mother was mortally ill, urging me to fly home with Tevis directly. Tevis and I, after having arranged for a family member to care for children and the home, caught the earliest flight to Montréal. Mother was lying in bed when we arrived, and I had a doctor friend come out to the house.

Before leaving, the doctor called an ambulance to take mother to St. Mary's hospital. He whispered to us, 'it's her heart'. All six of mother's living children were at her bedside: four daughters and two sons. She spoke to us individually. At noon on April 20th, 1979, mother departed from this world, two weeks before her 92nd birthday of May 3rd, 1979. My sisters looked after the funeral arrangements. We had the D'Allaire Funeral (the same funeral directors that assisted at my father's burial in

---

[3] "Man of the Century," p. 553.

[4] "Man of the Century," front flap.

Hon. Paul I. B. Staniszewski

TWO POLISH SOLDIERS OF FREE POLAND THAT TOOK PART IN THE ROUT OF THE BOLSHEVIKS (COMMUNISTS) IN 1920. COLLEAGUES OF S. BOGUSLAWSKI.

MY FATHER JULIAN (ON THE LEFT) WITH FRIEND; CONSCRIPTS IN THE RUSSIAN TSARIST ARMY --1905 IN MANCHRIA FIGHTING THE IMPERIAL JAPANESE

MOTHER, FATHER, EUGENE, JOSEPH, REGINA, AND VERA (CIRCA 1920)

PAUL; FIRST COMMUNION; 1931

PART OF THE PROCESSION OF OUR MONTRÉAL ST. MARY'S PARISH OF "CORPUS CHRISTI"
(CIRCA 1931)
IMPOSSIBLE TODAY BECAUSE OF THE AUTOMOBILES, TRUCKS ETC.

ON 13-APRIL-1940, AT MONTRÉAL WINDSOR STATION
POLISH GENERAL HALER, WELCOMED BY THE GUIDES, SCOUTS, AND POLONIA.

Hon. Paul I. B. Staniszewski

THE FIRST CONVENTION OF THE CANADIAN-POLISH YOUTH CONGRESS

PHOTOCOPY OF JANUARY 1946 OF
"THE DAWN" OFFICIAL MONTHLY OF
THE CANADIAN YOUTH CONGRESS

AS SECRETARY OF THE NATIONAL
CONGRESS, WELCOMING POLISH
SOLDIERS IN KINGSTON, ONTARIO

PHOTO OF JULIAN KAWECKI
MY COUSIN WITH THE POLISH AIR
FORCE IN ENGLAND IN WORLD WAR II

Wanda and Paul
on their Wedding Day

Paul in a Barrister's Attire
After Graduating from
Osgood Hall (Toronto)

Father and Mother with me
on my Graduation at The
University of Toronto

Huge Sign at 366 Runnymede Road
(High Park), Erected by John and
Mary Kudluk
Ukrainian Supporters of my Liberal
Candidacy

Hon. Paul I. B. Staniszewski

WANDA BY THE SHORE
OF LAKE ONTARIO

PAUL IN HIS COUNTY COURT
JUDGE'S ATTIRE

FROM LEFT TO RIGHT: JUDGE HAROLD LANG (SENIOR OF DISTRICT 1),
JUDGE BRUCE MACDONALD, SENIOR JUDGE SYDNEY CLUNIS, MYSELF,
AND CHIEF JUDGE ARTHUR R. WILLMOT.

03-July-1971
Tevis and I Married

ANDREA, BROTHER AMBROSE
(MCGEE HIGH, 1942),
PAUL AND CAMILLE-TORONTO HOME
1968

MICHELLE, KURT, ANDREA, TEVIS,
PAUL, GAYLE, AND CAMILLE

WINDSOR HOME: 1968-1991

Hon. Paul I. B. Staniszewski

PAUL ADDRESSING
WARSAW
CONVENTION ON
400TH
ANNIVERSARY OF
THE FOUNDING OF
ROYAL TRIBUNALS
OF THE KINGDOM
OF POLAND

GRANDDAUGHTERS
ALAINA AND JORDANA

GREG AND ANDREA,
HOLDING ALAINA AND JORDANA
CHARLTON

HEATHER AND KURT BAGNELL

GRIER AND BREAGH BAGNELL

LEFT: TEVIS, CAMILLE & EUGENE
MONTRÉAL 1997 LIBERAL VOLUNTEERS

ABOVE: PAUL & TEVIS IN
ZAKOPANE POLAND

ABOVE: PAUL & TEVIS

FORT LOUIS BOURG - CAPE BRETON N.S.

1961) sustain our mother's interment. Mother was an excellent seamstress, a very devout Catholic, and a Polish patriot.

The Funeral Mass was celebrated at the new Polish St. Mary's of Czestochowa Church. It was very moving and touching, bidding adieu to our 92-year-old mother. The interment was at the Côte de Neiges Cemetery located on Mount Royal in a grave next to father and Reggie's son Robert (my nephew).

Reggie prepared a reception at mother's home. It was sombre but realistic, that, not everyone reached the age of 92 as independently as mother did, with relatively good health all of her life. This was the last time I saw my favourite brother-in-law Frank as well, who passed away the following year.

Reggie, grieving and all alone in mother's home had begun to sink into a fearful state that her sister and niece could not comprehend. She could not bear to be alone; it seems that she was exploited with a promise to have her move in with either one of them, on the signing over of all her local realty and that of Val David, Québec to them.

On that dreaded night of October 19th, 1979 at about 8:00 p.m., I telephoned Reggie from Windsor; she did not answer my phone call. Worried, I phoned Vera who complained that her husband couldn't drive that far. I phoned my cousin Marcel Wichlacz who drove down to her, found the home in darkness, got no answer, and phoned me later to say that he was positive she was just sleeping. The next morning she was found dead, in her bed.

The shroud of death covered my sister Reggie on October 19th, 1979. I compared Reggie to the Greek Goddess Hera, consort of Zeus, guardian of the rites and sanctities of marriage. Some neighbours gossiped that it was an overdose, a suicide. She manifestly died, perhaps feeling betrayed, being unable to sell her inheritance except for a pittance and unable to abate her fear of living alone, her frailty precipitating her to join her son and her parents in their place of rest on Mount Royal mountain. Her soul left her exactly on the 11th anniversary of Robert's death, October 19th, 1968. She was buried in our parent's plot next to her son Robert.

After the funeral, the five surviving siblings of Reggie examined her holograph Will, which left the Val David, Québec cottage to one sister and the Montréal home to a niece. We drove to a classmate's legal office, René Talbot and discussed the matter at length. Then we signed an agreement that the five remaining siblings would share equally in any proceeds after disposing the two realties of the estate. What was important was that we all signed, and left the matter with the lawyer.

When we got back to Windsor, the Montréal lawyer called, to tell me that one sister and niece wanted the agreement back, which he refused. This intrusion was instigated by her husband. Naturally, litigation evolved (not in Court—but protracted lawyer's letters) attempting to settle. It was clear to us that Guy Morin, a brother-in-law who lived in a small wartime home, wanted to have the assets of Reggie go to his divorced niece. The property could not be sold so it dragged on for two more years.

I heard that Reggie hated to be alone before she died and wanted to live with Vera. This was torpedoed by her now deceased husband. It is fathomable that Reggie had negotiated a live-in agreement with her niece, conditional on Reggie leaving the house to her. She allegedly wrote a holograph Will in their favour.

The lawyers made a fortune for each phone call, letter, etc. Finally settled, five siblings' shared in the sale of the Laurentian cottage. The niece was awarded the Montréal home and contents, which included many of my personal books and Reggie's automobile. Our family was on 'haves' and 'have-nots'; the fires of enmity burnt beneath the ashes for a long, long time…

Letter to a Judge

As a County Court Judge, I occasionally received extraordinary letters from individuals who appeared before me in civil and criminal trials. One letter from an accused that I received in late mid–1970s was from A. J. B. (I employ initials, as it would be unfair to disclose names). From the seven-page letter, I quote pertinent extracts:

Dear Sir…

…I am writing this letter to thank you for saving my sanity and most probably my life…I doubt that you will remember me, but let me say that I will never forget you…on my bail appeal hearing, my attorney and others tried to discourage me from attempting to get a release on bail. This was because I was earlier refused bail, as I was on parole and three-and-a-half weeks later I was charged with a new offence.

As I stood before you…all I could think of was getting out…Through Alcoholics Anonymous, and the grace of God, I haven't had a drink for the past seventeen months, an incredible situation, which has given my life new meaning. For the last several months, I refrained from writing to you, fearing that it would be misinterpreted as an attempt to get on your good side.

I had the occasion to appear before you again about seven months later, at my divorce hearing. When you looked straight at me that day, I had the fearful feeling that you remembered me; that you probably were convinced that I was still living the same reckless, hopeless life. If this feeling was correct then Sir, then I cannot allow you to feel you made a bad decision at the bail hearing seven months ago. You did not! ...

This marriage is very sadly a part of my disturbed past...I can't begin to tell you of the new loving life that now exists between me and my four-year old daughter Tammy.

...the greatest reward sobriety has given me...It took me 13 years of drinking to climb out of my own gutter...I must say that you didn't change me, but made it possible for me to change myself; you threw me a rope when I was going down for a third time.

For that, I will be forever grateful to you. If you had decided against releasing me at my bail hearing, my mind would be twisted even worse than it already was —

I would hate policemen,

and I would hate you,

and I would still hate me.

I shall pay my debt, come out an ex-con, non-drinking, ex-alcoholic, with a miserable, confused past and a hopeful, promising future.

Thank you, good luck, and God bless you.

Sincerely,

A. J. B.

A Young Japanese Judge Visits...

In the early spring of 1980, I received a telephone call from a Japanese Judge touring the Michigan Law Courts. He asked me, in an extremely soft and polite voice, if he could please visit our Court and during one of our trials sit as a spectator. I replied that he was more than welcome to come by the next day to our Courthouse and that I personally would take care of him. Judge Hitoshi Murase and his wife, Hiromi arrived the following day at the Courthouse, profusely polite and thankful. I had both of them escorted to sit during a civil trial concerning a motor vehicle accident. At lunchtime, I invited them both out for lunch. I invited Tevis along and the four of us passed a very pleasant lunch at the famous "Auberge" restaurant. After lunch, Tevis kindly invited them to celebrate Easter dinner with our family, which they graciously accepted. Tevis drove back to her School Board office and we walked back to the Courthouse. I had an usher escort our Japanese guests to a Courtroom where a criminal trial had begun that morning.

The next day I arranged to reverse the type of trials our Japanese guests were to observe. At lunchtime, we ate at "Ye Old Steak House," a famous Windsor restaurant, owned by a Mr. K. Deeg who also owns "The Auberge." By about 3:30 p.m., I had the usher whisper to our Japanese Judge and his spouse to join me in my office. He told me he found it very instructive. I presented him with several textbooks — the Canadian Criminal Code, Probate Practice, several statutes of Ontario, and the manual of motor vehicle law. He was most grateful and appreciative.

On Easter Sunday (April 5th, 1980), they joined us for the dinner Tevis prepared with the help of her mother and our three daughters. After a sumptuous dinner (as par for our household!) our family presented them each with elegantly hand-decorated, multiple coloured Polish Easter Eggs.

The Murases were enchanted! They bestowed on us a picture with a gold background and a Japanese cultured garden is embossed in dark and gold-pinkish colours. The picture has pink flowers, a peacock, and two dark thick trees. We were captivated by its exquisite charm.

Some time later, we received a long letter of appreciation for our hospitality from Japan. The Japanese Judge thanked me once again for allowing him to observe our Court and for the texts, which he was reading. They wrote to us a second time — much later — from Japan, with their address enclosed. We attempted to write back but our letter was returned marked "wrong address."

There are people who come into your life and stay a while. Others go, but leave footprints on your life that you never will forget. I have been blessed with both...

Inquiry of a Possible Propinquity with an Ambassador

On having learned from our local paper that a new Ambassador to Great Britain from Communist Poland was an S. Staniszewski, in 1982, I wrote a letter to His Excellency Stefan Staniszewski, Polish People's Republic Ambassador to Great Britain, at London, England.

I sent my felicitations to the new Polish Ambassador on his appointment in these unsettled times. I further wrote that since our surnames were the same I wondered if there was any possible affinity, and I hoped that he might respond whenever he had a free moment. Then I went on, to briefly outline the roots of my father. I wrote hoping for an answer, either way, ending with the usual protocol salutations.

I never did receive a reply. Perhaps some present Polish diplomat of Free Poland can help me locate Stefan Staniszewski, Polish Ambassador to Great Britain, 1982.

French Immersion 1982

In March 1982, a French immersion course was arranged by the Commissioner of Federal Judicial Affairs. It was held in the Laurentians at Hotel La Sapiniere at Val David, Québec. That same hotel had a sign I saw (at age 13) at its entrance in the summer of 1939 which warned, *"No Dogs or Jews Allowed."* Thankfully, no such sign appeared in 1982.

Before the outbreak of World War II, anti-Semitic, atrocious, and cowardly acts were perpetrated against the Jews in the Québec Laurentians. At Val David, Québec a synagogue was desecrated with a large black swastika painted on its walls. In St. Agathe, north of the synagogue, bilingual placards appeared all over which read, *"Jews scram while the going is good."*

Many more anti-Semitic acts that were cowardly were committed in August 1939. These nefarious acts were ascribed to the French-Canadian fascist (group) gang of Adrian Arcand, who was helped by some of the locals. Even a monsignor Bazinet formed an anti-Semitic committee.

Norman Lester, who authored in 2001 — "The Black Book of English Canada," describes Adrian Arcand as Québec's minor Nazi leader who was financed by officials from the Federal Conservative Party (English). Adrian Arcand was not a Nazi; he was a "fascist," and "fascism" by force implanted its dictatorship in 1922 on a Catholic Italy. For some strange reason that I don't comprehend, this fascism was alluring to Québecers like A. Arcand, some clerics like monsignor Bazinet, and a multitude of others. For Norman Lester to invent a story that the Federal Tories financed Adrian Arcand's French-Canadian Nazis is historically unfounded, libellous, and preposterous in my humble opinion!

Val David, Québec was the village in which my parents had a summer cottage. The village was ever changing and developing, with a newly built suburb mushrooming.

On our daily breaks, many of us would walk across the snow, pass the village church to the abandoned sawmill, which had previously been operated by the Mayor of Val David, Québec. The Mayor died, I am told, in the mid–1950s. The mill died with him. His son is now the sole policeman of Val David, Québec.

Our professors loaded us up with homework, which the others and I could not always complete. Among some of the Judges I made acquaintance with were Ray Stortini, Mendes DaCosta, and Judge Karen Weiler, the youngest and most intelligent of our group.

She was appointed to the Ontario Court of Appeal. Several days later an anecdote circulated stated that two Judges took a day off and spent a day skiing at Mont Tremblant, about 30-odd miles north of Val David, Québec! I wondered how they had time for such frivolities if this was indeed true, as I could not begin to keep up with our assignments.

One day, as our evenings were free and no entertainment was listed on our agenda, I took it upon myself to remedy this situation. Since I knew that the hotel normally operated a party room for dancing and libations which was called "Cave Aux Vin," in their cellar — with the help of Judge Karen Weiler, a few other Judges, and their wives, we made arrangements to have the "Cave aux Vin" opened and hired a few musicians to perform one evening.

The combination of the French music, songs, (wine) and dancing made us feel like we were in a "Cave Aux Vin" in Paris, France. The accordionist sprightly played Viennese songs, tangos, waltzes, and popular jazz. The melodies seemed perpetual. Obviously, the wine helped and the dancing was boundless. Judge Karen Weiler's negotiations for the evening celebration were appreciated by all.

Many years later, we had another French Immersion course for Ontario County Court Judges and Justices of the Higher Court once again in Val David, Québec at the Hotel "La Sapiniere." This time no Judges went skiing, but we did have the "Cave Aux Vin" opened once again, which gave us all a much-needed break from our intense lectures. *Vivre la Cave Aux Vins!*

Poland's Solidarity Movement

Suppression of Poland's Solidarity Trade Unions resulted in Windsor's Polish community launching a $100,000.00 fund-raising campaign. The Solidarity Trade Union grew from a group of strikers in the shipyards of Gdansk, led by L. Walesa (after 1989 he was elected Poland's first president in a Free Poland). In mid–1980, this movement swelled throughout Poland. It gained many concessions from the Communist regime, including an independent, self-managing Solidarity Trade Union. Finally, Moscow now called this "non-Communist workers movement" an anathema. The Soviets left the job "of suppression by force" to its Warsaw's Communist rulers.

In mid-December, the Communist regime struck; 50,000 solidarity activists were arrested throughout Poland. A day later, martial law was proclaimed. The Polish Communist regime started to normalize things by 1982 ...seven years later Communism in Poland collapsed.

Emergency Relief Fund for Poland

The Holy Trinity Roman Catholic Church (Windsor, Ontario) organized an emergency relief fund for Poland. The fund came into being in Windsor on hearing martial law declared in Poland and the brutal Communist suppression of the Solidarity Non-Communist Union and its millions of followers.

The initiative for the drive was that of Monsignor Lawrence Wnuk, P.A. He called a meeting on January 23rd, 1982 of about 60 parishioners and members of associated Polish societies, businessmen, and professionals including myself. As a patron with their Excellencies, Bishops Sherlock, and Gervais, and B. Newman MPP, the goal of the committee was to raise $100,000.00.

The fund would buy medicines, food, and clothing from Western countries. Distribution would be to the starving and destitute in need of warmth, and medical supplies. Local Parishes, Caritas, and the Red Cross were the active distributors insuring that there were no political interferences. Many parishioners had relatives in the "old country" and that gave them great incentive to be profoundly charitable. The committee doubled in number and effort.

Although I attended my Court duties diligently, I devoted all my spare time—evenings and Saturdays to the drive. I was assisted by the clerical staff of one law firm with the mundane but important task of mailing requests. By early February, the committee had collected about $77,925.00. I personally had mailed numerous letters to local and Ontario Judges, lawyers, M.P.'s, and friends. The Jewish businessman's association was extremely generous and the "Windsor Italian Business Club" surprised me with their generous support. Throughout the campaign, I also lunched with numerous lawyers and/or local businessmen appealing for aid for the Polish Relief Fund.

In a booklet commemorating the 75th anniversary of the Holy Trinity Church in Windsor, on page 18, right side column, in Polish it recites, *"...at a special parish meeting we organized an emergency relief fund, for Poland, which was co-chaired with Reverend Monsignor Lawrence A. Wnuk, P.A. and with great diligence by Judge Paul I. B. Staniszewski. $213,000.00 was collected for medicine, clothing, and food."* This fund was successful, not only because of numerous donations by Polish people, but also by many Canadians of various other ethnic origins.

Our Archbishops and the Diocese of Hamilton added $100,000.00 to our campaign. Local parishes and convents helped us collect such a large sum. A small discord occurred when a prominent Polish-Canadian businessman unsuccessfully tried to make a lowball donation and met with the entire committee's acrimony...

My 58th Birthday

With our three girls in tow, Tev and I attended midnight Mass (Minuit Chrétien in French-to me is more colourful) at our church, on December 24th, 1982. We all participated in the solemn Mass and received Holy Communion.

The celebration of the Mass was sung in Polish, sanctimoniously in the symphonious Latin canticle of old. I reminisced when the Polish Christmas carols were sung. My thoughts went back to the Christmas Eves in Montréal in the 1930s and Toronto in the 1960s, hearkened me to the same imposing, religiously rousing Polish Christmas carols.

Judge Bruce MacDonald

In June 1983, we lost an outstanding brother, Judge Bruce MacDonald. As a roving Judge, he tried a multitude of serious criminal cases in numerous Courts spread throughout Ontario. One of his most famous cases was that of a robbery of a Windsor bank. There were five accused, including a woman.

A decade later, two defence lawyers became prominent Judges, one in Toronto, and the other in Windsor. Judge MacDonald's charge to the jury was 153 pages long. The jury, after long deliberations and asking several times for the re-reading of parts of the testimony of specific witnesses, finally rendered a finding of guilty against the five accused.

Judge MacDonald, after hearing submissions of Counsel for the five accused, sentenced the gang leaders 15 to 20 years and fined them $75,000.00. The lesser accomplices were given lighter custodial sentences. Within days, an appeal was filed. The greatest delay was caused in the Court reporter's having to transcribe about nine copies of 14 volumes of the trial's proceedings. The Court of Appeal some months later dismissed the appeal and upheld the sentences imposed by Judge MacDonald.

Judge MacDonald retired having reached the mandatory age of 75 in 1978. He received a then meagrely pension (as the French would define "soupe maigre"). For subsistence, he was compelled to assume the monthly presiding over of the Small Claims Court in Windsor, Ontario and in five Essex County towns. The remuneration was at a low "per diem" basis. He also lectured at the local Law School a few days of the month.

In World War II, the Judge had been a colonel in the Scottish Regiment. In 1944, he sat as president of the Allied Court of Inquiry of the German army war atrocities. After the cessation of hostilities, the massacre of about 48 Canadian soldiers was unearthed. The Canadians were Prisoners of War and were slaughtered by *Hitler Youth Corps* [special units with fanatical Nazi bigotry and savagely indifferent to killings]. The commander of this barbarous unit was Major General Kurt Meyer.

A sensation took place, with our Judge acting as prosecutor; General Kurt Meyer was the accused. After a lengthy trial, Meyer was found guilty and sentenced to death. Kurt Meyer served nine years of his life sentence in Canada, as the Cold War commenced with the Soviets erecting their Iron Curtain. General Kurt Meyer died in 1961 at the age of 51. Judge Bruce MacDonald made proud his city of Windsor, Ontario. His contributions are an inspiration to all Canadians. He will be loved and remembered as a caring husband, a practicing Christian, an auspicious Crown-Attorney, a righteous Judge, and as a *dauntless* Canadian officer.

"Verba Docent; Exampla Trahi..."

In 1983, Reverend Monsignor Lawrence A. Wnuk, P.A. was our parish priest, and he celebrated the 50th anniversary of his ordination in 1933 to the priesthood in Gniezno, Poland. His curriculum vitae, I shall humbly only try to sketch. Before the German Nazi subjugation of Poland with Soviet Russia's deceitful partnership, the Monsignor was a devoted priest ministering several Polish parishes in Western Poland. The Nazis commenced their diabolical policy of ethnic cleansing. Western Poland was incorporated into Greater Germany; the deportations of non-Germans were implemented.

Our Monsignor was arrested and transported in freight cars with Poles, Jews, and invalids to Central Poland, then called "Government General," and administered by the infamous General Frank; the allies at the end of the war had him hanged for his crimes. Monsignor was imprisoned in the town of "Piotrków-Trybunalski," (noted for the founding in the 16th century of Poland's Royal Tribunals and Courts). After some months, he was released.

Two years later, in 1943 with the Nazi's need for labourers, he was snatched, as he was over 6-feet tall and looked healthy and strong. He was transported to the infamous Auschwitz death camp, where millions were gassed. He still sustains the number imprinted on his hand by his "benevolent" jailers.

In 1944, after having toiled exhaustively at hard labour, along with many other prisoners, he was transported to Buchenwald. With Germany on the brink of defeat in early 1945, some hundreds of prisoners were compelled to march on foot for hundreds of miles; less than 310 prisoners survived out of the originating 800. Father Wnuk, in the most hideous and inhumane of conditions, sustained his faith in God and man's dignity in an inhumane atmosphere of horrid degradation.

After liberation by the Western allies and the surrender of Germany, Soviet Russia inflicted Communism on Poland. Father Wnuk refused to return to a Communist Poland and became a Chaplain at an allied detention camp near Soest, which was in the British occupation zone of Germany. In 1951, he was sent by his superiors to Hamtramck, Michigan U.S.A. to preside over a Polish parish. At that time, the Bishop located only Michigan-born priests in Michigan (commencing in the 1970s, priests were so scarce that this tenet has been nullified). In June 1957, his superiors sent him to Chatham, Ontario Canada.

In Chatham, with borrowed money and cooperative parishioners, a church was built and ready for 1957 midnight Mass. By June 1961, his superiors transferred Father L. A. Wnuk to the oldest Polish parish in the London Diocese "Holy Trinity Church" in Windsor, Ontario. In spite of multitudinous duties and exigencies, a virtuous Priest finds time for prayer, meditation, and the station's of the cross, applying an ancient proverb, "Verba Docent; Exempla Trahunt."

After dedicated watchfulness to the spiritual, including visitation of the sick and the material needs of the parish, Monsignor L. A. Wnuk concentrated his efforts on the youth and children of Holy Trinity Church. The Monsignor was inspired to sponsor some Polish Ursuline Nuns to Windsor. He advanced his case with local politicians, Federal Ministers, and Immigration officials. This took years.

After many promises and delays, finally in late 1965, 10 Ursuline Sisters were granted permission to settle in Windsor, Ontario. The Nuns injected energy and faith to Holy Trinity Church; they organized both a Polish preschool and a Saturday Polish school. Both are thriving today.

The Monsignor helped his people assiduously at the Immigration Board, Canada Manpower and Consulate when and whenever asked. His mastery of the German language helped many Poles in the Windsor area and the County of Essex receive compensation from West Germany, mostly because they were constrained into forced labour.

Under his direction and patronage, some of the funds or scholarships were established: The Copernicus Fund at the University of Windsor; scholarships for the Catholic University of Lublin, Poland; the Polish Relief Fund (1982 raised $213,000.00); the Polonia Park Housing Development; and the Stanley Grabowiecki Fund. Fifty (50%) percent of the monies raised went to the churches in Canada and fifty (50%) percent to the churches in Poland. The Monsignor was decorated by Free Poland with one of its highest decorations.

A Greek Odyssey

For the summer holidays of 1984, Tevis and I decided to explore Greece. I managed to squeeze in a few quick lessons in the Greek language, which came in handy. One of the highlights of the trip was sailing on a cruise ship from the port of Piraeus in Athens.

On first seeing the "Stella Solaris," I was deeply moved by its grandeur, splendour, and stately magnificence. It was about half the size of the Dutch liner "Voldendam," but more august and majestic. On entering the ship, we were not disappointed. Our room was large with a porthole from which we could view the deep, greenish-blue Aegean Sea. Our first stop the next day was to be Istanbul, Turkey's capital (formerly Constantinople), capital of the Byzantine Empire until 1453 when the Islamic Turks conquered it.

We sailed through the Aegean Sea in a northeasterly direction. We were invited to a captain's cocktail party several hours after lunch. The activities on the ship ranged all the way from arts and crafts to Greek dance lessons.

The following morning our ship docked in Istanbul. Upon landing, there was an announcement made warning us to beware of child pickpockets. Sure enough, when we descended from our bus, our group of 50 tourists were surrounded by 100 local children, who swarmed around us yelling, waving a small religious picture of Jesus.

Our first stop was at the St. Sophia Cathedral. It had been employed for centuries as a Moslem Mosque. We toured "St. Sophia" as it is now named by the Turks. The refurbishing of "St. Sophia" was incomplete but some paintings of Christian Saints' were restored, as was a large Byzantine painting of the Virgin Mary.

We did not have the opportunity to tour the gorgeous Blue Mosque located next to St. Sophia, but we purchased postcards of its magnificent exterior and interior. We hurriedly viewed the Istanbul Museum a short distance away. It was rich in contents, (e.g. there was a large bust of Alexander the Great), but layers of dust and a lack of English labelling on the displays made it a futile tour for us, as we were not versed in the Turkish language.

The next port that "Stella Solaris" docked at was the Port of Pergamum—"Dikili" in Turkish—in the southwest of Turkey. In ancient times, this city-state rose to power. Our guide indicated to us that at one time, the Pergamum Library boasted over 200,000 volumes, surpassing even the library of Alexandria. The city, situated between two streams, rose to 1,300 feet surrounded by a commanding wall. We browsed around small stalls outside the site and purchased a Pergamum statue.

The following day our ship approached a lovely, sunny, small corner of Greece comprised of about twelve islands called "the Dodecanese," situated off the Asia Minor coast. Rhodes, known as the Island of Roses, where "Stella Solaris" ultimately anchored, was the largest island of the twelve Dodecanese Islands. Our tour guide related to us how in the 4th century B.C., the island grew in wealth through trade with Syria, Cyprus, and Egypt. The citizen armies of Rhodes defeated invaders and constructed the legendary 105-foot high bronze "Colossus of Rhodes."

Some years later, shaken by an earthquake it disappeared into the sea, never to be seen again. Rhodes was "sold" off in the Byzantine era to the Knights of St. John of Jerusalem. They built almost impregnable fortifications throughout the island. In 1522, the Knights lost to Islam's Suleiman the Great's forces and reverted to Malta.

We briefly toured the Grand Master's Castle and saw the still visible remnants of its fortifications. We viewed the street of Knights, dedicated to the seven nations that comprised the Knights of St. John of Jerusalem. The Turks occupied the island until 1912. Many Mosques still stand and attest to the long Turkish presence.

In 1912, Italy occupied the island; in a local museum, we were surprised at the sight of a 20-foot huge, richly decorative Japanese vase, displayed prominently in the centre of the museum. We were apprised that the colossal vase was a gift from the Japanese Emperor Hiro Hito to Italy's dictator Mussolini. When World War II hostilities ended, Rhodes reverted to Greece. We briefly visited the town of Lindos on the other side of the island. Crowning the town is the Acropolis of Lindos. From this vantage point, there is a breathtaking view of "St. Paul's Bay" (Pelagos) where St. Paul dropped anchor on his pilgrimage to Esphessos.

The following day, after having cruised in the obscurity of the night, we docked at the Port of Knossos, on the island of Crete (Heraklion). Crete is the southern most of the Greek islands. It boasts mountainous and fertile terrain, with many varied attractive beaches. We decided to embark on a short taxi tour of Crete.

At a certain spot along the winding scenic road, our driver slowed down and pointed out the lovely bodies of naked young women and men, relaxing in the mid-day sun on a local beach. We toured the "King Minos" palace at Knossos. According to legend, Minos was a "God" born in Crete, who around 2000 B.C. founded the Minoan dynasty.

The Byzantines captured Crete in 961 A.D.; later the Venetians occupied it for 500 years, only to be displaced by the Turks, until Greek independence. In World War II, German paratroopers and Stuka bombers caused the British and some Greek personnel to abandon Crete, with heavy casualties and the loss of several destroyers. The Greek government, with British help, returned after the collapse of Hitlerism in May 1945.

The last of the islands we experienced in our odyssey was Santorini (its ancient name Ihiri). As our cruise ship, "Stella Solaris" entered the bay, we saw the towering cliffs of this volcanic island frame all sides of it. Perched on the top of its breathtaking cliffs is the town of Thira. Small buildings dotted the cliff top from afar resembling snowcaps on a Himalayan mountain range. The ascent to the town could be travelled either by cable car or by mules. We chose the former!

Back on our ship once more, a party awaited us. Greek dancers in multi-coloured, National costumes danced and sang Greek songs. We were treated to a feast of a Greek dinner, of roast lamb, vegetables, Greek wine, various local torts, cookies, and the infamous Greek coffee, whilst the Greek singers and ship's staff all sang Greek songs of farewell and au revoir with fervour. The dinner party broke up around 10:30 p.m. As we docked at Piraeus the next morning, our waiters said to us in Greek, "Ees-to-Epa-ne-Theen" ("Hope to see you again").

Back at the "Lido" hotel, we had one more day to shop in Athens. Our Greek tour guide invited a few of us to go and see the Parthenon, an architectural masterpiece of ancient Greece.

The guide relayed to us that it was built by Ictinus in the oldest Greek form, "The Doric." Built between 447 and 432 B.C., inspired by Pericles to glorify Athens within the temple was a costly statue of *Athena*, "Goddess of Wisdom."

This Parthenon remained virtually intact for 2,000 years. But in 1687, in a war between the Turks, who held Greece, and the Venetians, a cannon-shot fired by the latter, exploded a powder magazine stored in the Parthenon and shattered it.

How blessed I felt upon leaving Greece — *living with a real life Athena* — my dear Tevis and having the joy of seeing Athena's statue up close — *at long last…*

Remembrance of Christmases Past…

That next Christmas, Michelle, one of our youngest daughters, enclosed with her Christmas card some recollections of our past Christmases as a family, which I lovingly share with a smile…

"At 56 Edgehill Road in Toronto, I had an earache, and as I lay in bed thinking of Santa Claus, dad arrived and carried me down the stairs in my pyjamas to see Santa Claus. A neighbour dressed up as Santa Claus, to my horror gave my aunt a potato that he fetched from his huge sack. At that sight, I became scared of Santa for a long, long time. I was only five or six years old."

"A Court constable rang the bell at our Windsor home. I answered the door and he gave me a gift-wrapped shoebox and said Merry Christmas to the Judge and family. He added that the box contained a duck! As I was alone in our huge home, I softly uttered, 'Merry Christmas' and 'thank you' on shutting the door. I walked cautiously down the basement stairs and gently placed the 'box' outside the garage wall facing the Detroit River. I was convinced that it had to contain a bomb!

Later, when dad and Tevis arrived from Christmas shopping, I informed them where I placed the 'bomb.' Dad retrieved the Christmas present, which turned out to be a fresh duck. They both said that I read too many novels, both mystery and spy, and was bewitched with Sean Connery-007 movies."

"The Annual Ritual of Selecting the Perfect Christmas Tree."

"They all looked perfect lined up on the lot. We chose the nicest one. When we brought it home, we had difficulty carrying it into the house even through two wide front-open French doors. When the tree was standing up, many previously unseen bare spots appeared...but thank God, for string...I can only imagine if duct tape was available! Then again, if dad had only bought a more expensive tree stand ... Well, then *where* would we hang all of our Christmas cards? I mean, the purpose of all of that string was dual-holding up the Christmas tree AND to hang our Christmas cards."

"Never let your parish priests come to your home on Christmas Day...Why? Camille, Andrea, and I had not yet unwrapped all of our Christmas gifts from Christmas morning. When our parish priest arrived, well, talk about *a strong* handshake. He shook the *demons* out of your hand...we all learned to take our rings off before the *Almighty*, which brings me to another event of Confession before Christmas."

"We never wanted to go to Confession because dad always said that all of us would each have at least one big transport truck full of sins, and our priest would know it was the Staniszewski sisters, because we were the only ones who confessed in English. Our penance was surprisingly light for all those massive sins: ten Hail Mary's and three Our Fathers."

"One Christmas week, we had a couple of feet of snow. After the three of us girls shovelled our driveway (at 5420 Riverside Drive; Windsor, Ontario), Andrea, Camille, and I climbed up on top of the garage roof with the help of a ladder. Then we all jumped together off the garage roof into 12-foot snowdrifts.

We enjoyed playing in the snow. Our neighbour, Mrs. Eisen, was looking out of her kitchen window just in time to see us jumping. Some time later, I conversed with her. She told me that she calmed her husbands poor nerves with these words, 'Look honey, it's those fun loving Judge's daughters again...don't worry...they are only jumping off the roof and waving at me!'"

Nuptials of our Daughter Andrea

On our return from Greece, Tevis and I were overjoyed to help with the many preparations that weddings require. Our youngest, Andrea was to be married in August 1984. We had two bedrooms painted and redecorated for Camille, who was coming from Vancouver for three weeks and for Andrea who gave up her apartment to spend the week before the wedding with us at home.

There was a flurry of activity; the girls attended several wedding showers, fittings for the four bridesmaids, wedding rehearsals, and a formal dinner at the groom's parents. The night before the wedding, the four Staniszewski sisters went out on the town. Later that night, we took pictures of Andrea sleeping it off, on her last night before leaving us forever to live in wedded bliss. Our household was bursting at its seams; Andrea, Camille, Michelle, and Tev's sister Lally and her husband Terry all came to stay with us.

The day of the wedding, the bridesmaids congregated, their flowers arrived, and a photographer took pre-wedding pictures. Tev drove the bride, Camille, and I to the church. The nuptial ceremonies were held at the "All Saints" Anglican Church in Windsor, Ontario. The groom was Anglican. It turned out to be a sunny day, devoid of the dastardly humid Windsor summer days. After the wedding, the bride and groom changed their attire and departed for a golfing honeymoon at Honey Harbour — Georgian Bay, Ontario. The next afternoon, we entertained about thirty people for brunch at our home. Some guests stayed until evening.

When Andrea and Greg returned to their lovely brand new apartment, their sisters and friends had played a prank and moved all the furniture around. They also took every label off the canned goods in their kitchen cupboards and put sneezing powder in their freshly made-up bed! At the writing of this book, they have been married for 17 years and have two beautiful children — 12-year-old Alaina and 9-year-old Jordana. Gregg, Andrea's husband, is a pharmacist and a wonderful husband. They make Tev and I proud.

Rocky Mountains

Our plane landed in Calgary, Alberta in late July 1985. We boarded a bus that drove us to the year-round tourist town of Banff. Banff is located in the southern part of the Banff National Park. As the bus drove on, we gazed on the "passage" and deeply sensed as if we were travelling through the biblical Garden of Eden. There were thick, tall forests, with the ever present, jagged, snow-capped chains of huge mountains. We passed interspersed meadows and the serrated Rocky Mountains, grasping the heavens. The stirring scenery brought back memories when I, as President of the Canadian Polish Youth Club, toured the Canadian Polish Youth Clubs in Western Canada, and called Alberta "God's Country."

We came primarily to visit Tevis' son Kurt and his spouse Heather. They lived in a cozy apartment; Kurt held an important position at the world renowned "Banff Centre." We spent the greater part of the day with Kurt and Heather. Around midnight, we meandered back to the Banff Park Lodge. We discovered another jewel of the West; the drinking water was refreshingly succulent, as its source was from mountain springs. The next day after breakfast, Tevis planned our afternoon activities by telephone with Kurt. At a nearby restaurant, we had mushroom soup, sandwiches, coffee, and cookies for lunch. The mushrooms we had in our soup, precipitated a memory.

I recalled how my late father, every fall in the Laurentian forests north of Mont Tremblanc, Québec, picked mushrooms he called "podpienki," which were wild edible mushrooms that had sprouted around old fallen logs and attached themselves to stumps.

These Banff mushrooms were akin in taste to the Laurentian mushrooms that my father had picked throughout the 1950s. My stepson and his wife took us in their vehicle for a grand tour of the surrounding Rocky Mountains. We passed by several cerulean lakes, partially encircled by thick, dark forests, or by shores of jagged massive stone, which soared toward the sky.

Banff was filled with tourists. The greater part were Japanese; Americans were less numerous. We all went to Mass at a magnificent little church in Banff known as St. Mary's church. It had brilliant stained-glass windows. Tevis and I took Communion together. We were driven to the town of Lake Louise, which lies within the boundaries of Banff National Park. Lake Louise, adorned with the rays of the eastern sunlight, appeared like a million lit sparkles glittering over and over its azure apex.

The lake's shore had indescribable wondrous beds of huge red and pink Poppies, interspersed with smaller yellow Poppies. "We could have spent twelve months in Banff and yet not be appraised of this entire wondrous province." Before coming to Alberta, I was appraised by the fact that there was no provincial tax levied in Alberta. About 40-odd years earlier, the "Leduc Oil Discoveries" commenced Alberta's oil companies to make Alberta oil rich and Canada's "Saudi Arabia."

Pilgrimage to Vancouver

On August 1st, 1985, we flew from Calgary to Vancouver. In the 1940s, as President of the Canadian Polish Youth Congress, I had arrived at Vancouver by a C.P.R. train (thanks to my father being an employee). The train trip through the majestic Rocky Mountains, its jagged peaks, and sky-coloured lakes, imbedded a lasting impression of a part of Canada I had not known.

When we were in Banff, Alberta, our relatives informed us that some Albertans blamed the Canadian Pacific Railroad for the most trivial mishap that they encountered in their lives. My relatives mused that perhaps this minority rebuked all of their disasters because of the binding of the east and west together in 1885, by the Canadian Pacific Railway.

We stayed at the Holiday Inn Hotel in Vancouver, B.C. That day the temperature registered 17-degrees Celsius and it rained off and on all day. Tevis was in touch with her only sister Lally and her better half. For our daughter Camille, I purchased a ring with "Amorite" (a mineral fossil). It is the official stone of British Columbia.

We ate a pleasant dinner with Camille and Peter, her suitor, at a seafood restaurant in Vancouver. He declined to join us in a small glass of wine. The following day, Camille, having lunch with us (without Peter present) told us that Peter was divorced, and a reformed alcoholic. She was silent as to his age.

Later it was disclosed that he was 15 years her senior. Tevis and I were silent, wanting the best for her of course, but not wanting to interfere with her life. Driving back to our hotel that day, we passed through a down beaten area of Vancouver where there were aimless individuals sprawled on the sidewalks, addicted to various drugs — alcoholics and drug abusers — dancing to the drums of certain death.

I asked myself — why is there a complete vacuum of help for these ill-fated citizens? Where are the medical people, their clinics, hospitals, and institutions? Why are our laws not instituted to humanely and properly deal with this blight upon our democracy? Maybe only angels of mercy like Mother Theresa are all that these subdued addicts can hope. Perhaps religious missionaries should also help these lost souls, not only in the Vancouver area but also throughout all of Canada's areas where this human disintegration is simmering.

We visited Tevis' sister and her husband in Delta. Tevis and her sister Lally are inseparable. At lunchtime, Peter told the family, casually, that he and his sister had over twenty-five (25%) percent interest in a successful Scottish distillery, which was founded by his grandfather, and that the distillery was still active. Peter roughly estimated that the distillery was worth over $10 million Canadian dollars. I wanted to be overjoyed for Camille, to think that she had landed a millionaire, but at the same time, I was also sceptical. In time, the Scottish distillery story proved to be a fairy tale.

Windsor 1985

On arrival home from Vancouver, B.C., I sadly learned of the demise of Windsor's Chief Crown-Attorney, Brian McIntyre — a just and upright prosecutor. He had passed away at an early age and left behind a wife with two children.

In mid-August 1985, I attended our Canadian-Polish church. The church was replete with parishioners. The high Mass was celebrated to commemorate "newly resurrected Poland's miraculous victory at the Vistula."

The Bolsheviks, having by 1919 crushed the Tsarist's armies, east, north, and south, turned against newly revived Poland in order to join the powerful Communists in Germany. The Bolshevik hordes, led by the infamous Leon Trotsky, almost reached the German border.

The Polish volunteer army cut the enemy's left flank and routed the invaders. This celebration, from 1945 to 1989, was forbidden, as a puppet Communist regime ruled Poland those 54 years.

On returning to work that fall, I began to feel disturbingly anxious. The number of cases, the variety, and the often perplexity of cases increased daily. One morning I presided over four divorces and over a dozen hotly contested family law motions that same afternoon. That very week I made an appointment with my family doctor and had medication prescribed.

Canada's Fragile Sovereignty Endangered

We learned on March 21st, 1987 that Walter L. Gordon, an outstanding Canadian patriot, had passed away in a Toronto hospital at the age of 81. The former Liberal Finance Minister was at the forefront of reinforcing economic, social, cultural, and political sovereignty of Canada. His career began at an early age with his father's large accounting firm. He examined the economic prospects of the firm's clients and became concerned that Canada's sovereignty was in peril by its dependence of direct foreign investments. In 1955, he was appointed Chairman of the Royal Commission on Canada's economic prospects. His report launched Canada's review of its economic independence, especially from the U.S.A.

As Liberal Finance Minister, in Lester B. Pearson's government, he introduced a budget containing a thirty (30%) percent tax on foreign takeover purchases of Canadian stock. The Toronto Stock Exchange dropped dramatically. At the news, the corporate government welfare bums (as they were dubbed by the left-wingers) raised such a vocal national effluvium, that the tax was withdrawn. However, the collapse of the Foreign Investment Review Agency (F.I.R.A.) was averted. Gordon established, "The Committee for an Independent Canada," founded in 1970.

In the 1970s, Walter Gordon published his book, "Storm Signals," a warning to all Canadians. His lectures were numerous on the subject of the erosion of our sovereignty and multiple subjects stemming from its corrosion. His published lectures commenced in 1976 and past 1981, and helped to distribute his message. The "Council of Canadians" in a way replaced Walter Gordon's "Committee for an Independent Canada."

Eric Kierans in his last book, "Remembering" wrote, *"Walter Gordon had been far closer to the truth than I in 1963."* He was telling us that the U.S. government meant to use...these corporations, these mighty engines of enlightened capitalism, as a wrecking ball on the economies of trading partners, especially...Canada. U.S. corporations were not merely economic arms, they were political arms of American policy, and all the pious claptrap about the non-political nature of foreign investment was revealed for what it was...Ottawa should have told the Americans to get lost.[5]

At an Ottawa National Liberal Convention in the mid–1960s was where I first met Honourable Walter. L. Gordon. The minority government was led by Lester B. Pearson, who was awarded the Nobel Peace Prize, for solving the Suez Crisis. Walter L. Gordon and many others convinced the delegates for the implementation of "The National Health Act." This revealed Walter L. Gordon's care for social reform and not only for Canada's economic independence. However, the right wing of the party, possibly led by Mitchell Sharp, delayed implementation of the Health Act by one year.

We developed a genuine political friendship. Walter L. Gordon was a guest speaker at several of our Toronto Liberal High Park meetings. I admired him for his courage and above all his resolute defence of our Canada's economic, social, and cultural sovereignty. What amazed me was that although he was ridiculed as a Renégade from "The Establishment Class," by most Bay Street moneyed moguls, Walter L. Gordon effectively toiled for the National Health Act, Welfare Legislation, and other reformist, social, and cultural policies.

He was satirized as Canada's superman in one of "Time" magazine's issues. Eric Kierans, in his recent book "Remembering" ended his work writing, "As a Liberal, I reject any global order or commercial world view. Globalism and corporatism block intellectual growth and cultural

---

5 "Remembering" — Eric Kierans. p. 100.

political freedom. An open-ended future for mankind demands the pluralism and diversity that are the hallmarks of true Liberalism."[6]

The Canadian Patriot Paul Hellyer

At the time of this writing, Paul Hellyer was the leader of the Canadian Action Party (C.A.P.), a vigorous new Canadian party devoted to maintaining the political and economic sovereignty of Canada. He maintains that the country is in crisis because of the Free Trade and NAFTA agreements. Foreign investors have the same and sometimes more rights in Canada than Canadian citizens do.

Hellyer's party feels it is only a matter of time before Canadian cable, phone, airline companies, and banks etc. are gobbled up by American and other foreign interests. As an example for Canada, is the present free Democratic Poland's law that forbids the sale of its realty or vacant lands, permitting leasing for a fixed, reasonable time, to foreign citizens or corporations.

I met Paul Hellyer in Toronto before the election of 1957. He always struck me as a politician that placed the interests of Canada ahead of anything else.

In 1997, (a decade after the demise of Walter Gordon), Paul Hellyer brushed aside his retirement to rescue Canada and founded the Canadian Action Party. With the release of the 1995 federal budget, Paul Hellyer's long support of his party ended. He feels that the budget cutbacks ruined our national health care system, caused the continuing tuition increases, and weakened our controls of the environment. This budget and its stringent cutbacks destroyed Canada from a progressive, middle power, to a mediocre one. C.A.P. is striking forward. In the last federal election, seventy candidates were in the fray. Mr. Hellyer hopes that C.A.P. will play a pivotal role in offering Canadian voters who want to "Save Canada," a genuine alternative when the next election rolls around.

Paul Hellyer held senior posts in the governments of Lester B. Pearson and Pierre Elliot Trudeau, where he rose to Deputy Prime Minister. As Minister of Defence, he is perhaps best remembered for unifying our three separate armed forces.

---

[6] "Remembering" — Eric Kierans. p. 269.

Some recent discourses of Paul Hellyer were on "Globalization and how it's Killing Canada" and "Canadians' Choice: NAFTA or Medicare Can't Be Both." A slogan of C.A.P. is "Oh Canada or No Canada." Since 1971, Paul Hellyer has published 10 books. His latest book, "Goodbye Canada" is slated for a fall 2003 release.

Franciscan Father Conrad Morin

I abstracted parts of the following from an article of the Montréal Star, circa 1946, with the help of my niece Helen Morin-Chien. Father Conrad's brother was my sister's husband, G. Morin. In a little village in Yorkshire, recently an English mother sat down and wrote a letter to a Canadian priest thanking him for having saved her boy.

"My son has told me of all the sacrifices and hardships you had to endure to help him to live," wrote Mrs. Florence Castleton of Southfield, Yorkshire. *"Truly some mother must be proud to call you 'Son.'"*

The letter is one of several similar ones prized by Franciscan Father Conrad Morin, born at Sherbrooke, province of Québec and holder of a decoration awarded by the British Government, for his work among escaped prisoners-of-war near Rome during the German occupation.

Recently returned after having been a professor at the Franciscan college in Rome since 1937, Father Morin has been recovering in Montréal from physical debility, brought about by overwork and lack of proper food. An infection, aggravated by his physical condition cost him the sight of his left eye.

The story of Father Morin's work among the escaped prisoners-of-war and among Italians and Jews fleeing certain death or compulsory service in German factories was like an Allied underground novel. It started after the surrender of Italy, when the Germans took over military occupation of most of the country and started rounding up thousands of allied prisoners-of-war who were released, or just walked out of camps as soon as the surrender was announced.

There were about 2,000 of these escaped prisoners, mainly British and Canadian soldiers and airmen in the Rome area.

Father Morin said that for most of them he sought refuge with friendly Italian families or hid them with friendly farmers in the countryside. Speaking English, German, Italian, and French, Father Morin circulated among these men, bringing them food, money, clothing, and books in spite of the enormous difficulties of obtaining these things and ignoring the death penalty promised to anyone helping a prisoner to escape.

Italian civilians often gave their own scanty rations to help feed the escapees. He himself would not attribute his illness directly to his work among the prisoners, but friends who knew the situation said that the giving away of the greater part of his own food over a long period was the main cause of his physical breakdown.

A cheerful, active man, Father Morin, although he gained about 22-pounds in two months upon his return to Canada, still showed signs of his severe ordeal. He said that he wanted to rest up and eat "grand Canadian food." He worked for the Canadian Family Institute at the U. of M. until he passed away, in the spring of 1987.

Puerto Vallarta

On July 10th, 1987, with both of us stressed to the max, Tevis and I arranged with a local travel office for a week's holiday on the Mexican Pacific coast. Our hotel was Hotel Bougainvillaea's Sheraton, on the Pacific Ocean in Puerto Vallarta, Mexico. We landed at about 2:10 a.m.; the temperature was 20-degrees Celsius.

Since there was a lack of cabs and large buses, we arrived at our hotel at 3:30 a.m.; too tired to unpack, we managed to undress and put on our sleeping attire. We viewed from our window the Pacific Ocean swell; its supple, endless waves touching the shore tenderly, disappearing only to be substituted by another wave, and on it went, endlessly. I gazed at this view for a long while, which lulled me into a deep restful sleep.

There was a high, thick wall around the entire front of the hotel, also extending to its rear area, except for the ocean's aperture. As we lounged by the pool the following day, we noticed a uniformed man with a revolver in a holster, make his rounds approximately every half hour. All of the guests were warned not to stroll outside the perimeter of the wall after dusk.

We often spent the days reading novels, history books, etc., sitting on the chaise-lounge feeling safe in the rear area of our fortress "Hotel Bougainvillaea's." Tev read two novels in three days.

Out of curiosity, I made enquiries as to where their Court House was located. Hesitantly the reply was, "The jail and the Court House were over 70-kilometres south. No buses travel there, only police cars. Civilians rarely go there." Here I was, supposed to be resting, and my interest inherently trickled over to the judicial system... thank God that Tev was there with me, and didn't allow me to spend another moments thoughts on it... we shared wonderful meals together, entrancing romantic evenings, pleasant walks, sunbathed, and returned to Windsor both greatly rejuvenated and refreshed...

Strasbourg, France

In May 1988, I received an invitation from our Toronto Senior Judge to attend a seminar in Strasbourg, France open to French-speaking Judges. The seminar was to be from July 9th, 1988 to July 16th, 1988. The international European situation was on the verge of the collapse of Communism. The strikes in Gdansk, Poland filtered into the rest of Poland. Pope John Paul II, on his visits to Poland, had deliberately undermined the Autocracy of Communism. All Communist-dominated eastern countries were making noticeable rumblings to regain their freedom. By November 1989, after the collapse of the Berlin Wall, freedom catapulted throughout Eastern Europe to the Baltic States, the Ukraine, through Soviet Siberia, and to the Pacific Ocean.

At first, I planned to visit Poland with Tevis after the seminar, but friends and Canadian Foreign Affairs officials in Ottawa, Ontario did not advise such a venture. I agreed to attend the Strasbourg Seminar and decided that I would bring Tevis along with me, paying for her expenses. By mid-June, our Montréal travel agent had all of our flights, hotels, etc. arranged. Since our plans had changed to visit Poland at the end of the seminar, we decided to fly from Strasbourg to London, England and spend several days in England and Scotland.

By mid-June 1988, I received a letter from Montréal and a parcel enclosing a 700-page French book entitled "Canadian and European Perspectives of the Rights of an Individual Person" (Vue Canadiennes et Européennes des droits et libertés). This book was authored in 1984 by a series of lectures conducted by "The Canadian Institute for Advanced Legal Studies." The Institute had held successful conferences in Louvain-la-Neuve, Belgium, Palo-Alto California, Cambridge England, and recently in Canberra, Australia.

Apart from our Canadian Judges and lecturers, there were numerous Judges and lecturers from France, Belgium, Holland, and England. The

Advocate General of the Court of Justice of the European Community also took part.

The Right Honourable Lord Denning of England and Brian Dickson were patrons. The Right Honourable Paul Martin was a supporter of the Institute. It was difficult for me to read the book sent to me in mid-June, as this was the busiest Court time for me as a Judge.

On July 6th, 1988, we boarded our overseas flight, arriving at the huge Paris Charles DeGaulle Airport (I could not suppress my resentment to Charles DeGaulle's name being attached to the airport) reminding me of his explosive and inflammatory words in Montréal in 1967 that to this day diffuse a level of disharmony in Canada. The General was abhorrent of the English and their American cousins, and had become an "Ishbosheth" shamed at the loss of France's Colonial Empire after the end of World War II. Insolently he sowed discord, hoping French Québecers would stampede to become an "independent vassal of Gaullist France."

We were driven by airport bus to where an awaiting "Air France" jet plane, which flew us to Strasbourg, the capital of Alsace-Lorraine. This province was first annexed to Germany at the end of the Prussian-Franco War (1870). After Nazi Germany's short rule from 1940 to 1945, Alsace was returned to France.

In 1949, Strasbourg became the seat of the "Council of Europe," "The European Parliament," "The European Court of Human Rights," and others. The University of Strasbourg was founded in 1538 and has always had an excellent reputation internationally. We checked into the "Hilton International Strasbourg" on July 9th, 1988. The manager informed me that I was automatically registered with the "Strasbourg Judges Conference." The lectures, receptions, banquets, and breakfasts took place at the Hotel Hilton Strasbourg, and the "Palace of Music." Ninety-one Judges attended the seminar and forty-three academics, in addition to officials of several provinces and the federal ministry.

The Hilton Strasbourg proved to be a magnificent hotel, very modern with all the amenities of a North American hotel. Since this was Sunday, Tevis and I took a taxi and attended Mass at the Strasbourg Cathedral; a magnificent structure, built between the 11th and 15th centuries, it was said to be a notable example of Rhenish architecture. What struck me as odd was that the participating faithful numbered at most 80, in a Cathedral that could accommodate well over 500.

On the evening of July 10th, 1988, there was a reception and a banquet for all the participants of this seminar. The reception was sponsored by the Canadian Deputy Minister of Justice jointly with the Canadian Cultural Affairs Consular of our Embassy in Paris. The opening banquet followed one hour later. The Honourable D. H. Carruthers, President of the Canadian Institute and his co-chairman, the Chief Justice of the Superior Court of Québec, greeted the participants to "Les Journeés Strasbourgeoise 1988"; a gourmet four-course dinner followed that only French chefs can prepare!

On July 11th, 1988 during the afternoon session, a Canadian Senator introduced "The proposed Meech Accord" and its application to the Charter. A government of Québec Minister enlarged on this topic. This politically (explosive) topic was handled well by the approach of the Francophones outside of Québec. This was propounded by a lady Dean of Law at the University of Moncton. The point of view of Canadian women was handled by a lady professor from the University of Calgary. This, in my opinion was the most intense part of the seminar.

Early that evening there was a reception held conjointly with the Counsel of Europe and Strasbourg's City officials.

At dinners, we always sat with the French-speaking Judges and their wives. Tevis had to struggle with the sparse French that she knew. Every morning we had a buffet breakfast, which gave my wife an opportunity to meet more of the Judge's wives. One day, Tevis and several of her new friends decided to go on a guided tour of Strasbourg.

On the morning of Bastille Day (July 14th, 1988), my wife and some of her lady-friends took a bus to Germany to Baden and the Black Forest (which the French army command thought was impenetrable in 1940). In fact, that was the point where the German tanks had penetrated France, causing it to collapse in about five weeks. The ladies were able to speak English with one another on their outing, which was a respite from the formal dinners where French was spoken exclusively.

During the evening of "Bastille Day," caravans of French soldiers in tanks, jeeps, motorcycles, and open carriers drove down the main streets of Strasbourg. The "Marseillaise" was heard as the troops rolled by; children waved French flags. Some of the streets had German names like Kehl Street and Av. Herrenschmidt.

In the region (province) of Alsace, we noticed that there were many German named cities like "Kayserberg," "Lichtenberg" etc. At the Hilton

Hotel there was a festive evening held for France's "National Day" — fireworks, dancing, and singing. As all the local French stores and restaurants were closed, Justice Rouleau suggested a good German restaurant nearby that had remained open. We feasted on a gourmet dinner and saluted France's national holiday with a round of libations...

Returning to the seminar the following day, our Judges were confounded to be made aware of a new medical-legal issue.

A five-page copy of a 1986 recommendation to the Parliament of the Counsel of Europe was distributed. The legal recommendations and laws were on the use of human embryos and fetuses for diagnostic, therapeutic, scientific, industrial, and commercial purposes. Laws were recommended, which included, the right to a genetic inheritance by the following techniques:

A)   Fertilization In Vitro — man has achieved the means of controlling life in its earliest stages.

B)   All technological opportunities in science and medicine to be governed by clear ethical and social guidelines.

Further recommendations forbade the creation of identical human beings by cloning or any other method. Research on a human embryo was one of the most controversial issues of international bio-ethical debate at that time and probably still is, next to the science of cloning.

We were all presented with a copy of, "The Universal Declaration of Human Rights." I shall cite, for interest's sake, a few of the 30-odd articles contained in this declaration.

"Whereas it is essential, if man is not to be compelled to have recourse, as a last resort to rebellion against tyranny and oppression, that human rights should be protected by the rule of law."

Article 3

"Everyone has the right to life, liberty, and security of person."

Article 23

(1)   "Everyone has the right to work, to free choice of employment and favourable conditions of work and to protection against unemployment."

(2)   "Everyone, without discrimination, has the right to equal pay for equal work."

(3)   "Everyone has the right to form and to join trade unions for the protection of the interests."

On the third day after our arrival, there were no afternoon lectures so Tevis, I, and two other couples took a bus to Boersch and had lunch at Schaetzel Cave (built in 1722). We viewed the beautiful countryside from our window. With lunch, we both enjoyed a glass of the local "Pinot Noir." Upon leaving, we received a booklet on the wines of Alsace.

Early one evening, Tevis and I walked to the L'orangerie, a magnificent palace built by Napoleon, for his Empress Josephine (1763-1814). On the way from our hotel, we were lost. I asked a passing-by lady, in French, for directions to the famous L'orangerie.

She looked at me intently and asked, "Parlez vous allemagne?" In French, I apologized and said unfortunately not. She then proceeded to give us directions in perfect French. I thanked her and we located Josephine's summer palace.

We were disappointed, as we could not visit inside, as visiting hours were over. We were able to view the garden however; although attractive, it lacked the opulence of the well-groomed gardens we had viewed at some of the English Royal castles.

At a Plenary Session the following day, the Canadian Charter of Rights and Freedoms was dissected from sections one to fifteen. Comparison and study was made of the Parliamentary Assembly of the Council of Europe's "Universal Declaration of Human Rights," which consisted of 30 articles. These were studied and compared to Canada's Charter.

On the last night of the seminar at our hotel, there was a gala banquet and dance sponsored by the President, the Honourable D. Carruthers, and co-President, Honourable L. Poitras. The banquet was a French gourmet extravaganza. We sat among other Judges with the Rouleau's, Karen Weiler, and Janet Scott. We all had a wonderful time, full of laughter. We danced, sometimes fast, and other times relaxed with the slow-dancing music.

Some years later District Court Judge Karen Weiler was appointed to the Ontario Court of Appeal; she proved to be an excellent choice. District Court Judge Janet V. Scott passed away some years after 1988.

The next day, July 16th, 1988, having made previous arrangements, we flew to London, England from Strasbourg. We encountered flight difficulties at Strasbourg's airport. The first plane was grounded as a heron flew into one of its jets. An hour later, onboard another plane, we had to change planes to Paris. Although we missed the connecting British plane, an Air France flight carried us from Paris to London. We arrived...sans baggage.

We stayed in the airport hotel...sans elevator. The airline gave us paper pyjamas, a small tube of toothpaste, and a toothbrush...Not a good beginning! The next morning our luggage arrived. We moved to the Novatel London Hotel. We found the accommodations to be excellent. The next day we left on a four-day bus tour of England and Scotland.

The first stop was Shakespeare's birthplace, Stratford on Avon. I was very much moved. I could not believe we were walking on the same turf that the great Shakespeare (1564-1616) must have walked on. We admired the newly built theatre—a replica of the theatre in Shakespeare's days—over 400 years ago. Just like déjà vu, the plays we read became reanimated in our minds: Julius Caesar, Macbeth, Othello, The Merchant of Venice, King Lear, Hamlet, and Romeo and Juliet.

He is no doubt England's greatest dramatist, surpassing ancient Greece's literary giants like Plato and Herodotus. We cherished every moment being there. Later on, we had a walking tour of the walled city of Chester and visited Chester's Cathedral. We enjoyed the customary English tea with all of our meals. The next day we were driven to Liverpool; due to scars of the 1940s, it was not as enchanting as the Lake District. From there, we were driven on to Edinburgh.

We went on a walking tour of Edinburgh Castle and joined in on an evening of Scottish dancing. Unlike Tevis, I found "haggis" very delicious. We were entertained with highland dancers, bagpipes, and multiple Scottish jovialities. The next day our bus drove us to Abbotsford and we toured the home of Sir Walter Scott.

A long time ago as a student, I was deeply moved by one of his famous poems "Soldier Rest."

"Soldier Rest! Thy warfare o'er sleep

The sleep that knows not breaking

Dream of battlefields no more..."

After being driven to the Scottish border, we arrived at Gretna Green Village in Dumfries and Galloway in Scotland, about two-kilometres from the English border; eloping lovers had been allowed to be married here without residential qualifications or the consent of their parents from (1754-1856). After 1856, one of the parties had to have resided in Scotland for 21 days prior to their marriage. The services were usually performed by the local blacksmith until such a time when these marriages were made illegal in 1940.

We were driven through the Northumberland Park where impressive remains of Hadrian's Wall were still well preserved. Hadrian's Wall was built by Emperor Hadrian (of Rome) between 122 and 126 A.D. to fortify the northern boundary of Roman Britain. Fragments of the wall remain and some stone houses; the wall was 75-miles long. After touring the magnificent gardens of the hotel, we stayed at a hotel in nearby Darlington. The following day we arrived at England's "medieval city," the city of York. We went on a conducted tour of York Minster Cathedral. We stopped at the Belvoir Castle of Duke and Duchess of Rutland.

After lunch and tea, we arrived at the famous Cambridge University. After several hours touring Cambridge, our bus drove us to our Novatel Hotel in London.

I was tired when we arrived and spent the next day at the hotel; however, we did manage to tour "Windsor Castle." We walked through lengthy aisles with exhibits on both sides, lined with ancient military hand swords, sabres, bagpipes, and assortments of collections of Royal decorations, medals, tiny silver pots, and ornaments. There were exquisite diamond rings and one of a kind necklaces inlaid with precious gems; there were selected treasures of fine art from the numerous castles of the British Isles. Later on that afternoon, Tevis went off on her own to shop at Harrods's, Fraser House, and Harvey Nichols.

We left the next morning on an Air Canada plane, and hours later, we were joyful to be home.

Autumn Leaves

It was the eighth anniversary of my sister Regina's death in 1988 (we fondly called her "Reggie"). One of her favourite songs was "Autumn Leaves." At the age of 15, on her own, she had entered a local Montréal radio station's singing contest. She did not win; it was her life's dream to become a famous singer. After her only son died in a motorcycle accident, she spent her summer weekends at mother's cottage with Mary Gresko. Her dream finally came true of singing, if only at area bistros and local retirement homes.

In mid-September 1988, I was invited to a luncheon at the Windsor new Polonia Centre to meet Poland's newly ordained Cardinal Glemb. He was in his mid-40s, and possessed a broad worldly view of religion, politics, philosophy, and history. He reminded me of the brightest Jesuit lecturers I had at Loyola College in Montréal. After spending some time with Cardinal Glemb, discussing the problems of enslaved Poland, I donated a sum of monies in support of his work in Poland.

A few years later, the Polonia Centre was in financial straits. One of the members rallied many parishioners to each write a $10,000.00 cheque, which was to prove to the (Québec-owned) Bank National that the arrears on the mortgage could be paid. The Polonia Centre was $8-million dollars in the red at that time; not surprisingly, they failed at their efforts, largely due to the incompetence of certain individuals I fear. Sadly, it was turned into a French-Canadian Centre.

A day prior to Armistice Day, we attended High Mass, sung in Polish with the ancient Latin music that I loved so well. There was a small reception at the church. We met the priest from Poland who was in the process of building a new church in Karszice, Poland. They collected a neat sum, including a generous donation from me.

The next day, November 11th, 1988, we watched the impressive ceremony in Ottawa commemorating Armistice Day on television. The gun salutes, the official orations, the sight of the mother who lost two sons, the organized laying of the wreaths, the mournful playing of the Last Post, the bagpiper's melancholy melody, and the march past of the veterans all deeply moved me... Armistice Day was revered by us religiously every year; November 11th, 1918 is also the day Free Poland was resurrected.

My Daughter Camille's Wedding

Camille Ellen was a special kind of daughter. She was always the first to volunteer to help. Whether it was help with the dishes or the many other chores around the house. All the girls helped with the maintenance of the house-painting, planting tulip bulbs, and shovelling snow, etc., but Camille was always the first to chip in and to do the job attentively and with zeal. She excelled in high school and university, receiving above average marks for her general B.A. She left home after school to go out on her own and took a position with a dental firm in Vancouver, B.C.

In 1989, Camille wrote us a long letter, stating that on Valentine's Day she had become engaged. In her letter, she stated that she wanted to be married in Windsor by a Judge because Peter was a divorcee (We had met him briefly on our last trip to Vancouver in 1985). He had told the family at that point that he held a substantial interest in a Scottish distillery, which over time proved to be untrue. I asked my dear friend Judge Ken Ouellette to perform the ceremony.

Previously, Tevis had organized a wedding reception at our lovely home for a girlfriend of hers; Camille desired the same arrangements. The wedding was set for Saturday, May 27th, 1989 at our home on Riverside Drive East in Windsor, Ontario. Since Judges are precluded from performing a marriage on Saturdays, Camille and Peter were married earlier and my colleague Judge Ken Ouellette repeated the ceremonial words for the family gathered on Saturday, May 27th, 1989.

Camille wore a gorgeous gown that had been made especially for her in Vancouver—adorned with lace, silk, and small pearls. It was an intimate reception—approximately 60 guests took part. Tevis engaged a pianist to play on our grand piano and decorated our home with lovely flower arrangements.

The caterer's fare was Belgian "Haute-Cuisine." The bride and groom spent their honeymoon night at the local Hilton Hotel. The next day, they flew to British Columbia for their honeymoon. At that time, I worried how things would work out, as I was unsure of Peter's sincerity towards my daughter, but Tevis and I gave them our blessings and wished them well. Peter subsequently passed away in 1995.

We cannot protect our loved ones from making mistakes, or painful choices… however; we can continue to love them when things don't work out.

Judge James B. Trotter (1923–1989)

I met Jim in the mid–1950s as he, Senator A. Roebuck, and his nephew shared office space with the firm in which I was a partner. Members of both firms used to lunch together often at "The Savarin" on Bay Street.

He told me one day that he suffered the opposite of diabetes. He discovered this while writing a law school, exam paper. He started to fall asleep and upon eating a chocolate bar, he was stimulated enough to be able to finish his exam paper. He sought out and received medical treatment for this condition. We developed a warm, personal friendship. I was an usher at his wedding.

Jim Trotter was born in Brandon, Manitoba and graduated from the University of Manitoba and Osgoode Hall. He practised law in downtown Toronto. After being married, he continued faithfully to look after his elderly mother's needs. He was a man of great heart and a champion of the oppressed.

Jim was first elected to Queen's Park (Parkdale) in 1959. He was part of a handful of Liberal members who sat in opposition to the Tory (blue) machines of Leslie Frost and John Robarts. He served as Housing Critic and Health Critic. He was held in high regard by the Liberal leader Nixon.

Jim was defeated in 1971 and returned to the practice of law until September 1975 when he was appointed District (County) Court Judge. At the following seminar, some of his friends advised him to ease into the job cautiously and easily because of his health concerns. "No way" was his answer!

In 1978, Judge James B. Trotter presided over a case where charges had been laid under the *"Combines Investigation Act."* Judge James B. Trotter dismissed testimony from The Imperial Oil Ltd. officials as "bureaucratic nonsense," and convicted the oil giant of squeezing an independent gas station operator.

His many colleagues praised Judge James B. Trotter for the care and attention he paid to his duties as a Judge, for the human aspect of justice he dispensed, and its impact on all of the lives affected by his judicial decisions. Judge James B. Trotter died on June 1st, 1989 at the age of 66. He is remembered fondly by us all.

My Last Months of Judgeship

My health began to deteriorate in 1989. I was hospitalized for a short time out of town. In 1990, we sold our Windsor home on Riverside Drive located on the Detroit River. The 12-room house was far too spacious for Tevis and me alone, as the children were all gone now. We had no "Private for Sale" sign up, as there were buyers constantly at our door; we sold our lovely home to a manufacturer of car parts for a substantial amount of money. Talk of the sale price spread like wildfire throughout the legal sector and some errant "busybodies" of Windsor.

Due to the perseverance of the then Liberal Attorney General of Ontario Ian Scott Q.C., on September 1st, 1990 all of District Judges (including myself) were appointed Justice of the Ontario Court of Justice (General Division) now referred to as the Superior Court of Ontario. The Attorney General abolished the salutation of "Your Lordship" to "Your Honour."

The pressure and stress increased as the new Chief Judge tried to assign two-week trials a distance out of town. I was a Supernumery Justice also, and apart from surrendering my upper level office, library, paintings, and being de-escalated to a basement office, I had to spend precious time learning the new computer software that we were required to work with. I had the added stress of settling into a new home in Tecumseh, Ontario.

We employed the services of a real estate agent, and after driving my wife and I around in her brand new Cadillac for several weeks were shown a new property; we liked it somewhat, but decided we'd sleep on it. The real estate lady phoned us back that same evening to inform us that the builder had received an offer on the lot that we had liked, and if we were serious about the property, she advised us to act immediately by putting in a counter offer of an extra $1,500.00.

New at this game, we "bit and bought." Later on, when we had ample time to think about it, I said to Tevis how stupid I felt, falling for the pressured sale. We found out the day right after the purchase—that there were no sidewalks on either side of the street, definitely a minus!

On my 65th birthday, I automatically became a Supernumery Judge and soon after a Justice. This extended my judgeship to the age of 75. The obligations of my duties as a Supernumery Justice were reduced by approximately five months.

On my resignation in 1991, our Judges sent me off with a formal dinner and goodbyes and a bust of my likeness, which my wife had commissioned the famous local sculptor Christopher Reeves to create, with the idea in mind to donate it to the Court House down the road. That was not to be, as allegedly some "Ishbosheth" of the then Windsor Law Association (on a technicality) opposed it. The bust presently sits at the University of Windsor's Leddy Library, graciously accepted by Dr. R. W. Ianni, President of the University in 1996.

The problems at the Court House went on. My doctor prescribed medication, rest, and advised me to abandon my judicial position. After a few months of prolonged melancholia, I applied for a resignation (on medical grounds) to our then Federal Minister of Justice, Kim Campbell. I was successful and after 22 years of Judgeship, I was granted the use of "Honourable" preceding my name and surname for life.

In retrospect, I am extremely thankful to the two Senior Judges that I served under, for their assistance in discussing difficult parts of trials and applications of case law. Their advice always proved helpful. It was a canon of law that Judges were forbidden to discuss problems arising from their work with any persons, except "brother" Judges.

I am also sincerely grateful for the many other Windsor and Ontario Judges that volunteered their sound advice in similar situations I found myself. I have fond memories of all of our Judges, but especially Senior Judge Carl Zalev; Judge Wellie Hollinger etux, now retired in Pembroke, Ontario; Judge Richard Huneault etux, now retired in Sudbury, Ontario; Justice Anthony Cusinato etux, in Windsor, Ontario; Justice Ken Ouellette etux, retired in Windsor, Ontario; and Justice Robert Daudlin etux, in Tecumseh, Ontario. I now understand that all new appointees, before they are to dispense justice, have courses they must attend preparing them for the real thing.

This recent approach was written up in-depth in a national daily newspaper. In my case, I received (on the 12th year after being sworn in as a Judge) a booklet entitled, "A Book for Judges," written at the request of the Canadian Judicial Counsel! *Better late than never as they say...*

Canada—Saguenay Flood Relief Fund

In the summer of 1996, following my "almost falling through the cracks," I convened an Ad Hoc Committee, to aid the victims of the recent Saguenay-Lac-Saint-Jean devastating floods in Québec.

The Mayor of Windsor, acted an Honorary Patron, Mr. P. Boucher of the P. B. Group of Companies and Mr. Clare L. Winterbottom, President of "Anchor Lamina," both well-known industrialists and philanthropists, were directors.

The three of us shared all the expenses dispersed in that campaign. It was requested that all donations be made to the Canadian Red Cross.

At the end of our drive, the manager of the local Canadian Red Cross sent us a letter of thanks of the help raising the $29 million that was raised across Canada. A marvellous achievement (he added).

Chapter Four

Retirement

O ur first trip together celebrating my retirement was on August 4th, 1990. Tevis and I flew to Miami, Florida's Airport, where we were bussed to Fort Lauderdale. We boarded the cruise ship M.S. Norway of the Norway American Line late that same afternoon. (The famous liner "Isle De France" had been sold to the Norwegians who refurbished it and re-named it—"M.S. Norway.") We sailed all night long under a blanket of stars...

Except for the officers, the crew was composed primarily of Philipinos and Indonesians, a group of neat, polite, and friendly individuals. At 7:30 a.m. on the third day of the cruise, the ship docked at Philipsburg, St. Maarten. This is a bi-national island, amicably divided into a Dutch side and a French side.

We boarded a tender (a nautical vessel) with dozens of other passengers and landed in Philipsburg. The place was crowded with wool and linen shops, cheese, Dutch chocolate shops, and other speciality vendors. We spent two hours trying to make our way through the many shops, but overwhelmed and exhausted, returned to our ship early. It was not a very fruitful expedition for us.

The next day, August 8th, 1990, our ship docked at St. Thomas, U.S. Virgin Islands. It appeared that the financial tentacles of corporate American "Disney" et al were planted in the U.S.-owned St. Thomas. Recommended shops were posted on our cruise liner the evening before.

Tevis spent some time shopping and procured some good buys of summer clothing and other miscellaneous items for our grandchildren. We returned to our cruise ship by tender once again.

On the fifth day of our cruise August 9th, 1990, we spent all day at sea. After lunch, we viewed a newsreel, "The Gulf War and The Collapse of Communism in Eastern Europe." The fall of Communism in Eastern Europe in the newsreel brought instant joy to me as a Canadian of Polish heritage! The Empires of Britain and France went to war in 1939 with Germany for Poland's independence.

With Hitler's armies collapsing in 1944, Poland was (without any consultation) abandoned to Soviet Russia, which ruthlessly imprisoned it with a brutal, barbarous, autocratic Communism. The Polish people survived the Nazi's six-year occupation and forty-five years of savagely imposed Communist rule.

We attended a formal dinner in which the ship's Captain was our host. Only one officer spoke to us in English, thanking us for choosing their cruise line and wishing us well. Not a word was said about the Gulf War or disintegration of Communism. The captain recited part of a poem about travellers:

> *"Some ask why we travel*
>
> *With all we have at home.*
>
> *I guess, just as our forefathers*
>
> *We have had an urge to roam."*
>
> (Barbara Burr)

The officer was given a standing ovation for his sentiment. After more than a week at sea, away from the comfort of our own beds and our home, we were happy to arrive back in Canada on August 13th, 1990. *"There's no place like home…"*

The Demise of Tevis' Mother

In the early months of 1991 Mrs. Mary Roy MacLean, my mother-in-law, fell seriously ill while visiting her daughter Lally in Delta, B.C. She was diagnosed with congestive heart failure, and the doctor suggested that Tevis be sent for immediately as death seemed imminent. I was left in the care of our cook, who prepared my dinners. Tevis and her sister Lally cared for their dying mother. Their mother deteriorated until April 12th, 1991 at which time she slipped away quietly, at peace at last.

The girls had her body flown to Windsor, Ontario where she was laid out at a Windsor funeral parlour and interred next to her dear husband, Daniel MacLean at the Windsor Memorial Gardens Cemetery. Tevis and Lally were devastated.

Mrs. Mary MacLean was a sanctified person, a religious and devout Christian of the Anglican faith, always active in her parish of St. Aidan's. She was a dedicated wife, a devoted mother to her daughters, and loving grandmother to her grandchildren. She smothered her grandchildren with affection, especially Kurt, one of her favourites. She will be cherished in the memories of her children and her in-laws.

On the anniversary of both Mr. and Mrs. MacLean's birthdays, flowers abound, and every Christmas holiday our family lays out a seasonal Christmas spruce blanket over their graves in memoriam…

The Wedding of our Daughter Michelle

In mid-August 1991, we flew to Vancouver, B.C. to attend our second youngest daughter's marriage to Darrel Beaven. As parents, we assured Michelle that we would bear the costs of the wedding. The marriage took place on a three-story vessel. The officiating Priest arrived by noon, as had the 50-odd guests.

Congratulations, hugs, and kisses by relatives of both sides were exchanged. The bouquet tossed by Michelle was caught by a guest, a young girl. The vessel set steam and meandered amidst what seemed like Norwegian fjords. A champagne toast was made for the couple, wishing the traditional Polish toast of 100 years of life and love. Our vessel meandered past rock walls, twisted and buckled by the primitive forces that had created these magnificent mountains.

Our vessel twisted by a few waterfalls that gushed out of glaciers; it was a first for Tev and I—a marriage and reception on a vessel—it was quite lovely. The groom had thoughtfully arranged for a white limousine to have several of his relatives driven around for a tour of the Vancouver area. By 9:00 p.m., Michelle and Darrel had already departed for their honeymoon to San Francisco and the Napa Valley.

We stayed on for a few days at Tev's sister and brother-in-law's home in Delta, B.C. The hotel that we had stayed at in Vancouver was so isolated from everyone; their warm reception was comforting. They took us to Stanley Park, showed us around the White Rock area, and entertained us at many excellent restaurants.

After a few days, with great sadness, we left our gracious hosts. It had been a magnificent trip all around — a charming fairy tale wedding, and a relaxing, enjoyable holiday.

My Sister Wanda

Wanda was my youngest sister. She completed Marianopolis College in 1951 with a B.A. and married Stanley Rozynski in 1953. Stanley, like our siblings was a Montréaler. Stanley began painting and sculpturing at an early age. His first sculpture was exhibited at New York's "Living Arts Centre." Wanda and her husband moved to New York in 1956 to study pottery and sculpturing. On completing their studies, both returned to Montréal in 1960 and opened a Studio-Gallery on Mansfield Street (downtown Montréal). This consisted of a pottery gallery and a pottery school.

Wanda spent the next six years making pottery during the day and teaching students in evening classes. In the meantime, Wanda's husband spent his time creating sculptures, mainly in clay. In the mid–1960s, Eaton's of Montréal held an exhibition of Canadian ceramists, among which were 35 displays from Wanda. Prestigious "Ogilvy's of Montréal" accepted Wanda's vases for sale in their stores. Wanda took part in over 20 exhibits in Canada, the U.S., and Switzerland. In addition, her work is represented today in numerous public and private collections, including the permanent collection of the Confederation Art Gallery and Museum in Charlottetown, Prince Edward Island, which was purchased by the Department of External Affairs. Her works were exhibited in New York; Sarnia, Ontario; Syracuse U.S.; London, England; and Ottawa, Ontario.

In the spring of 1966 Wanda and her husband moved to Way's Mills in the Eastern Townships of Québec, located approximately 100-miles from Montréal and 8-miles from the American border. They converted the school building into a summer school of pottery; 10-weeks of summer were devoted to instructions in pottery to a limited number of resident students. The property was located off the banks of the Niger River and was encompassed by 2-acres of beautiful flowers. In the winter of 1974, Wanda accepted a position of Secretary in the County of "Barnston Quest West." This area's history goes back to 1680, when settlers from the colonies were attaining "free" lands.

By 1871, the new immigrant Irish outnumbered French-Canadians by fifteen (15%) percent out of a census population for Barnston West of

2,500 souls. In 1996, a hardcover anniversary book was published by the "Barnston Quest West" community, where the Mayor then, Michel Belzil, in his introductory message on page one wrote as follows, *"The creation of this souvenir album 1996 is evidence of the pride of a community where Francophones and Anglophones live and work together in harmony."*

There were many articles written concerning Wanda's work, including the Montréal Star, December 3rd, 1964. The article entitled *"Fabrics, Pottery...Exhibited by Québec Craftsmen..." "The Work of Wanda Rozynska, a Montréal Potter, is attracting much attention, especially her wine sets of bottle and goblets. Mrs. Rozynska and her husband Stanley, a sculptor in terra cotta...(She) said 20 potters lived for 3-weeks in North Hatley taking lessons from Shimaoka, one of the leading Japanese potters who came especially for... her seminar."*

In the publication, "Vies Des Arts" of Sherbrooke, Québec, 1982, Jacques Renaud wrote an article on my sister:

"Wanda Rozynska's school at Way's Mills...list of students came from...Connecticut, the Prairie Provinces, the Maritimes, from the Sherbrooke area, and even from as far away as Europe, especially West Germany... I've noted the unified architectural effect of the Rozynska Pottery School...The same sense of Greek beauty, pure in form, free and expansive, yet terrestrial and solid...It isn't often that pottery touches us with its beauty, by a genuine air of silence and of spiritual awareness, yet this is the case with Rozynska..."

Sadly, in January 1988 my dear sister Wanda was stricken with crippling Rheumatoid Arthritis. By early 1989, she was able to limp onto a plane and fly with her husband to Florida, to bask in a warm climate for her health. This meant the end of pottery, which was a great blow to her, and a whole lifestyle adjustment.

Not to be beaten by illness, she and her husband developed their present 2-acre garden over time, so that by 1986 the magazine "Plein Air," a popular Québec publication published at Laval, Québec, published a lengthy article on their amazing garden. The article included 11 colourful illustrations along with comments of how masterfully pottery and sculpture were arranged together, accentuating the respective flowerbeds.

You can't keep a good Staniszewski down!

Stanley (Buddy) Rozynski grew up only a few streets from our family's home in Montréal. He credits the most important influence in his early years as being his older cousin, Louis Dudek (who was to become one of Canada's greatest poets). When Stanley's cousin moved to New York for his M.A. and Ph.D., they corresponded regularly.

Mr. Dudek often sent books to his cousin in Montréal, Québec and when he visited Montréal, they went for long walks to exchange ideas.

Louis Dudek's works in poetry are acclaimed today in English Canada. He was a professor at Montréal's McGill University, and received the "Order of Canada." Buddy first met Wanda at a Polish Youth Picnic at the Rozynski's farm (outside of Montréal being the property of Stanley's grandfather). They married 18 months later, on June 13th, 1953. He met his eventual mentor, the sculptor Michael Lekakis, in New York through his poet cousin. Stanley created innovative sculptures using as much as a ton of clay at times. His works have been exhibited at the Galerie Libre in Montréal. Some of his finest work may be seen in their garden at his Way's Mills home, where it harmonizes perfectly with its surroundings.

Meech Lake

The press reported that Prime Minister Brian Mulroney, with the recommendations of the Charest Committee, had prepared a revised version of "Meech Lake" with new Constitutional changes. The ousted Bouchard and the vociferous Pequites condemned the revised "Meech Lake," which had a clause to do with Québec's "distinct society." Mulroney's plan was to hold a National Referendum on the new set of proposals. I joined the Windsor area "Yes" Committee as the Liberals, in opposition, supported Mulroney's appeal to all Canadians.

I took it upon myself to organize a satellite committee to the Windsor "Yes" Committee. Thanks to the kindness of Windsor's famous restauranteur Mr. Kurt Deeg, we had a place to hold informal meetings over coffee. I engaged a very efficient secretary to take notes of our discussions. The Windsor "Yes" Committee was chaired by our Mayor Michael D. Hurst, with M.P.'s of the three parties, including the well-known local philanthropist Charles Clark, Q.C.

At our first meeting in early January, with about 24 people in attendance, I was elected chairman. I distributed the government's bilingual pamphlet of proposed Constitutional changes. At the discussions of each meeting, there were constructive suggestions to compile a letter to the Federal Government of a précis of our collective view and suggestion. Contributions were made from all who attended. I make special mention of Kurt Deeg, Harry and Wanda Zekelman, Monsignor L. A. Wnuk, Professor Jean-Pierre DeVillers, and Reverend Father U. Paré for their input.

Herb Gray and I spoke at several meetings, including the Polish Windsor Hall. At my own cost, I placed a large ad in the Windsor Star urging to vote "YES" on October 26th, 1992. The "NO" national vote ended the Constitutional proposed changes.

When our legislatures had a vote in Manitoba, Elijah Harper NDP member (a one-man filibuster), like the infamous "Liberum Veto" in 17th century Poland, defeated any proposed law or legislations. Clyde Wells, Premier of Newfoundland, killed the vote of legislature and Canada's proposed Constitutional changes.

From Mayor M. D. Hurst, I received, as chairman of the Windsor area "Yes" Committee, a letter of thanks for my help and dedication to the campaign. About four years later, Ralph Klein, Premier of Alberta, was reported to have understood that Québec is a "distinct society" (Globe & Mail, December 19th, 1996).

Caribbean Cruise

In February of 1993, Tevis, my brother John, and I decided to go on a seven-day Eastern Caribbean Cruise with the Holland American Line, on the M.S. Westerdam. After we flew from the Detroit Airport and arrived at Fort Lauderdale, Florida, we were bussed to our luxury ship. We spent two full days at sea; we all found it very relaxing. I lost about $70.00 to the one-armed bandits, and we all ate very appetizing meals prepared by some of the leading chefs of Europe. At the Queen's Lounge on board, Tevis and I danced to soft music; we avoided the loud lounge where "Rock & Roll" thundered and blasted one's eardrums.

The ship stopped briefly at St. John, before arriving at St. Thomas, U.S. Virgin Islands. We learned that St. Thomas, U.S. Virgin Islands once served as "home port" to numerous infamous pirates. It is said that the shops that line the harbour were formerly used as pirate warehouses for the "loot." The island now is full of duty-free goods, being sold by merchants who could be called by some *"successful apprentices"* of the previous infamous pirates! After our cruise ship was at sea another full day we arrived at Nassau, capital of the Bahamas, located on New Providence Island (During World War II, King Edward VIII [ca 1898–1972] abdicated from the British throne to marry a divorcee).

He was made Duke of Windsor. He later became Governor-General of the Bahamas and resided there with his American wife until the end of the war.

While shopping, my brother and I became separated in Nassau. I lost my bearings and wandered into a public square with over 200 people milling around. I could not find my brother for the life of me... In Polish, I shouted "Tatus" (father) repeatedly. People around me began to look at me strangely; suddenly from amidst the sea of bodies my brother appeared, and I was lost no more!

The best way to see the Bahamas is by water. It is a quiet and relaxing way of life on the islands, with many scattered beaches. We enjoyed many amazing panoramic views by climbing "The Queen's Stair Case" to the ruins of Fort Fin Castle. Back on the ship, the three of us feasted on a French culinary dinner. The next morning we docked at Fort Lauderdale, Florida and parted ways with my dear brother—quite the memorable family holiday!

Parkinson's Disease

Around about March 1993, a local Tecumseh family doctor, Dr. Phil Fioret, diagnosed me as having Parkinson's disease. This was concluded merely by observing a slight tremor in my extended left hand and by slightly twisting my wrists. He did not send me to a neurologist for thorough testing. He prescribed (Eldopa) Levodopa / Benseraside, which I took until the late fall of 1993.

Dr. Fioret moved to the U.S.A. sometime in the summer of 1993. He was replaced by a younger doctor, a Dr. Reginald Klassen, at the same office in Tecumseh that was previously occupied by Dr. Fioret. Dr. Klassen, without as much as a check-up or any sort of examination, automatically continued to prescribe the same Eldopa medication.

When I wrote to my druggist's pharmacy in Windsor, Ontario, the clerk sent me a printout of my prescriptions from February 20th, 1993 to January 26th, 1994. The clerk wrote a note, which said, "Sorry that is as far back as our printout goes," *disclosing only one prescription of Eldopa on September 14th, 1993*. My suspicions were aroused; my wife Tevis' and my recollections were that I was on Eldopa since about March 1993. Some time in late autumn of 1993, I contacted a friend of mine (dating back from my high school days in Montréal), a Dr. Michael Kovalik. I asked my friend to arrange for an examination by a neurologist in Montréal,

Québec. Tevis and I travelled comfortably by first-class coach with VIA Rail to Montréal. It was a sad trip for me, as the last time we had been in Montréal was at my older sister's (Reggie Carboneau's) funeral in 1980. She had endured an unfortunate married life with a French-Canadian who was a cripple, suffering from occasional epileptic seizures.

After only two years of marriage, she separated from him, as no divorce law existed in Québec at that time. As the train crossed into Québec, passing the Poplars, Elms, Maples, Spruce, Oak, and Willow trees, with the staccato noise trains emanating, it felt to me as if these very trees were standing in a mournful salute to the memory of Reggie, her son, my father Julian, and my mother Rose.

To all of the Staniszewski's buried at Côte-des-Neiges Cemetery, atop Mount Royal overlooking Montréal, Québec, I reminisced that thousands of kilometres separated my parents from their parents and their families in the graveyard off the banks of the Berezina River, no longer a part of Poland. They were laid to rest thousands of kilometres apart, only to have their souls meet eternally in some far off heaven.

Tevis and I saw Dr. Kovalik, who had arranged an appointment with a Dr. Howard Wein whose office was located on St. Zotique Street in the depths of east Montréal, Québec. The thing I remember most about this appointment was that it cost me more than $100.00 to get to Dr. Wein and back to our hotel "The Queen Elizabeth." Much later, I received the report of Dr. Wein's tests, and his conclusion was that my tremor "while similar to Parkinson's, was caused by drugs that were prescribed."

In or around the summer of 1993, I sent an enquiry letter to the Royal Ontario College of Physicians and Surgeons about the diagnosis I had received of Parkinson's from Dr. Fioret, followed up by Dr. Klassen. I enclosed a copy of the report of Dr. Wein, the Montréal neurologist, to the Ontario College of Physicians and Surgeons.

I visited a Windsor neurologist around the same time, a Dr. Hiren Desri who, after examining and testing me for over one hour advised me not to take the Eldopa pills as he felt I was not suffering from Parkinson's disease. Within two days of not taking the pills, I felt like a new man! I was able to walk briskly, bend over, and touch my toes; I immediately became less depressed and more active. The Ontario College of Physicians and Surgeons answered my one and only letter to them on November 1st, 1993; amongst other things, they enclosed a brochure entitled, "The Complaints Process."

In their preamble of their pamphlet, "The Complaints Process" was the following: *"Most importantly, the college thrives to make sure that you get the best medical care possible. Patients, who are concerned about their care, may complain to the college"*... *"If your complaint involved a serious problem with your doctor's conduct, or the care you were given, the College can help you get the facts."*

The pamphlet is then followed by a short paragraph entitled, *"You Have the Right to Complain."* This is followed by a long paragraph entitled, *"Telling Us about Your Complaint."* In law, this would be a nauseating scheme for a prospective "plaintiff" to reveal his claim (or case) on discovery, if a "complaint" degenerated to a litigious Court case.

The pamphlet's next paragraph, *"Letting You Know,"* *"Where the Complaint's Committee has arrived at a decision, it will do so in writing. The Complaint Committee is made up of three doctors, and one who is a member of the public. Their decision can be appealed to the Health Discipline Board."*

In my humble opinion, this is a self-regulating system comprised of physicians and surgeons; it should not possess the absolute authority of making a decision in a Judicial Manner. This would also seem to be contrary to Section 7 of *"The Charter of Rights,"* which read as follows, *"Everyone has the right to life, liberty, and security of the person, and the right not to be deprived thereof except in accordance with the principles of Fundamental Justice."*

"...You can lead a Judge to water, but you can't make him drink..."

In the fall of 1993, I wrote to a medical colleague of mine that I had been told I had 5 to 10 years left to live at the time of my diagnoses of Parkinson's (in the opinion of my two Tecumseh doctors, Dr. Fioret and his replacement Dr. Klassen).

In the late spring of the following year, I attended, at the request of Dr. Klassen, several meetings of a support group for Parkinson's disease. This took place at the Concorde Centre (formerly the Polonia Centre) in Forest Glade, Windsor, Ontario. I felt out of place being there, as I was not remotely afflicted by any of the symptoms of the other attendants.

After having been thoroughly examined in December 1993 in London, Ontario by a Dr. P. E. Cooper—in his assessment he wrote, *"I would agree with Dr. Desai that there really is not enough present on physical examination to make a diagnosis of Parkinsonism. Mild cog wheeling is something that can be seen in patients. He does not have the bradykinesia or rigidity that I would associate with this condition."*

Upon reading his full report, I consulted Counsel, as I felt aggrieved; I suffered from fear and insomnia, because in my mind what transpired was an act of gross error and negligence.

I chose Mr. L. Paroian as my Counsel for two reasons: First, he was one of the first to welcome me warmly at my Judge's swearing-in ceremony in February 1968 at the Windsor County Court House, and he showed an exuberant affinity to new Canadians of Central European ancestry. Secondly, he was a senior partner of a large law firm that had the reputation of handling difficult and complex litigation, more specifically "medical malpractice."

After a few lengthy meetings with Mr. L. Paroian and some of his colleagues, I retained his firm. A Notice of Action was issued December 5th, 1994 at the Court House of Chatham (as their civil caseload was lighter than Windsor's was). A Statement of Claim was issued January 3rd, 1995.

The service on both defendants took almost a year-and-a-half, as both doctors had moved outside of the Windsor area. Dr. Fioret was located in some small coal town in Kentucky, U.S.A., and the other defendant, Dr. Klassen was then residing in the province of Manitoba.

Dr. Klassen telephoned me (he said from London, England), and chastised me for suing, saying that he was only trying to help me. The statement of defence was finally served on my lawyer's firm as late as April 24th, 1995.

The defendant's lawyer was the firm of McCarthy & Tétrault of London, Ontario, referred to as the "champions of the elite." They were commonly used by large banks, insurance companies, and corporations such as Chrysler, General Electric, Sears Roebuck, Coca-Cola, Bell Canada, and CBC, etc. They were the Goliath of law firms of Canada.

My Statement of Claim was for $500,000.00 for general damages and $100,000.00 for estimated special damages, interest, and costs.

The claim was based as caused by the negligence of:

I.   Dr. Fioret, inter alia: a)   failed to make proper examination

                                b)   misdiagnosed the plaintiff and
                                     improperly prescribed ProLopa

II. Dr. Klassen, inter alia: a)   failed to make proper examination

                                b)   misdiagnosed the plaintiff and
                                     improperly prescribed ProLopa

I found the Statement of Defence to be novel. I only set out a brief outline here:

Dr. Fioret alleged that I was referred to him by a psychiatrist in 1991, which was false in itself as he was my family doctor since 1990. Furthermore, why would a psychiatrist refer me to my own family doctor?

He said that I complained of tremor, rigidity, akinesis (rigidity of movement); (I complained of a sore throat only), and he said that it was consistent with Parkinson's Disease for which Dr. Fioret prescribed Eldopa (he didn't testify that it was two years later—not until March 1993—that the prescription for Eldopa was written).

Dr. Klassen fared worse than Dr. Fioret did. In his pleadings, he got his dates mixed up. Dr. Klassen pled that by September 1993 I was no longer on Eldopa, yet the medical pharmacy printouts do not support his claim demonstrating otherwise.

Mr. L. Paroian and two others (certified as specialists in civil litigation by the Law Society of Upper Canada) met with me several times; I vividly recall that on or about mid-summer of 1996, they discussed several problems in my claim—the statute of limitations being the greatest problem; that and one of my medical reports was ambivalent. I suggested that we engage a medical expert, and they commented that the cost would be prohibitive. I informed my lawyers that I would seek a second opinion.

Mr. Paroian warned me that the McCarthy & Tétrault do not settle cases. Although the O.M.A.'s motto is *"protecting the public – guiding the profession,"* my experience is that they drag you to the Court of Appeal even if you win a modest amount from the jury. If they are not successful at Osgoode Hall's Court of Appeal, they will then drag you to the Supreme Court of Canada!

I advised my lawyer, Mr. Paroian and his associates to discontinue this action without costs, which was completed by mid-February. I must express my sincerest thanks to Mr. L. Paroian, Q.C. for not sending me an account; lawyers like Mr. Leon Paroian are all, but extinct in the legal profession.

As a post-script to this abandoned suit against two medical doctors, I cite this article from The Globe & Mail, Saturday, August 24th, 1996:

MS's College Fires its Disbarred Lawyer

TORONTO — "The Director of Legal Services for the College of Physicians and Surgeons of Ontario was fired yesterday after a television report revealed he was disbarred a decade ago.

The college, the regulating body for doctors, was not aware that Duncan Newport is not entitled to practise law until he was confronted about his credentials by Global News.

Mr. Newport was disbarred by the Law Society of Upper Canada after admitting he forged documents and misappropriated hundreds of thousands of dollars of his clients' money, the report said.

The college investigates complaints against doctors. Spokesman Jim MacLean said a major part of Mr. Newport's job involved deciding which doctors would face disciplinary proceedings.

Mr. MacLean said the revelations are embarrassing to the college and he hopes that 'It never happens again...'"

Book on the Canadian-Polish Congress

I recall that in the fall of the mid–1990s, whilst visiting friends in Toronto and attending a Toronto Symphony Concert, I telephoned my old scoutmaster (now retired) in Toronto, and we arranged to meet in central Toronto.

Our rendezvous place turned out to be the home of an elderly Polish writer, B. Heydernkorn. After exchanging pleasantries, they both spoke of the need for the publishing of a book on the history of the Canadian Polish Congress; I had been present at the 1944 founding convention and some time later, I had been appointed General Secretary.

I agreed to finance the book. I sent the writer, Mr. Heydernkorn all the materials, photos, etc. in my possession as well as several long letters about the first installation convention of 1944. I also sent him historical background on my election as President of the Canadian-Polish Youth Congress in 1946 and my countrywide rail tour from Ontario to Vancouver to visit many of the Canadian-Polish Youth Clubs, arranged and financed by my father.

I related to him my belief that the Canadian-Polish people of the day were equally bound to Canada as well as to a Free Poland. This small book, written in Polish, was published three years later.

Mediterranean Cruise

We began our wonderful 1995 autumn trip at the "Hotel Excelsior Roma" in Rome. This hotel was old but extremely elegant; our bed linen was as white as the driven snow, pure cotton with a high thread count, and very gentle on one's skin. I was particularly enraptured by this seemingly small detail, as I spent a lot of my time in bed at the hotel.

Since we were located on Via Veneto, one of the main streets of Rome, Tevis was able to go out on her own, spending afternoons at leisure window shopping and browsing. An Italian doctor (who barely spoke English) relied on a small dictionary to communicate his explanations to me. He appeared to reassure me that I would recover from my ailment once I was on board the cruise ship. I paid him several hundred Canadian dollars for two, 10-minute visits (Months later, O.H.I.P. refunded me only $30.00 of my claim).

We left the hotel on Sunday. Tevis and I were sadly unable to visit the Vatican, nor to attend a kindly pre-arranged visit with His Holiness, Pope John Paul II. However, I was happy to board the ship and to see our beautiful quarters—a stateroom with a window, king-size bed, double closets, sitting area with loveseat and chair, dresser, radio, and TV.

We were at sea the entire first night and again the following day. On the morning of the October 2nd, 1995, we docked at Valletta Malta. Malta is a tiny island, once a fortress of the Knights of Malta—population 350,000. Tevis signed up for a city tour; I demurred, instead passing my time browsing in some shops.

On October 5th, 1995, we anchored at the Italian island of Sardinia at about 10:00 a.m. and boarded a tender from our ship to Alghero, Sardinia. We signed up for a wonderful little tour of the town on a miniature train that meandered up and down the narrow cobbled streets. At a tourist office in Alghero, I inquired about the possibility of visiting the Island of Elba where Napoleon I, in 1814, was forced to abdicate and live in exile.

By early 1815, he had returned to France where his armies were defeated in 1815. He was exiled at that time to St. Helena, a drab island off the west coast of Africa. As to the Island of Elba, I was advised it would take two days by vessel to travel. The island was easterly of the French island of Corsica and close to Italy's western town of Piom Bino.

On October 6th, 1995, we arrived in Minorca, one of the Spanish Balearic Islands where we set out on a walking tour of the town of Mao.

It was a delightfully rich town and area—you felt immediately how strong the Spanish peseta was and how progressive their economy was; very different, Tevis mused, from the time she had first visited Spain in 1961 under Franco's regime.

On October 7th, 1995, we arrived in Barcelona, the capital of Barcelona in the Province in Catalonia Spain. We had signed up for a tour of the city, which we enjoyed immensely; we found the city stately, extremely clean, and affluent. Almost all of the buildings and homes had been painted a stark clean white for the previous year's Olympics.

Barcelona prospered under the Romans; it was captured by the Moors in 713 A.D. who imposed their Moorish architecture on the city; it was captured once again by Charlemagne in 801 A.D., less than a century later. In the Civil War (ca 1936–1939), it was the seat of the Socialist-Communist government.

On October 8th, 1995, we arrived at Marseilles, France and entered the city on a shuttle bus provided by our ship. A guide informed us that Marseilles is one of the principal French seaports. It was established on the Mediterranean by the ancient Greeks (ca 600 B.C.). It is linked by a canal to the Rhone River, a major 500-mile-long river.

It issues from the Swiss Alps and flows southward through France to the Mediterranean. The city possesses heavy industries, food processing plants, and shipbuilding yards.

One of our last full days at sea was October 11th, 1995. There were festivities held aboard ship and a gala evening was thrown. On October 12th, 1995, we docked at Livorno, Italy, a lower middle-class, shipbuilding town, which never fully recovered from World War II's air bombings. I had wanted so much to go to see Florence but the bus left at 8:00 a.m. and we missed it.

The next day we arrived at Naples—we had some hilarious experiences trying to cross the streets (as no traffic lights were in operation). Two kind Italian policemen helped us safely across two streets. We were later advised that the Mayor, who had been allocated money for refurbishing city lights had instead spent the allotted monies for billeting foreign soccer teams, as in his mind the international play-off soccer game was more consequential!

On October 13th, 1995, we docked at Civitavecchia, Italy, the port closest to the city of Rome. After the usual turmoil of packing, we were bussed to the airport. The plane stopped at Milan, as a few more passengers alighted. During the long flight home, we marvelled at how luxurious our experience of travelling by ship had been on this occasion. Our ship had visited so many cities in the western Mediterranean in only 12 days. There was no need to cart luggage, as tourists travelling by bus or train are obliged to.

Tevis and I both agreed this was the best trip we had ever had. After changing planes briefly in Toronto, we landed at the Windsor airport and were safely home.

The Black Triangle

Upper Silesia in Poland, Czechoslovakia, Northern Bohemia, and Saxony Germany had been thrust into living conditions of disastrous, heavy air pollution by their evicted Soviet occupiers.

For over 40 years, the Soviets built large industrial complexes in total disregard for the environment; the poisonous pollution that was a by-product of the plants was imposed on the local people. A World Bank report estimated that in order to meet environmental standards, Poland would have to spend $20 billion (US).

In Upper Silesia, 300 children suffered from severe lead poisoning because of the polluted air and water. The infant mortality rate was sixty-five (65%) percent compared to a low fourteen (14%) percent in Sweden.

In two successive years ending in 1995, this horrific situation prompted me to donate about $40,000.00 through the Canadian Red Cross, along with others, to have countless Polish children spend weeks in a supervised clean air environment during two successive summers.

The President of the Polish Red Cross, in a letter, acknowledged with thanks my contribution to help the Polish children; he also enclosed a copy of their program. He described in his letter of thanks the most endangered part of Poland — the town of Bytom, which is situated next to the coalmine "Rozbark"; it had in operation the huge "White Eagle" steel works and two electricity power plants, which continuously contaminated the surrounding areas with a nitric of various dangerous compounds. There was also a huge railroad crossing, in the centre of town, where coal-stoked locomotives would pass several times a day.

This densely populated area was saturated with all kinds of pollution, composites of sulphur, carbon, and nitric monoxides in addition to heavy dust particles suspended in the air, which greatly influenced breathing and lung conditions such as asthma. Soil and sub-soil water of the surrounding areas was contaminated as well. The local authorities made plans to move most of the inhabitants of Bytom.

In December 1997 at the offices of the Canadian Red Cross of Windsor, the President Robbi Howett arranged a reception on my behalf. Many people gathered that evening, including Mayor M. Hurst.

After congratulatory speeches from members of the Red Cross and Mayor M. Hurst, I was presented with a large mounted citation from the Red Cross for my support of the International Youth Development in Upper Silesia, Poland, and a plaque recognizing my assistance to the International Red Cross Youth Development. CBC Television covered parts of the reception on the evening news that day.

The Long Ordeal…

In December 1995, I still was complaining to my new doctor, Dr. A. Hammer of diarrhoea. I was referred on to a Dr. L. Brown. After an x-ray, Barium test, and a colonoscopy, I was told that the diagnoses was "Diverticulitis" for which there was nothing to worry. By February 1996, I had lost about 15-pounds. The doctors, who were treating me, in retrospect, seemed to me to be "alchemists." I had stored away all of the empty prescription bottles that were dispensed to me, in case I should ever be in need of them.

In September 1994, a year after it had been established that I did not have Parkinson's disease, to my alarm my new doctor was still treating me for Parkinson's disease! Thanks to my wife's sane intervention and two competent V.O.N. nurses, I was sent to a hospital of choice by my then family doctor, Dr. Hammer (I was only half-conscious).

My dear Tevis filled me in later after this long ordeal, which started on March 16th, 1996 and ended April 23rd, 1996. She revealed to me that she was told that there was no bed for me (at the hospital that my family doctor Hammer had sent me to). I was then transferred by ambulance to Windsor's most westerly-located hospital (by whose authority I never found out).

Tevis was told that I "almost fell through the cracks," and that especially one medication that I was on three times daily, was not being regulated by my doctors Dr. Hammer and Dr. Yaworsky, though I was supposedly being "monitored" by quarterly blood tests. This negligence resulted in a build-up of drugs that was poisoning me slowly and surely!

At the last hospital that I was taken to by ambulance (half-conscious), an Eastern Indian doctor, Dr. Rai, misdiagnosed my condition! As a result, I was held in solitary confinement for several days and nights.

During the long tortured nights, I sang English, French, and Polish songs—*always ending with a plea for my release*. Release from solitary confinement finally was granted after five long days, which seemed to me in my mentally agitated state, like an entire month. My guardian angel, Tevis visited me every day, rain or shine, and helped save me from impending extinction. I hold true that I did not "fall through the cracks"; I was allowed to slip through them by the negligence of my attending doctors. I was told later that Dr. Rai had plans underway to send me to an out of town "nut house." Thanks to Tevis' bedside vigils and her long talks with me, I became lucid and signed myself out. A nurse prepared a script for me and I walked out of that inferno on April 23rd, 1996.

The Paul I. B. Staniszewski Bursary

On January 17th, 1996, I formally presented the bronze bust of myself to the Leddy Library of the University of Windsor; Dr. R. W. Ianni graciously accepted the gift. Later, at a gathering of friends and professors and Dr. R. W. Ianni, I hosted a light luncheon at the University Club. After the repast, I presented the University of Windsor with a $25,000.00 cheque earmarked for a bursary to be known as "The Paul I. B. Staniszewski Bursary" with three awards annually of $500.00 each to be given to whoever demonstrated sincere financial need.

One subject to be encouraged was "Canadian History." The Fathers of Confederation left education in the governance of the provinces. In Francophone Québec and some areas in New Brunswick, Canadian History rightly starts with the establishment of New France. Most of the other provinces teach that it occurred after the Plains of Abraham. In addition, another reason for my creation of this bursary was done because of the drop in students registered at our local university (1996) by three (3%) to four (4%) percent.

My Disabling Car Accident (Part I)

On Wednesday October 23rd, 1996 whilst standing in my own driveway in Tecumseh at about 10:15 a.m., I was knocked to the ground and injured. I had been on my way to a printer that morning regarding the "Canada Saguenay Flood Relief Fund," as I was its Convenor. This unfortunate accident was precipitated by the sudden backward movement of my car, at that moment operated by my visiting brother John, while I was placing files in the back seat of my car.

After being driven to the Emergency Department at Hôtel-Dieu Hospital in Windsor, Ontario, my head was x-rayed, an intern found no injury, and they said I had to be driven home. From October 23rd, 1996 to October 25th, 1996, I couldn't bear the pain I was experiencing, especially my left front temple.

On the 25th of that month, my new family doctor, Dr. F. DeMarco, instructed my wife Tevis to purchase a non-prescription painkiller, "Robaxacet." The pills did not help; the horrible headaches persisted. I averaged two to three hours of sleep a night. I called my family doctor on Sunday morning and spoke to his associate doctor on call. I was prescribed a painkiller (Ketorolac Tromethamine 10 mg).

I was advised to see my own doctor on Monday, October 28th, 1996. On that date, my family doctor ordered a CT scan. Following the CT scan, my doctor said something to the effect of—"blood on the left temple," and that I was to be admitted to the hospital immediately. The diagnosis was that of a subdural haematoma; Dr. Chakravarthy, a neurosurgeon, operated on the left part of my skull on November 1st, 1996. I underwent a shunt insertion, which I was later told would allow the drainage of accumulated blood. I spent five days in the Intensive Care Unit. On November 9th, 1996, I was discharged.

Tevis remarked that after November 9th, 1996, I did not eat well; I was incontinent, unable to walk, falling, unable to shave, despondent, and deteriorating in both health and strength. Six days following my discharge, Tevis drove me to see Doctor F. DeMarco (about November 15th, 1996). My only memory of that visit was that I could not lift myself up onto the examining table; I was very unstable on my feet and I needed assistance to place both feet inside the front seat of our car. On the November 16th, 1996, Tevis wrote in her calendar "failing, hallucinating, incontinent." On November 17th, 1996, she wrote "worse."

Two V.O.N. nurses visited our home on November 18th, 1996, and after consulting with my doctor, he immediately ordered my return to Hôtel-Dieu Hospital. I was taken there by ambulance.

On November 18th, 1996, I was transferred to the cardiac ward where I was diagnosed with an arrhythmic heart and was placed on a drug, Solatol-160 mgs. On November 23rd, 1996, I was transferred to the general ward. On November 29th, 1996, I was discharged home after two days of physiotherapy. On November 29th, 1996, with great difficulty, Tevis dressed me and drove me home.

It took me all the way until about mid-May to partially dress and even then I needed help, as I couldn't bend to tie my shoelaces, pick up anything from the floor, or even bend to connect electric plugs.

From November 9th, 1996 on, I couldn't prepare my own meals. I rinsed a few dishes on January 2nd, 1997, but with great exertion. Sleeping patterns became poor since the accident; I woke up nightly at 3:00 to 4:00 a.m. I tried to read or watch TV, but with little success. Often I remained awake all night long until Tevis woke up around 7:30 to 8:00 a.m. and had breakfast with her.

Once in mid-December 1996 we went out together to see a lawyer to make an accident statement to my insurance representative. When we returned home, my knees went rubbery at the front door and I fell down several steps. Tevis, with some difficulty, struggled to get me back on my feet. In retrospect, the lawyer and insurance company agent should have volunteered to come out to our home instead of dragging a sick man out to them miles away.

On December 25th, 1996, we had family, including our two grandchildren over for dinner. I remained dressed in my housecoat, as I had felt exhausted since my hospitalization, and was in pain much of the time. I couldn't say Christmas Grace before dinner as I had always done in the past; I sobbed in frustration at the table and asked my son-in-law to say Grace in place of myself.

In keeping with our family tradition, Tevis did the best she could and shared the Christmas Host (Oplatek) with all present. Christmas dinner and the gift giving were all blurry and confusing. Overwhelmed, I soon retired to bed.

Since I had physical limitations and with my extreme weakness, I had to sit on a hard armchair or solid chair. If I sat on a soft sofa, I could not get up without assistance. This was to continue for years.

During this time, I also had a hard time swallowing foods, especially dry foods like crackers and toast.

Pills would become lodged in my throat and become difficult to swallow. I resorted to taking morning pills with mushy porridge. I would swallow my night pills, one by one, with other soft moist food or pieces of melted chocolate and water.

Doctor F. DeMarco arranged for an x-ray of my throat at the Hôtel-Dieu Hospital on January 2nd, 1997 at 9:15 a.m.; the results were negative. I hobbled around with a cane when the weather permitted with a home-care lady. If the weather was bad, I walked with a cane 30 times across the length of our house, just to keep active.

My shoes and slippers became too loose. This was because I had lost nearly 20-pounds in body weight from October 23rd, 1996 to January 1997 (Since the operation of November 1st, 1996, I had dropped to 178-pounds).

My family doctor gave me a prescription for pain. It eased the pain somewhat; however, I soon found that after a few days these pills constipated me, causing me further distress.

My nose ran constantly and formed a rough crust around my nostrils. I applied Polysporin topical antibiotic ointment twice a day. It helped somewhat, but did not eradicate the problem.

I still have problems with a sore tongue, which appears from time to time until this day. As I felt I was going downhill fast, I thought it best that I get all my documents in order, should anything happen to me, because Tevis would need to deal with the aftermath.

Before Christmas 1996, I revised my Will with my lawyer's assistance; he came out to the house. Later, I discovered that he inserted a clause to the effect that although we were friends, this would not preclude probating the Will, allowing him to charge the maximum fee allowable. You can guess what happened to that Will!

I gave Tevis a copy of a contract dated 1993 for an outside mausoleum at "Heavenly Rest Cemetery" for both of us, and that there were places for four more graves. The mausoleum is located between the grave of Paul Martin Sr., Liberal politician and Mr. Toldo, a great philanthropist of Windsor. There was also a copy of the details for a Judge's widow pension.

I am sure that this was all very hard for Tevis, but I felt that I owed it to her and to my family to set everything in order for my possible demise. I had the support of a homemaker on Tuesdays and Fridays from 10:00 a.m. to 2:00 p.m., and a nurse's visit and physiotherapy on Thursdays. After Christmas 1996, I procured a new Will with a different lawyer.

My diary entry concerning my required assistance at that time is as follows. A homemaker came twice a week. After the first month, she succeeded in assisting me to walk without a tripod-cane. I walked outside with a regular cane for a short distance, increasing a little each day. At first on my return trips, I would collapse onto a chair; slowly I improved. The homemaker must have come at least 90 more times.

Nurses came by weekly to check my blood pressure, weight, and general well-being. All of the assistance ended as of November 1997. As of the writing of these memoirs, three years and five months have passed since the filing of a claim, and discovery has not occurred yet.

With Ontario's new Insurance Law imposed, I am told the new government legislated law favourable to the automobile insurance companies; the Harris Conservative government preserved this law, being 100 (100%) percent pro-automobile-insurance companies. It was required that I be *first* examined by the insurance company doctors (cleverly referred to in the Insurance Acts as "The Accident Injury Management Clinic") as since the time of the accident, I was unable to drive a car.

My wife drove me to the insurance company's examination clinics in mid-May 1998, to be tested by the insurance company's orthopaedic surgeon and two psychologists. When I first saw the orthopaedic surgeon, he growled angrily at me barking, "You had your driver's licence taken away from you, didn't you?" I calmly retrieved my current driver's licence and threw it on his desk! He looked at it, and murmured something. Even a good insurance counsel would not insult a plaintiff in such a way, and if he did and was proven wrong, he would have definitely apologized.

When I saw the insurance company's psychologist, one of the first questions he had for me was, "Have you ever tried to commit suicide?" I never did, and to add insult to injury, he interviewed me in a tiny room with a female assistant that looked to me as though she was too stressed-out herself to document the volumes of written questions he had awaiting me! That poor woman left early and I had to answer the questions alone for several hours, in that small dark room.

At the end of such a long time sitting, I had great difficulty standing up, and painfully manoeuvred myself out of the office of the psychologist; I had spent about eight hours being interrogated with one 40-minute break. I literally fell into the arms of my wife Tevis where she was waiting for me patiently in the waiting room. She helped me to get into the car, soothed my rumpled nerves, and drove me home. Here it was now mid–1998—no discoveries, no trial dates. I can only discern the lawyers' old tactics I know so well, of wearing your opponent down.

The pro-auto insurance companies "Accident Injury Management Clinic," reported to Tevis and I that all three of the Insurance doctors minimized the extent of my injuries, and my then present debilitating condition. Ever since the accident, I do not drive the car for all practical purposes. I walk mostly with a cane every morning when I am able.

When weather is inclement, I use the treadmill in our basement. The pro-auto insurance company's law displaced the old common law that a plaintiff after discovery, at trial has to prove his injury claim with a jury. This system, similar to the code of Québec, is that the defendant takes a first examination of a plaintiff! Why are our lawyers, presently protected from being sued themselves, silent on this erosion of our democratic laws? As a former practicing lawyer and a Judge myself, I have many comments about this newly designed system, none of them good.

I was examined by the neurosurgeon for an updated report for my insurance claim, after a two-and-a-half hour wait sitting in a crammed waiting room. I was also examined in several different stages by a psychologist, B. O'Rourke, referred to me by my lawyer. In the summer of 1999, I was examined by an orthopaedic surgeon. While being examined I had several seizures, but persisted in allowing him his observation of me and we completed the examination.

Twice in 1999, my Examinations for Discovery were cancelled. The following year mediation was arranged. After hours of wrangling between my lawyer and the insurance lawyer, who had a company insurance man advising their lawyer, for what sum he could settle, the mediator (a lawyer) was chosen and remunerated by the opposing automobile insurance company. I did not find out about the cozy arrangement of the so-called "mediator" being paid out of the pocket of the defendant's automobile insurance company. No agreement was reached.

In 1997, I still required the help of a nurse's aide twice a week and a V.O.N. every Wednesday. The nurse's aide mainly took me for walks, gradually increasing the distance. She also prepared lunch for me. This was all discontinued by October 1997.

I worried, waiting for the results of a bone marrow biopsy performed on my spine. After a few weeks, I received good news—no cancer. I was prescribed iron pills to strengthen my blood.

The Federal Elections of 1997

The press revealed that G. Duceppe became leader of the "Québec Separatist Bloc" (the "Trojan Horse") mothered by Mulroney's ex-Minister and ex-Ambassador to France, who now led both the Bloc and the Separatists, determined to destroy Canada.

In spite of my weakened condition due to my seven-month-old, skull craniotomy and because of my accident on October 23rd, 1996, I was angered that G. Duceppe, a Separatist (and now leader of the Bloque Québecois), represented and was running for re-election in the Montréal-East "Laurier-St. Marie" riding for the Separatist Bloc.

My exasperation led me to gather all my strength to do what I could to stop this man—a former Catholic, turned Marxist, then Trotsky-ite, and finally a follower of Separatism. This was the riding where I was born, attended St. Mary's Polish Church, attended St. Anselm School, High School, etc. This was where my parents and siblings grew up. This was the heart of "Frontenanc's" Polonia.

This is the place from where hundreds of families sent their boys off to war. This is where our parents, patrons of St. Mary's Polish Church died. Parents of our friends, from the (French) St. Anselm Church died, and the parents of our friends from the Ukrainian and Lithuanian Churches died. The hundreds who died, or were maimed went to war for Canada from this riding in World War II. This was of utmost importance to me and I felt a personal responsibility to take action on behalf of all those who had gone before me and couldn't.

Soon after the Federal Election was announced for June 2nd, 1997, I asked my doctors' permission to go to Montréal to assist the Liberal candidate in my former riding where had I lived—to try to help Canada and Québec rid itself of the Separatist illness that can potentially destroy the Canada and Québec we all treasure. Both doctors categorically refused to give their permission. My wife was also against my idea of going to Montréal. I decided to go, to try to do my best to dislodge this "deceptive" Separatist's leader of the "Bloc" in Ottawa, and strike a shot for Canada.

Against the wishes of my doctors and Tev, on May 6th, 1997, I packed a light bag of essentials, including my numerous pills, and vitamins. Tevis reluctantly made reservations with the Northwest Airline in Detroit, Michigan to fly non-stop to Montréal. The next day, a friend drove me to the Detroit Airport. He would not let me carry my light valise from his car to the airport.

The Hotel Patrie had been recommended by someone from the Liberal candidate's office and on landing at Montréal's Dorval Airport; I hailed a cab to take me to the Sherbrooke Street East, which was a run-down, mini-scale hotel. At once, I recognized this as an old two-story home refurbished into a place that passed itself as a hotel. I signed in as Paul Morin, no address given, nor asked.

My sixth sense made me feel as though City Hall had allowed certain "friends" to convert this old house and run a so-called "hotel," entrapping foreign tourists and uninformed individuals like myself. Given a key to the only room on the first floor, as I entered a young Haitian lady was leaving, having just completed vacuuming the room. The rug was a dirty grey and the whole room was dismal. It was most shocking to see the microscopic washroom.

As I gazed unhappily, I saw a tiny sink and a diminutive shower with an old discoloured piece of plastic drop-cover, acting as a shower screen. With difficulty, I peeked into the shower and concluded that a person the size of Mahatma Ghandi could not shower in this cubicle! A few hours later, I moved to the Crown Plaza Hotel.

I phoned our Liberal candidate's office and arranged to meet with him, the staff, and his workers. His office was only five or six blocks away. A cab was required for transportation every time I went anywhere in Montréal. My cab drove me to 1160 Sherbrooke Street East, Liberal headquarters of David Ly, Liberal Federal candidate for "Laurier-St. Marie."

On arrival, I met the campaign manager and numerous workers. I was most impressed by the arduous hard work of the candidate; trilingual, he spoke French, English, Cantonese, and Vietnamese. The campaign chairlady had prepared a heavy daily schedule for Mr. Ly. He was to visit hospitals, schools, and speak at Ethnic and Francophone luncheons and banquets. Ly also spoke at Gay & Lesbian clubs; he worked every day non-stop from 8:00 a.m. to 10:00 p.m. After a few days at the office, I concluded that the "chiefs" were doing all the work but many of the "Indians" were just hanging around.

I was allowed the use of a small desk, telephone, and telephone book. I compiled a list of all the schoolgirls and schoolboys I had known in the Frontenac District and those from the Canadian-Polish youth clubs with who I had been involved. I sat there and looked up their telephone numbers and addresses. I found out as I went down my list, that many had moved outside the province and that several old friends had died during World War II.

I brought and gave a list of 29 names of my relatives, their addresses, and telephone numbers to the office. A few lived in the riding, the rest in greater Montréal and the Eastern Townships.

Our matriarch sister Eugene (80+ years young in 1997) volunteered to phone voters from David Ly's office; being trilingual, she had no difficulty in communicating in French with voters. My nephew Gilbert was also a great help by having his son and three other unemployed young men work for the Liberal candidate.

For the last three weeks of the campaign, they put up the political posters of David Ly. The campaign manageress was very pleased with these volunteers. Part of their task was to replace the signs they had already put up, as they were torn down regularly by the Bloc's workers.

Among my greatest disappointments was a close Montgomery Street neighbour. He said he couldn't help out, but gave a suspicious alibi. Then there was the Canadian-Polish owner of a deli, who complained that when he had placed a Liberal candidate's sign in his window, his electric power had been cut off. He went on to recite other unpleasantries he suffered. I concluded that some Montréal ethnic citizens were living in terror and real fear of the ugly head of Separatism choking their democratic rights. Separatists forget history—the ethnic people, though a minority, have fought the worst of tyrannical oppressors. Their resilience and courage cannot be overcome—time is on their side.

Whilst in Montréal for that short time, I telephoned a Montréal High School classmate of mine—René Talbot—who had acted as lawyer for our family years ago. It seemed that he now had two partners. My great error was to make my telephone inquiry in English. A female voice barked out that, he was her uncle and that he was now retired.

When I asked for his telephone number, she replied in an almost shrilling voice, "You can look him up in the phone book," and hung up in my ear. The telephone book had 20 listings of René Talbot! The next day I had my matriarch sister mail a letter with her return Montréal address to the law firm, with the envelope inscribed in French, "Attention de René Talbot."

The letter was never returned-no answer from René. Could this be an example of tampering with Canada's mail by the unlawful acts of some Separatists? It's bad enough to prohibit a schoolmate from contact with another one after a 30-year period—does Separatism want to build this kind of country?

The evening of May 7th, 1997 after dinner with three workers, I unpacked, took my prescribed pills, and went to sleep at the Crown Plaza Hotel. After a light breakfast, I arrived at David Ly's headquarters by taxi. I had a sore neck, shoulders, and back. I could not walk the several blocks from the Crown Plaza Hotel.

I met Sam the Greek and his wife, both very brave and active Liberals. Sam donated sandwiches, fruits, tea, coffee, and pop to all of the workers in the Liberal committee room. I was advised that on May 8th, 1997, at 6:30 p.m. the campaign would be launched. The guest speaker was to be The Honourable Federal Minister Stephane Dion and candidate David Ly. It was urgent for me to get as many of my relatives as I could to come out.

My matriarch sister Eugene did just that. I also invited Mrs. Gresko and her companion and a few friends from Montgomery Street, Bercy Street, and Hogan Street; remnants of "the Frontenac Area" of days long past. Prior to my arrival to Montréal, whilst speaking to my sister Eugene by telephone on May 3rd, 1997, she advised me that the Honourable Paul Martin, Minister of Finance was to address the Polish community celebrating the "Constitution of May 3rd of Poland" at the Polish Hall "Dom Polski" on May 3rd, 1997.

I called David Ly's office at 5:30 p.m. and advised his campaign office to have Mr. David Ly attend if he could. Later, I found out that candidate David Ly did attend. Furthermore, he was introduced by the Minister of Finance to the audience. Mr. David Ly made a speech at that time as well, the theme being: "How much we as immigrants owe to Canada." The audience responded warmly to both speakers.

On the evening of May 8th, 1997, David Ly's headquarters was filled with over 400 to 450 people. We shared refreshments—courtesy of a Polish European Deli; Vietnamese food was served, courtesy of the candidate. The speakers were inspiring; the launching of David Ly's campaign was a great success. The keynote speaker was the Honourable Stephane Dion. He spoke in French and inspired everyone present to work for a Liberal victory in David's riding.

After the meeting, some members of my family assembled in my huge room at the Crown Plaza Hotel; there were about twelve present. Mary Gresko sang some multicultural songs; her escort sang love songs and beautiful Yiddish songs. French and Polish songs were also sung. The party broke up circa 10:30 p.m. and happily, I slept well that night!

One afternoon, together with candidate David Ly and a Globe & Mail writer and photographer, we attended a luncheon for a combined "Mothers' Day and Fathers' Day" at the Dom Polski on Frontenac and Ontario Streets. After a short speech in Polish exposing the Bloc candidate as a "cry baby" whose goal for a Separate Québec, if attained, would transform it into a vassal of (Gaullist France) not much different from the former colony of New France, I introduced David Ly, who spoke about the unity of Canada and Québec. Great applause followed.

Most of the attendance consisted of seniors and eighty (80%) percent of them did not live in the riding Laurier-Ste. Marie. However, most were inclined to vote Liberal.

On the morning of May 10th, 1997, infused with Gaul and vigour, I was so excited about the progress of recent events that I celebrated by taking a long hot bath, having forgotten about my craniotomy operation of November 1st, 1996; it took me 30 minutes to grapple myself safely out of the bathtub!

I packed my clothing and my cache of medicines and flew home from Dorval on Northwestern. I was picked up by a friend in Detroit and arrived home exhausted, but with a happy mind.

Back to Montreal...

Apart from being distressed that the Bloc leader was running in the riding where I was born and bred during my formative years in Montréal, I also desired to help our Liberal candidate, as it took me back to some of my financial difficulties as Provincial Liberal candidate in Toronto in the 1960s.

The Liberal Party contributed about $2,000.00 to my campaign; my campaign committee raised another $2,000.00; the balance of expenses I had to scrape up from my own pocket—sometimes up to $10,000.00. I did not want this misfortune to happen to David Ly, so in order to help the Montréal Liberal candidate in a practical way, I helped by providing the services of relatives and friends. I was in contact by mail and telephone with the campaign chairman in the riding of Laurier Ste. Marie after May

10th, 1997. I was also in touch with the campaign manageress who kept me abreast. Tevis and I also contributed to several local Liberal Ontario candidates in our area.

On Saturday, May 17th, 1997, I had arranged a small luncheon for the Honourable Herb Gray, with local Canadian-Polish leaders. This was at an Italian Restaurant on Ottawa Street in Windsor, Ontario. The next day, the latest poll was heartening, Tories — twenty (20%) percent, Liberals — thirty-four (34%) percent, and Bloc — twenty-seven (27%) percent. I pressed my nephew in Montréal to acquire additional volunteers for candidate Ly. By May 19th, 1997, Bouchard nosed in to help G. Duceppe — announced rallies at Joquiere, Rimouski, and Montréal. By telephone, I urged relatives and friends on to work even harder than ever, in David Ly's Montréal riding.

Although doctors once again advised me not to travel, I arranged with Air Canada to fly to Montréal, Québec on May 29th, 1997 and return on June 3rd, 1997. Tevis came with me and I made hotel reservations once again at the Crown Plaza Hotel. After unpacking, Tevis and I taxied to the Liberal Committee room. I introduced my wife to all present, including Sam (le Depaneur), and took pictures of the candidate and his workers.

Back at the hotel we arranged for the printing of a two-page, Staniszewski Reunion formal menu, "Staniszewski and Family — 97 — Reunion," June 1st, 1997 at the Crown Plaza Metro Centre, Montréal, Québec. Tevis and I telephoned and invited over 30 relatives, 11 of who were of French parentage. We had the hotel order 30 red and white carnations for the Sunday dinner.

The Liberal candidate David Ly was our guest of honour as were his two lady campaign managers. I arranged for a photographer. This was perhaps the last time there will be such a reunion.

The next day at the rally at St. Hubert, my daughter Camille, who arrived from Vancouver, took pictures and succeeded in getting two very good shots of our Prime Minister, Jean Chrétien.

That afternoon I visited with Mrs. A. Riendeau (campaign manageress) and several friends, including a Polish pastor. We also had a "Vote Liberal" picture taken in front of our old ancestral home at 2557 Montgomery Street. An elderly Chinese gentleman who now lived there, posed with me. We never did get a copy of that picture.

My attendance stirred up the curiosity of an officer of the Sûréte de Québec who lived a few doors north of 2557 Montgomery Street. I introduced myself, saying that I lived there about 50 years ago. He replied in Joual, "Funny, I never saw you before." I asked him where he came from. "Chicoutimi" he replied.

I thought to myself he, like L. Bouchard, came from the same area "Le Reyaume du Saguenay," and as pre-Plains of Abraham French called it, "The Domain of the French King."

After the 1759 Debacle, the French army, equipment, squires, wives, and children deserted their people, and fled to France, and Québecers "Habitant" were all abandoned. One wonders whether "Je me souviens" is remembering a battle lost by France or remembering the abandonment of "Les habitants" and the Priests to fend for themselves?

On June 3rd, 1997 we flew back home and were astounded by newspaper election reports in both language papers, stating that David Ly got only 1,100 votes. I wrote to the chief electoral officer who, in his last letter to me dated September 8th, 1997 wrote, "I am supposed to hear from the returning Officer for Laurier Ste. Marie and the media consortium co-ordinator. No word yet (June 2001)."

It was later confirmed that David Ly received 11,062 votes and was in second place after the Bloc. In a French morning paper, Liberal David Ly was listed as coming in 10th place! I was promised by the National Returning Officers' Bureau, the telephone numbers of the local Returning Officer and Newsman of the riding. *Peculiarly,* I never received their phone numbers.

I am proud of the fact that my relatives and myself contributed in some part to David Ly arriving at second place in this skirmish.

My Disabling Car Accident (Part II)

In my diary on January 1st, 1997, I inscribed that my wife dressed me fully (as I could not even tie my shoelaces). She drove me to 47 medical appointments that year.

On January 6th, 1997, with great difficulty, I was driven to see my family doctor, Dr. Frank DeMarco. I presented him with two full pages of my physical complaints, keeping a copy for myself. These complaints included painful sores in my mouth. In a report to my solicitor, dated

October 14th, 1997, my doctor Yaworsky alleged that on January 8th, 1997 he saw me and that my wife had to drive me to his office.

In Dr. Yaworsky's report of only two sentences on January 8th, 1997 he wrote, *"That Mrs. Staniszewski noted that her husband was self-sufficient and made a turn-around...he is writing some memoirs... his wife noted he is not outwardly agitated, but his mind is restless."* That's the whole report—that I made a "turn-around," approximately two months after my busted skull and the craniotomy operation. Perhaps Dr. Yaworsky was apprised of the fact that liability was admitted and perhaps painted my recovery as occurring earlier than it was.

Dr. Yaworsky went on to write on page two of his report—that in the spring of 1996, I had a *confused state and landed in Windsor Western Hospital.* Dr. Hammer, my family doctor admitted to my wife that he and Dr. Yaworsky failed to check blood levels of a medication I was on and that as a result I "fell through the cracks" with an overdose of a prescriptive drug. It was strictly required that my two doctors send me for a blood analysis to gauge my ongoing medication blood levels, at least every four to five months.

They did not do so for over an eight or nine month period and during the spring of 1996, I was prescribed three of these pills daily. By June 1997, I was taken off Dr. Rai's "Epival" for epileptics. I voluntarily discharged myself on April 25th, 1996; Dr. Rai prescribed Epival—750 mg a day and Chloral Hydrate, a sleeping pill.

It is noteworthy that Dr. Yaworsky in his report of September 14th, 1996 never mentioned that in 1994, Dr. Fioret improperly diagnosed me as having Parkinson's disease. This case was lost because of the two-year statute of limitations, which barred our suit. However, the only negative medical report sent to my solicitors was that of Dr. Yaworsky. My solicitors would not even allow me to read it in order not to upset me. I questioned Dr. Yaworsky's motive, as my solicitors said in effect, *"If he is your doctor, I wonder who your enemies are?"*

In 1997, my wife drove me to about 30-odd medical appointments and a few dental appointments. I have diaries up to mid–2001—a long catalogue of pains, weaknesses, unable to do even the simplest chore in our home. To this day, I must lie on the floor next to my desk to fetch what I drop; my wife has to help me, with difficulty, to get me up. Since the summer of 1997 to 2001, in order to swim in our pool I have had to wear a life jacket.

The medical reports of seven doctors (specialists) along with the last one completed on July 15th, 1999 were generally supportive of my claim except Dr. Yaworsky. The three reports of "The Accident Injury Management Clinic," were in my opinion, naturally biased in favour of the defendant's insurance companies.

I was promised "examinations for my discovery" on two occasions in 1999 and 2000. I spent hours in preparation for examinations for discovery, which were duly cancelled.

I have never gotten over this dreadful calamity to this day. It's a modern day update of the old "Cain and Abel" story of the Bible, except that I (Abel) miraculously survived my brother's (Cain's) blow that robbed me of over four years of tranquil life!

Our suit was for damages, interest, and costs for $200,000.00. In mid-meditation, the defendant automobile insurance company changed lawyers; that was after March 2000. I sought advice from Mr. Strosberg L.L.P., who is a senior partner of the lawyer I retained. He agreed with Mr. Holland, my lawyer's handling of my claim.

After March 2000, there were several "mediations." During these "mediations," I was never asked if I had recovered fully, nor asked to report on the agonies that I struggled with daily. The defendant lawyers and mediator depended on the voluminous medical and hospital reports. In my humble opinion, Dr. Yaworsky was their weapon, undermining the medical reports that could have assisted my case.

My crucifixion that began in late October 1996, four years later had been reduced by fifty (50%) percent. I sought the advice of H. Strosberg L.L.P. He believed that my lawyer Mr. Holland was on the right track.

I signed a temporary agreement, which a mediator and my lawyer hammered out. I would receive about $14,000.00, and half of the original claim costs would be paid to my lawyer's law firm. The automobile's insurance lawyer rejected that.

By January 30th, 2001, I felt I had no recourse but to give up. I settled for a third of my original claim, thanks to some subtle pressure from another lawyer—"mediator." From that paltry sum, Sutts and Strosberg, L.L.P. held back $20,000.00 for their costs and disbursements.

My wife Tevis, in one of her diaries of February 2001, wrote, *"Things are not and never will be the same."* These eventually proved to be premonitory words!

The Soviet Massacre of Polish P.O.W.'s

Norman Davies in his book "Europe a History," published in 1997 in London, England, on pages 1004-1005 describes the murder on March 5th, 1940 (by a signed order by Stalin and his people's commissars) to shoot 26,000 Polish prisoners of war by the NKVD.

This massacre was completed by June 6th, 1940. These prisoners had been captured during a joint German-Soviet military invasion of Poland the previous fall that ignited World War II. They were held in three separate Soviet prisoner camps. Nearly all were Polish Reserve—officers, doctors, lawyers, professors, engineers, scientists, policemen, architects, priests, etc. They were separated from a larger pool of P.O.W.'s. Driven in small groups to secret killing grounds, bound, and blindfolded, they were shot in the back of the head and buried in mass graves.

Norman Davies further writes, *"Whilst the West was transfixed by the 'Phoney War' their Polish allies were being systematically and cynically murdered by the Soviet NKVD as a result of their governments 'Treaty of Friendship and Demarcation with Nazi Germany.'"*

In June 1941, when Hitler's armies were hurled against the Soviets, Stalin signed an alliance with the exiled Polish government, freeing about two million Poles from all Siberian arctic "work camps." A Polish independent army was organized to help fight the German invaders of Soviet Russia.

In April 1943, during Warsaw's Ghetto uprising, the Nazis released a news film showing the bodies of thousands of murdered Polish officers unearthed in the Katyn Forest. The Nazis said it was a Soviet crime. The Soviets said it was a German crime!

The London Polish-Government-in-Exile, in desperation asked the Red Cross for an enquiry. They were denounced by the Soviets who withdrew diplomatic recognition from the Polish-Government-in-Exile.

The British enquiry found that the Soviet guilt was a near certainty. However, to preserve the Allied Alliance *"so every effort was made to suppress the facts"* (by the British). *"The official line in the U.K. has been to pretend that the whole affair was a fake... Any other view would be distasteful to the public... since it could be inferred that we were allied to a power, guilty of the same sort of atrocities as the Germans."*[7]

---

[7] 1950–1952 U.S. Congressional Committee.

Despite the unanimous findings of a U.S. Congressional Committee in 1950-52 (10 volumes), in part seven of a U.S. Congressional Committee on page 2,157 cites — *"Stalin said to Sikorski that maybe these officers escaped to Manchuria."* On page 1,942 of the same U.S.A. Congressional Committee, the Russian professor and doctor who prepared a report that the Germans were the killers, *"repudiated his report as he knew the crime was committed by the Soviet NKVD."*

In a publication of 1994, entitled "Special Tasks" by Pavlek & Anatoli Sudoplatov — "Appendix Five" reveals finally that the Soviets did commit the barbaric, uncivilized massacre of about 26,000 Polish officers, prisoners of war, and civilians.

A Top Secret Letter was revealed written by Leonid Beria to Joseph Stalin dated March 5th, 1940 (six months after World War II had commenced) recommending the execution of these captured Polish officers (I am merely paraphrasing this letter of execution).

This letter was endorsed for action by Stalin, followed by his grovelling commissars, Kliment Voroshilov, Molotov, A. Mikoyan, Kalinin, and Kaganovich. This letter clears up over a half of a century of the Russian-Soviet government's formal denials.

The letter listed "military and police officers in camps as counter-revolutionaries..." 14,736 former officers, landowners, policemen, police, settlers, etc. and 10,685 formerly in Western Ukraine and Belarus, officers, spies, saboteurs, factory owners, and resistance members.

All of the above were hardened, obstinate enemies of Soviet authority... Supreme penalty shooting... examination of cases were carried out without summoning those detained. The Communists during the Civil War (ca 1917–1920), started eliminating enemies like the Tsar and his family, landowning nobility and families, businessmen, and opponents like the White Armies in the Civil War.

This reign was carried on secretly by their secret police. They kept this heinous policy until Communist Russia collapsed in 1991, causing most of its satellites to re-establish their freedom. To Poland and to Poles abroad, this massacre will live as one of the greatest atrocities suffered in World War II. The Katyn atrocities, though not as diabolical in magnitude as the Holocaust, where six million defenceless Jewish children, men, and women were callously exterminated by the Nazis, still burns in Polish hearts.

In the last volume of the American congressional committee, investigating the Katyn Forest massacre (volume 10), an incomplete list of about 3,000 Polish officers' names and ranks were catalogued. I recall reading in shock, the list and finding three Lieutenants with my surname "Staniszewski." Poles outside Poland erected monuments in Canada and probably the U.S.A.

In Polish history, such atrocities go back to the 13th century savagery of the Mongols, but at the same time Poles do not forget that two million of their people died by execution, death camps, and starvation at the hands of the Nazis. After the fall of Communism in Russia some years later, Yeltsin, Russia's President, admitted that the Katyn massacres in March—May 1940 were committed by the Russians.

I might add that I read the 10 volumes of the U.S.A. Congressional 1952, and they lay the blame on Soviet secret police acting on Stalin's order and his commissar cronies, yet a British foreign minister was still proclaiming in 1989 that the faults were unclear.

For 50 years in Soviet Russia and Communist-dominated Poland "Katyn" remained a non-subject. The "Black Book of Polish Censorship" classed Katyn as an event that could not be mentioned, published, discussed, etc. Possession of the "Lista Katynska," a roll call of the victims published abroad was a criminal offence.

On April 13th, 2000, a bulletin from Warsaw announced that Russian President Putin (a former NKVD operative in East Germany) offered Poland's president help to investigate the notorious massacre of Polish officers and civilians in 1940, as a way of mending strained relations between Poland and Russia on the 60th anniversary of this massacre. Poland officially now a member of N.A.T.O. however, treated Putin's suggestion as "a fine gesture."

Now that Russia has abandoned Communism, although it has full government control of all the media networks and seems to be sliding towards an autocracy, I am waiting to hear if apart from investigations, democratic Russia is prepared to compensate the relatives or their descendants in any way.

"After 1939, Nothing is Inconceivable ..."

In 1985, at my request, I received a copy of the U.K.-Polish agreement (from the British Foreign Office) dated London, August 25th, 1939. This was one day after August 24th, 1939, when the infamous Soviet-Nazi pact was signed.

The post-Munich world was struck like lightning. Six days later, Hitler's armies hurled their Blitzkrieg without a declaration of war (copying an old Oriental type of sneak attack) on isolated Poland, with the Soviet Red Army in the east poised to invade as well.

In the August 25th, 1939 agreement signed by both parties, the first four articles dealt with the agreement of mutual assistance in the event of hostilities. Article 5 read, *"The contracting parties to give each other mutual support and assistance immediately on the outbreak of war..."* The British waited until September 3rd, 1939 to declare war on Germany.

Article 7 of said Mutual Assistance Agreement—I quote, *"Should the contracting parties be engaged in hostilities in consequence of the application of the present agreement, they will not conclude an armistice or treaty of peace except by mutual agreement"* (At Yalta in 1945, there was no agreement when Poland was deliberately surrendered to the slavery of atheist Communist Russia). Thus, Poland lost the war in 1939 and at Yalta in 1945.

Conventional prudence failed as to foretell the unravelling of World War II and that which followed. The French Army was held to be invincible. The Maginot Line was impregnable and the Royal Air Force could not stand up to the German Luftwaffe.

Germany would never fight a two-front war. The Soviet army would collapse in one month against a Nazi Blitzkrieg. The United States would stay neutral. Pearl Harbour was invulnerable. The bestiality of the Holocaust would never be forgotten nor the slaughter of millions in Europe and Asia (ca 1939–1945).

The atomic bomb would never be used and its secrets never to be divulged to the Soviets. The U.S. loss of about 50,000 soldiers and defeat in Vietnam War. The collapse of Communism in Russia and Eastern Europe (unforeseen). The American Airspace and the first walk on the moon. The recent greed and fraud of some Western leaders of multi-national corporations like Bre-X and Enron. The attack on New York's Twin Towers (September 11th, 2001). The U.S. and allied attack on terrorists in Afghanistan and elsewhere. Foreign policy, world balance of powers, and their interrelationship, is not something set in concrete. It is in constant motion, surging like tides of an agitated sea.

Banff 1998

On Thursday, October 23rd, 1998 after the usual pre-flight arrangements, Tevis and I flew to visit my stepson and his family. We flew to Calgary via Toronto. A special bus took us to Banff. The highway was in excellent condition. What struck me most was after the bus passed the suburbs of Calgary and its Olympic ski structure, there were no dwellings to be seen.

We peered at the Rocky Mountains, some covered by green forests, others with snow on their peaks, others bare, except for their craggy grey rock formations seemingly reaching into the heavens. One felt as if our bus, whilst carrying us, was meandering through an embellishment of bliss.

At 6:00 p.m., we were met by Tevis' son Kurt and family. All of us had tea at their new home. Tev helped her grandson Grier with math. I took my nightly pills and we were all in bed by 10:30 p.m. Because of the loss of time, I did not sleep well. I read a little about the sparkling array of jewel-like lakes, glittering against the backdrop of the Rocky Mountains. I read about geologist J. Hector, in 1858, who was kicked by a packhorse while crossing a river, thought by his guides to be dead, which turned out to be not so. This incident gave the river and the pass at its head the name—Kicking Horse Pass.

I also read that the Banff National Park was established in the same year that the geologist J. Hector was exploring the Bow Valley. The park expanded from 10 square miles to the present 2,580 square miles. Lake Louise, which is northwest of Banff, is referred to as an Alpine gem.

The next night, Tevis and I slept in the master bedroom. When its curtains were unfolded, the three-story home was thickly surrounded by hundreds of statuesque pine trees, taller than their home. To the left of the trees, one could see part of a huge green-coloured Rocky Mountain. I was later informed it was part of the Northquay (Norkway) Mountain.

After breakfast and the grandchildren were driven to school, Tevis, Kurt's better half Heather, and I went to downtown Banff. One must admit that the many lofty peaks of the Rocky Mountains reminded me of the Mexican Sierra Madres; the Tatra Mountains of Poland, although majestic, were still smaller than the Rocky Mountains. After a wonderful visit and some extraordinary sightseeing to the surrounding areas, we were on a plane back home to Tecumseh once again…

Canadian Deal Makers Defraud Polish Potato Farmers

This is a very complex story. It began in 1991 after the collapse of Communism in Europe when democracy and an ascent free market were restored in Poland. In Victoria, B.C. in the 1980s, Mr. Robert Palm, a preacher in Princeton, B.C., and Mr. Jason Dallas incorporated a company — "Advance Capital Services." Mr. Dallas indicated that the two men attended the same large Pentecostal church in Victoria, became friends, and later on business partners. The two were openly known to network at a circuit of Christian businessmen's luncheons, raising money for a string of ventures on the Vancouver Stock Exchange in the 1980s.

When the two men were frequenting Christian business meetings in British Columbia in the 1980s, Mr. Palm's blend of religion and business sense appealed to investors such as J. Hanson. A Coquitlam man recalled Mr. Palm said he was raising funds to further the Christian cause. Hanson invested $30,000.00 U.S.; he never saw the money again.

By 1993, Mr. Palm, Mr. Dallas, and their company were sued by a Kentucky man alleging that he was swindled out of $4 million U.S. dollars. They were also sued by a Finnish company that claimed being defrauded $2.4 million U.S. dollars.

In the early 1990s, Mr. Palm and Mr. Dallas suddenly appeared as international, global dealmakers in post-Communist Eastern Europe along with a flood of Westerners hoping to cash in on the ground floor. Poland at that time was a toddler in business dealings.

From March 7th, 1993 to May 1993, "Advance Capital" was seeking out a Polish medium. They got Poland's farm foodstuffs agency — Hod-Impex Co. Ltd. (which was a novice; especially on such things as, "pay on delivery to Advance Capital").

Seventy-seven smaller Polish firms had to scour the countryside to deliver over 165,000 metric tons of flour at $320.00 (US funds). The president of Hod-Impex described how Mr. Palm always started a meeting with a prayer. He was like a preacher or a clergyman. He brought Canadian Capitalism with a shrouded, hypocritical use of the cross and Bible.

After the Polish farmers (with Hod-Impex) delivered $37 million (US dollars) worth of foodstuff, and Advance Capital failed to pay, the shipments could not be halted, as they already had been received in Russian army camps and veteran's groups. On April 7th, 1993, Hod-Impex sued Advance Capital, Robert Palm, and Jason Dallas in the

Supreme Court of British Columbia. The plaintiff's prayer for relief is for a judgment for $37,263,232.10 (US dollars), six (6%) percent interest, and costs. If I can understand, the statement of defence is that the foodstuff supplied was wholly inadequate.

To clarify this lawsuit, only Robert Palm is presently living in British Columbia. This case has been adjourned constantly from its inception. On February 21st, 1995, this case was adjourned again. In my 23 years as a Judge, I have never heard of a civil trial dragging on unresolved after 10 years.

Mr. Jason Dallas in 1995 and a Ms. Jacobson checked into a Swiss hotel, fresh off a flight from London, when the police swooped in. When Palm was called by telephone, he said I couldn't help because it would only cause problems.

About a year later, Dallas was extradited to Poland. Dallas told his accusers that he did nothing but sign the original purchase agreement. He also said he is penniless, and is living off his 80-year-old mother's Canadian pension. Dallas also said that the Polish farmers would have been paid if they had waited longer. He further said Advance Capital had billions of dollars available from banks in Moscow and Uzbekistan.

The Polish prosecutors found that the United Bank in Russia and its affiliate Uzinkam Bank in Uzbekistan never existed. Dallas contests that this Russian bank was just about to get started when the scandal broke. Dallas said he had direct knowledge of $1.5 billion under our control in Russia, and the guarantee of the Russian parliament.

The Uzbek bank pledged 200 tonnes of gold to the Polish venture. He filed a letter supposedly from Uzinkam Bank to a printer ordering $28 billion dollars worth of promissory notes, signed and sealed by the Government of Uzbekistan. The signature proved to be illegible and unidentifiable. Dallas blamed the collapse of the financial empire because the Polish farmers were impatient, and thought that they could be paid in two weeks.

Hod-Impex was supposed to wait a year for payment according to Dallas. When Hod-Impex management insisted on payment, Mr. Dallas and Mr. Palm came up with all sorts of excuses, burying them with guarantees, promissory notes, and tons of gold. A letter of Mr. Palm claimed that $125 million dollars was about to be transferred by Guan G Xi Trust Investment in China.

The trial of Mr. Dallas in Warsaw dubbed as "The Potato Affair" grabbed headlines in Poland. It still serves as a cautionary tale in Capitalism. Mr. Dallas went through numerous Polish lawyers. He elected to defend himself, and at times, he stopped his trial to pray. He told the Court he had to fraternize with God.

After a very lengthy trial, he was convicted of fraud and sentenced to eight years in prison in Warsaw. On appeal, the sentence was reduced to five years. Victoria, B.C., January 19th, 2003: "After more than a decade of waiting, a group of Polish farmers finally has a court judgment—to allow them to collect more than $50 million from a Canadian fraudster. However, their lawyer admits it's still very questionable whether they'll ever see the money.

[In a scathing judgment Friday, B.C. Supreme Court Justice Allen Melvin ordered Victoria-based Robert Palm to pay more than $37 million U.S. to Hod-Impex, the Polish agricultural co-operative" (The Province, 2003).]

The Paul I. B. Staniszewski and Mrs. Tevis Staniszewski Fund

As I mentioned earlier, it was my parent's generosity to their fellow countrymen, which inspired me to set up bursaries to assist students in their pursuit of higher education. Three siblings in our family went on to obtain university degrees, and I went on to obtain a law degree as well.

In 1998, "The Paul I. B. Staniszewski and Mrs. Tevis Staniszewski Fund" was funded at the University of Windsor. My cherished friend, distinguished lawyer Mr. Leon Paroian, Q.C. added $500.00 to our bursary. Because of a matching fund from the Ontario Government through the "Ontario Student Opportunity Trust Fund" (O.S.O.T.F.) our bursary is now valued at $51,000.00. The same provisions of the 1996 bursary were added to the 1998 joint bursary of $51,000.00.

In 1999, I presented another bursary for Law students at "Osgoode Hall," York University. The bursary was named the "P.I.B. Staniszewski Bursary." The Ontario Government through the O.S.O.T.F. fund matched my $25,000.00, increasing my bursary to $50,000.00.

In the dialogue I had with Dean Peter Hogg, I asked him to make sure that the Law course in "Ethics" be emphasized to avoid future graduates from committing any form of fraud. I was shocked to read about a recent case of a lawyer in London, Ontario, who by fraud garnered over $60 million dollars. Ethic courses I stressed cannot be glossed over to avoid such catastrophes.

Dean Peter Hogg underlined some of the many challenges the Law school faces, such as faculty recruitment. Government supports are at their lowest. Student tuition was increased by seventy (70%) percent in the last five years; a further twenty (20%) percent increase is foreseen in the coming year. My bursary is being awarded to Osgoode Hall Law students residing in Ontario. They should demonstrate financial need and plausible academic achievement.

In the summer of 2000, I established a $25,000.00 (Cdn) bursary with the Catholic University of Lublin. The University's President was in Windsor and had an undertaking signed in Lublin of my bursary. Before 1970, his Holiness Pope John Paul II lectured here, at the only Catholic University in Poland.

Jumping for Joy?

A retired Judge and former Member of Parliament at the young age of 80 celebrated his 53rd wedding anniversary by making his first skydive. The Honourable John Matheson, of Rideau Ferry, Ontario parachuted out after his plane reached 3,300 metres. Matheson's wife, whom he married in 1945 didn't join him.

Judge Matheson was first elected to Parliament and served four terms. This incident was reported in the Globe & Mail of August 5th, 1998. In fact, The Honourable John Ross Matheson, whom I met at all of our judicial seminars, became very good friends and colleagues after his appointment in 1968.

Honourable Judge Matheson was a most interesting Judge and Parliamentarian. He was a colonel in World War II, and served overseas with the First Regiment R.C.H.A. He was wounded and invalided home in 1944. He was elected a Member of Parliament in 1961, Knight of Justice Order of St. John, Kt., companion of Most Honourable Order of Meritorious Heritage, Genealogist Priory of Canada, Most Venerable Order of St. Jerusalem, member of the Canadian Artillery Association, and numerous and many other prestigious associations.

In 1982, he authored "Sinews of the Heart" and in 1980 "Canada's Flag: a Search for a Country," a 275-page book of the struggle with five Conservatives, one New Democrat, one Social Creditor, and one Creditiste, which gave birth to our beloved flag.

The author was the most active chairman of "the Flag" committee, who with others overcame hundreds of hurdles until its passage and proclamation. Finally, Canada's Flag Day was declared on, February 15th, 1965, thanks to J. Matheson, M.P., which is a story unknown to many Canadians.

1999

On New Year's Eve 1999, Tevis and I stayed up 'til midnight and listened to Guy Lombardo's orchestra heralding the New Year with "Auld Lang Syne."

In mid-January 1999, at the local Windsor office of The Canadian Red Cross, I was personally endowed with a framed tablet, which thanked me for "my support of the Canadian Red Cross' Relief Effort to assist in the Québec victims of the ice storm of 1998."

In mid-February 1999, Tevis and I journeyed to Toronto by way of the Via Rail. Not withstanding the fact that we were seated in a Club Car, the train was replete with passengers, many being Americans.

A hockey game was to take place at Toronto's Maple Leaf Gardens; this "icon" was built almost 70 years ago. The previous hockey patron and owner of "The Maple Leaf Gardens" was now deceased—Mr. Harold Ballard. He served the enterprise of hockey ardently.

On arrival at the Union Station in Toronto, we checked in at the Royal York Hotel (In the 1930s, this hotel was considered the tallest building in the commonwealth). This hotel revived fond memories of decades long past, where the local Canadian-Polish community held its yearly "Spring Time in Poland" formal ball. The waltzes, mazurkas, and tangos oh!

After unpacking and freshening up, we decided to dine at the "Samovar." On one occasion when I visited Montréal in the late 1940s, Eugene, my matriarch sister and her better-half Frank, had me dine with them at Montréal's restaurant "Samovar." It was a long drive by cab to Toronto's "Samovar." The restaurant's food was only adequate, but this was supplanted by the melodies of Gypsy and Slavic songs, accompanied by Balalaikas. Later in the evening, a guitarist played background to a songstress who sang Spanish tangos and ardent love songs of the soul.

Near the end of the musical entertainment, a rendition was sung of "Sunrise, Sunset," a sad song from the movie "Fiddler on the Roof." The house lights were engaged cleverly and portrayed light and darkness. The music sustained us as our cab drove us back to our hotel.

The next few days, we took a taxi downtown and walked around a little. I found that I could not keep up with Tevis and had to stop every fifteen feet or so to catch my breath and rest. After a brief afternoon out, I needed to lay on the bed and rest before I could recover enough to go out for the evening. Nonetheless, we had a special time.

We arrived home on the 16th from the Windsor Railway Station by cab. A Canadian-Polish neighbour brought us some Paczki (Ponchkie), as it was Shrove Tuesday.

Three Deaths in Montreal

On June 4th, 1999, which happened to be my birthday, we decided to fly to Montréal, as three of our relatives were deathly ill. Also ill was a lady that was a very good friend of our family, going back to the 30s in Val David, Québec. The flight from Windsor was cumbersome, as we had to change planes in Toronto. Tevis pre-arranged for wheelchair assistance for me to proceed to the Montréal's departure gate. This was too far for me to walk.

On arrival in Montreal by cab, we arrived and checked in to the Park Plaza Hotel in downtown Montréal. We called all of our relatives to join us for dinner at our hotel that evening. My youngest sister Wanda and her husband Stanley "Buddy," who lived in the Eastern Townships 90-miles south of Montréal, joined us. My matriarch sister, my nephew, first and second cousins, and spouses also joined us. A head count I made concluded that there were nineteen relatives present.

We ate at the main dining room. Sadly, most of the talk at dinner was about our dying relatives and our lady friend. Everyone was sombre and pensive. The youngest great-nephew Shawn, only in his mid–20s, was the most tragic victim of the lot—stricken by cancer. Our gathering broke up early. I was happy that my 74th birthday never came up that evening, and was left between Tevis and me.

The next day we took a cab and shopped at Eaton's in Montréal (In the mid–1930s, I first saw Eaton's catalogues acquired by friends living in Val David, Québec. My sisters and mother shopped at Eaton's frequently). On August 19th, 1999, its shares dropped from $16.00 in 1998 to 0.71¢. This 133-year-old retailer, cherished by Canadians, was then being dragged to its final termination.

Apart from the management and other inner failures of Eaton's, its termination was inevitable with "Canada's Free Trade Agreement" (Due to the influx from south of our border of the Wal-Mart's, the Bi-Way's etc.). We purchased dressing gowns for Marcel and Guy; both were facing diagnoses of mastasized cancer.

My brother-in-law Guy, though knowing his cancer was spreading, refused any medical intervention. When we visited him at his home that day, he was in great spirits, liked the gift of the dressing gown, and showed no constraints. He died that fall.

We visited Marcel the following day in the hospital. He was not very talkative. He was spirited away by the grim reaper on October 19th, 1999. Our family lady friend, whom we visited briefly, passed away that fall as well. My great-nephew followed, dying on November 3rd, 1999.

Y2K

There were trepidations as we slid into the new millennium; the police feared riots, revellers planned where they could safely celebrate, others dreaded the "Y2K," which foreshadowed chaos to many. Ninety kilometres north of Toronto, a retired teacher built an underground shelter—900 square metres, implementing 42 school buses. This shelter was constructed to withstand whatever the millennium might have in store, including a nuclear bomb.

Panic spread that banks and investment accounts would vanish into a tangle of dysfunctional cables and chips. With the much-hyped arrival of New Years' Day 2000, no calamities of substance occurred and we sailed safely into 2000. Since early January 2000, with the cooperation of our parish priests and others, I made inquiries at the municipal, provincial, and federal authorities to assist the Canadian-Polish community to acquire a home for the aged, though not exclusively for Polish people.

On March 10th, 1900, an MPP promised to arrange all government parties concerned with our Adhoc Committee inquiry about vacant land. Our file is bulky with promises that are endlessly spun. The last spin was in early June of 2000.

My 75th Birthday

Weeks before my 75th birthday, we debated as to whether: hold a dinner for friends at a hotel, club, etc., or attend Stratford to enjoy a

Shakespearian play. We decided on the latter. I received many kind gifts and cards from family and friends, and from local politicians I received lovely scrolls. I was the most moved by the Apostolic Blessing Scroll I received from His Holiness, Pope John Paul II, which our retired Monsignor delivered to our home in person.

Tev treated me by purchasing the VIA Rail tickets and priceless front-row seats for a performance of Hamlet. We enjoyed the play immensely; it lasted three-and-a-half hours. Canadian Actor Paul Gross played the part of Hamlet. In a most difficult scene as the Prince of Denmark set to avenge his father's murder, his acting was nothing short of brilliant.

Tev and I saw Mr. Gross in a 13-week CBC TV series entitled, "Chasing Rainbows." In this series, he acted as a Canadian officer in World War I who returns to Montréal after the 1918 armistice, and we witness the slippery life that ensues.

The next morning, Tev wished me a "Happy Birthday." We enjoyed a small breakfast at the hotel. As Tevis packed, I searched the Yellow Pages for a bus service to Windsor. None exists!

I told Tev that I was adamant of not going back by train because of the long delay we had suffered on our journey there. I located a telephone number for an executive air flight. The price was exorbitant; however, I decided to go for it, rather than suffer more VIA rail delays, and I booked an afternoon flight to Windsor.

We took pictures of the crew; they took pictures of us in front of their plane. Our pilot was warned by radio not to fly over Dieppe Park because of demonstrations being held there against the O.A.S. meeting in Windsor, Ontario.

That evening, we had a wonderful meal at "The Keg Restaurant" in Windsor-Broiled Atlantic salmon and lobster, and for dessert a tiny lemon birthday cake with one sparkler (74 missing).

Tevis' Family Reunion

On July 19th, 2000, we flew Air Canada to Sydney, Cape Breton, Nova Scotia—Tevis' birthplace. Although the tickets were purchased in early July, because of some Air Canada employee's negligence, we had to accept four flight changes instead of two, according to the tickets we originally purchased. The change in Toronto was made less difficult as Tev arranged assistance for me. From Toronto, we flew to St. John's, New Brunswick, then to Halifax, then to Sydney. On arrival at Sydney, we checked into the modern "Hotel Cambridge," with a luxurious sitting room. The hotel looked over beautiful Sydney harbour.

When we had caught our breath and came down for a coffee, the restaurant was full and we exchanged hellos with Tev's relatives from Northern California, Minnesota, and their respective children. Excusing ourselves, we went to a restaurant across the street. We were about to order when Cousin Shirley and Bill and Cousin Aida from Florida, joyously greeted us and we met their children. Others, whose names I cannot recall gave us a sincere welcome.

The next morning, we could not rent a car (there were none available), so one of the many cousins drove us to Point Edward. In all, that day I met close to 100 relatives and/or near relatives of Tevis. Tevis and other ladies posted their family trees on some of the walls. Tevis' mother was one of the nine children born to Robert and Ada Grant.

Tevis' cousins, Lorna and Robin, months ago, compiled a Grant Family Cookbook with both new and old family recipes. At the reunion, these cookbooks promptly sold out.

The second day, July 21st, 2000, we acquired a rental car. Back at Point Edward, there were games and activities for all. Soup chowder was served for lunch. I gave the three main organizers, Ellen Beth MacDonald, Aida, and Shirley, a bottle of Mum's bubbly for their efforts. Later, I had Tev drive me to the hotel, as I was exhausted.

On July 22nd, 2000, we got up, had breakfast, and Tev drove us to Louisburg Fortress. The French originally built this fortress. By 1740, the garrison reached 700. The civil population rose to about 2,400. With three changing of hands between the French and the British, by 1763, New France ceded it to Britain. In 1928, the Fortress of Louisburg was made a National Historic Site.

The French blue and red uniforms to me seemed much more colourful than the British one of that era that one saw in Ontario. The high point of our visit was the marching past of French drummers and the French regulars, who on reaching the ramparts of the fort, on command, fired the cannon, and shouted "Vive Le Roi!" Tevis' family reunion was a great success, and I greatly enjoyed meeting all of her relatives.

Is This My Last Skirmish?

On January 3rd, 2001, I was informed I had to attend a "mediation" meeting concerning my accident of 1996. This was adjourned to January 16th, 2001, this time with an elder lawyer, D.C., to act as "mediator." I was exhausted at the time and was on antibiotics for the continuing sores in my mouth.

Lawyer D.C. put pressure on me, cajoled me, and flattered me. Under the guise of friendly advice, exhausted and defeated, I signed the settlement papers. Out of an approximate $100,000.00 settlement, my lawyer deducted $20,000.00 for fees and disbursements. I was told in 1998 by one of the doctors that my "Counsel" sent me to for an examination concerning my accident that my lawyer is swift in settling cases and avoids long, involved trials. This proved to be true!

The second last day of June 2001, we were surprised by our three daughters, Gregg, and two grandchildren. They all arrived around 5:30 p.m. in a long white limousine with a chauffeur. We were driven to an Italian restaurant on Via Italia in Windsor to celebrate our 30th wedding anniversary. A savoury dinner, with Mum's champagne for the adults, and chocolate milk for Alaina and Jordana, our grandchildren.

After the well wishes were enunciated and the cake was cut, we drove off to say hello to one of my daughter's (Camille, who lives in Vancouver, B.C.) girlfriends in Windsor. After that short visit at our daughter's insistence, we drove along "Staniszewski" Street, and then proceeded home. That summer, I was advised by the Consul General of the Republic of Poland that I'd be awarded Poland's "Knight Cross of the Order of Merit."

To celebrate our 30th wedding anniversary, we discarded holding a party. We made reservations at the famous "Manoir Hovey" at North Hatley, Québec.

To avoid wheelchairs for myself, we flew "Northwestern" out of Detroit, Michigan and reached Montréal's Dorval Airport in two hours. Since this was July 1st, 2001, "Canada Day," we received a small Canadian flag. We were met by a Manoir Hovey's taxi, which for $120.00, drove us for a two-and-a-half hour drive to the Manoir.

The following day, I called my sister Eugene, my sister Wanda, and her husband Buddy. The three of them came to visit after lunch. We enjoyed a long drive around the town of North Hatley (and Eugene's cottage where I had spent many lovely summers). The trees are now colossal! That fall, Eugene sold the place for almost half a million dollars. In concluding the tour, we all landed at our Manoir and had a four-course meal "a la cuisine Francaise."

Our wedding anniversary was the next day, July 3rd, 2001. The 100 red and white roses that I ordered for Tev were delivered. After breakfast, our relatives arrived bearing gifts.

We all had lunch in North Hatley. We visited Wanda and Buddy's beautiful home in Way's Mill, admired their many artefacts, and their embellished garden, which borders a stream. We went on a tour of the city of Sherbrooke, which dominated the eastern township. We also paid our respect at Eugene's husband's and daughter's graves.

That evening, we celebrated our 30th wedding anniversary with our families. The four-course meal "a la Francaise" and libations made for a memorable evening. We had another enjoyable day of sightseeing and a tour of the area, which is very hilly and reminded Tev and I of the hills of San Francisco.

In late July 2001, I underwent a colonoscopy and cancer was discovered on my right colon. Later, I was operated on by the eminent lady surgeon, Dr. B. Heartwell. Like an angel, she came every morning to check my healing. Sometimes young nurses came to check my incision. In September 2001, I commenced a six-month treatment of chemotherapy; at the end of the treatment, I was given encouraging words.

When I was first informed that I had cancer, I did not panic. I prayed that I should be like one of the few cavalrymen who survived the British charge of the Light Brigade; I did not moan the cry, "Is that all there is?" My Polish ethnicity and Roman Catholicism have imparted me with the moral strength to engage the cancer in a battle for life.

Since beginning the chemotherapy (September 2001), I drank eight glasses of bottled water every day. I walked in our neighbouring park for 30 minutes, and when the weather was inclement, I walked on our basement treadmill, at least five days out of the week. I ate a lot of fruit and legumes, with fish, chicken, and very little meat.

Between 9:00 a.m. and 11:30 a.m., I sat and wrote my memoirs and wrote some letters. After a light lunch, I slept every day for almost two hours. My cassette player was my constant companion in bed, as I listened to endless classical music to uplift my soul and inspire my body to heal — Bach, Beethoven, Chopin, multi-national songs, and my beloved Gregorian chants. After a few minutes of enchanting melodies, I would succumb to sleep. I squeezed vitamin E oil on my cuts and sores to facilitate healing. On July 29th, 2002, I went for follow up tests at the Cancer Clinic—A clean slate!

On June 1st, 2002, His Excellency Dr. Pawel Dobrowolski, Ambassador of the Republic of Poland, on behalf of the President of the Polish Republic, bestowed upon me the high distinction and decoration of "The Knight's Cross of the Order of Merit of the Polish Republic."

The Ambassador then briefly outlined some of my achievements: A son of Montréal, of Windsor, and of Poland; The first Federal Judge of Polish descent in Ontario, the Secretary-General of the National Canadian Polish Congress in 1945; President of Canadian Polish Youth Clubs; and the establisher of the Polish monthly "The Dawn."

The Ambassador referred to my support of many charitable causes and institutions including our Windsor Roman Catholic Polish Church. The Ambassador further cited my scholarships in several Canadian universities, as well as the Catholic University in Lublin, Poland. Due to my significant donation to the Polish Air Force, the Ambassador handed me a ceremonial Polish Air Force officer's small sword, with an inscription, and a letter of thanks from the Polish Air Force Commander—General Ryszard Olszewski.

Remission

When I met my Oncologist Dr. Yoshida, on July 27th, 2002 after a brief examination of my stomach and my neck, he told me he was pleased with the findings. I was in remission.

I would like to express hearty thanks, on behalf of those countless numbers of cancer-stricken patients in Windsor and Essex County, my family, and myself, to the boundless humanitarianism of businessman and philanthropist Mr. Tony Toldo. He generously and kindly contributed over $1.5 million dollars to the new Windsor Cancer Clinic.

This very large, modern facility vastly raises the spirits and hopes of many cancer patients. Mr. Tony Toldo, a very successful Italian immigrant businessman is in the forefront of philanthropic donations in our area. In 1998–1999, he donated $2.5 million dollars to our community. He supported the Windsor-Essex Regional Hospital, funding two Urology surgical suites. He also paid the community portion of the cost for the above operating rooms.

This compassionate man's humanitarianism is endless to this day. His "Toldo Foundation" will be carried on by his daughter, Donna Corlin. He also donated non-medical gifts to the Italian Senior Centre; funds to aid autistic children; the Windsor Symphony Orchestra, and to the Jewish National Fund. Since the spring of 1999, he has continued his humanitarianism up to the time of this writing. Tony is aware of his own mortality; he battled prostate cancer.

In the last two weeks of August 2002, we entertained a couple from Poznan, Poland. The husband is an Orthopaedic surgeon and his wife a Cardiologist. We drove them to view the sights and have lunch at several county towns: Amherstburg, Kingsville, Essex, and Comber. We also visited Windsor's Art Gallery, Reaume Park, and many other areas of interest in Windsor.

Our guests visited Niagara Falls for a few days and were thrilled, especially in the evening when the falls were illuminated and fireworks were displayed. On their return, we all enjoyed our pool and evening walks in Tecumseh's Lacasse Park.

By August 25th, 2002, they left to fly back to Poland. The reason for me sponsoring this couple's visit was as a gesture of remembrance of my friend, the late engineer Joseph Kicinski, who was a family friend when our family lived in Toronto. Joseph Kicinski helped me greatly when I was Toronto's President of the Canadian Polish Congress and in my Liberal Provincial Candidacies as well. Joseph Kicinski was the father of Dr. Andrew Kicinski, who visited us with his wife Roma.

After undergoing a colonoscopy, which was performed by expert Dr. Bachus, polyps were discovered. Weeks later, an Israeli female expert surgeon, Anat Ravid, successfully removed the polyps. All of my doctors, including Dr. F. DeMarco, I owe so much that words cannot be found to express my gratitude.

In the same month, I chose to help a Windsor-born piano virtuoso, Daniel Wnukowski, by assisting him financially to hold a piano recital. This recital was dedicated in remembrance of the 3,000 victims of the infamous calamity of September 11th, 2001. I was helped by a circle of friends, including Reverend Canon, Pastor P. Sanczenko, and others. The concert took place at the Capitol Theatre, September 8th, 2002. It was well publicized in the local and county press, radio, and television. Announcements appeared in the weekly bulletin of our parish.

Daniel Wnukowski amazed the audience with his outstanding musical interpretations and his incredible technical expertise. Over the years, Daniel had taken part in many international festivals. In 1997, in Poland, he played with the Warsaw Philharmonic, where he was tumultuously acclaimed.

In the year 2000, Mr. Wnukowski was distinguished as "Laureate" at the Polish National Chopin Competition. He held very successful piano recitals in Paris, France; Basel, Switzerland; Amsterdam, Holland; and Ottawa and Windsor, Canada. He is also a composer.

He won awards and praise for his work, "Like a Dove." On September 8th, 2002 at 2:00 p.m., the Capitol Theatre was completely filled. *"The concert opened with a quiet, contemplative rendition of the famous Bach chorale 'Jesu, Joy of Man's Desiring;' then followed four Brahms Ballades. These pensive works served to emphasize the serious nature of the disaster, which happened in New York nearly one year ago."* (This is a small part of a quote from an article of pianist Claire Durocher).

In January 2003, arrangements were made to have Mr. D. Wnukowski hold recording sessions at Toronto's Canadian Broadcasting Centre (CBC) Glen Gould Studio.

Epilogue

"Canada's Federal Budget of 1995 was...dictated...by Wall Street." Since then, we have seen the dismantling of our great system of healthcare,...public education, a disregard of environmental priorities,... and a dramatic cut in Canada's Armed Forces,...and reduction in public-sponsored scientific research...the unfortunate mess...was the abdication of independent power by Ottawa in favour of the rule of financial markets. Marcia Russell, a New Zealand author, wrote in her book, "Revolution: New Zealand from Fortress to Free Market." ...the rush to embrace changes we trampled into near oblivion, some old, hard-to-measure values...ETHICS and MORALITY."[8]

Under Canada's *"Free Trade" Agreement*, we are being taken for idiots. For instance, the soft wood export of Canada to the U.S.A. has been forced by the U.S.A. to pay a twenty-seven (27%) percent tax, which tax the U.S. pays directly to its private lumber corporations.

This transgression by the U.S.A. has not been reviewed by a Court of Law, but by a nameless committee made up of mainly U.S. financiers. It is my opinion that it is high time that the Canadian Government and ministers stood up to these actions, and pull out of some of the other parts of the "Free Trade" Agreement. After all, no commercial or any other agreement is ever carved in stone.

As to the possible ratification of the Kyoto Agreement, it is already too late for thousands like myself and me who are cancer victims. Recent statistics reveal that the area surrounding us (Essex County) as compared to the rest of Ontario has the highest rate of cancer victims.

---

[8] "Stop and Think" by Paul Hellyer of the Canadian Action Party, p. 21.

Perhaps the arguments against Kyoto should be tempered by the diminishing number of people being stricken by numerous other serious or fatal maladies. Is a healthy, unemployed person worse off than persons suffering from cancer, emphysema, severe asthma, chronic bronchitis, and many other respiratory diseases?

In my humble state of mind, I suggest that there be a review of Canada's economic agreements, such as "Free Trade," NAFTA, and the drive to Globalization. Along with the unprecedented purchase and sale of manufactured goods, foods, and other items, has come abhorrent infestations and mutations of all kinds; diseases such as SARS, Mad Cow Disease, and the West Nile Virus are a growing threat to us right here at home in Canada.

Monster Chinese Carp have surfaced, Zebra Mussels have multiplied to an all time dangerous high, and we are plagued by oil spillages from large ocean-going tankers off many of our pristine coastlines. And most recently, the threat of GMO's (Genetically Modified Organisms) has flooded the North American market. GMO is a more palatable term for "Frankenstein" food. Mankind has no idea of the long-term effects of the genetically tampering of crops. Only time will tell…

Our parliament must select a Royal Commission headed by a chairman who is a dynamic exponent of Canada's independence. Some countries *do not sell* their land to foreigners; they lease it instead. Canada seems to be swamped with non-Canadian enterprises.

To name a few, there is Arby's, McDonald's, Kentucky Fried Chicken, Red Lobster, fast-food outlets, and then of course Wal-Mart, Home Depot, Honda, Mazda, Nissan, and Saturn as well. The Japanese carmakers here admit to receiving auto parts from Japan. We also have dealerships of Mercedes-Benz, Volkswagen, and Volvo, among others.

After expenses and taxes, their profits go back to the countries of origin in most cases. One has only to travel throughout Canada to realize how we are swamped by foreign-owned investments.

Too many hotel chains are not Canadian-owned; large corporations of multiple varieties are foreign-owned; we have some foreign banks, such as Hong-Kong Bank, Ing Bank (Dutch), Swiss, and others. We import California wines and European wines and beers; foreign pharmacy chains abound, which also sell volumes of non-medical items; we import much of our food, including fruits, from the U.S.A. and from Mexico. In the stationary and office supplies area, we're swamped with "Staples—

Business Depots" and "Monarch Office Supply." Other foreign corporations, such as "Radio Shack" and "Blockbusters Video" peddle their wares in Canada.

We witnessed the horrendous protests against globalization, the "I.M.F.," and other functionaries of the free market in Seattle Washington, in Québec City, in Kananaskis Alberta, and one in Italy where a demonstrator was shot.

My message to these brave, idealistic young people is to conserve your energies and protect your lives; form a legal association with chapters worldwide, pool your resources, write bona fide letters of exposure, and protest against the tentacles of globalization. Collect your information and print your own newspaper pamphlets and booklets exposing this incursion. Call your own meetings and rallies; remember that the word is mightier than the sword.

Certain Canadian individuals—authors like Naomi Klein, Mel Hurtig, M. Chossudovsky, organizations, alliances, and the political party "The Canadian Action Party," led by Paul Hellyer could actively participate with one another to form a united front and develop a common sense strategy.

This would prevent future incursions by the multi-national corporations from reducing Canada to a satellite state, dependent on the excesses of the free market, and international bodies like the "World Trade Organization."

An example in modern times is how an autocratic dictator (had executed by his Secret Police NKVD) 33,368 Polish prisoners of war, 14,736 of which were Polish officers. This was kept secret for over 50 years. Stalin's written order was made in March 1940. It had a tribunal, without the presence of the victims, all condemned to be massacred by shooting them in the back of the neck (Russian NKVD style).

These Polish military officers and civilians were said to be sworn enemies of Soviet authority, full of hatred for the Soviet system. Most were said to continue their counter-revolutionary activities, and were carrying on anti-Soviet agitation.

There were Polish officers, spies, saboteurs, land and factory owners, priests, and prison guards etc. They were all hardened and uncompromising enemies of the Soviets. The supreme penalty for these "monstrous anti-Soviet deeds, committed whilst in Soviet P.O.W. camps, commenced in March 1940 and ended in late May 1940" ("Special Tasks,"

P. Sudoplatov, p. 471). The lie of Soviet Russia's innocence in this massacre lasted until this evil Empire disintegrated in the summer of 1991.

I was shocked when I read in the "Report on Business Magazine" July 2001, about "Canada's Global Business School" named Schulich School of Business. It was reported that this Canadian school's goal is to improve the business between Canada and Russia, and educate the Russian's corporate governance in executive education programs across Russia. A photo discloses ten provincial premiers and Canada's prime minister launching the economic school in Moscow.

Canada's Canadian International Development Agency (C.I.D.A.) contributed $3 million dollars to the school in Moscow. Do our provincial premiers and our prime minister think that the "Russian Bear" in time, if fed enough of "free market" will be gentler than "the elephant we have to the south of us" I ask?

Recently, I was extremely pleased to read how our Minister of National Defence, in reply to Mr. Felluci's (US Ambassador to Canada) speeches in Canada, urged that Canada's armed forces be strengthened.

Promptly our Defence Minister diplomatically expressed the view, that since some of an Ambassador's functions are to promote the sale of their country's "wares," it is still up to the government of Canada to decide our military structures. Is Ambassador Felluci a "persona non grata" and should he be sent back to President Bush for a new assignment, perhaps to Iraq?

Some Canadian corporations are like "angels" dancing on the head of a pin. In the United States of America, the massive loans to executives handed out by the likes of WorldCom, Adelphia, and Tyco resulted in the recently passed "Sarbanes-Oxley Act," which forbids most companies from making such loans. This will affect Canadian companies listed on U.S. stock exchanges. In Canada, granting loans to executives is an old practice among major corporations.

A Toronto company, "Martin Rea International Inc." gave $9 million dollars interest-free to its chief operating officer, Erich Ginsberger. It gave its President and C.E.O. Fred Jaekel a $4.5 million dollar loan, and Chief Financial Officer $2.25 million dollars. It was explained by a company officer that these loans are non-recourse loans. That means that if the value of the stock goes below the loan price, the executive effectively gets a write off against it.

The Globe & Mail, October 10th, 2002, p. B7, having printed a series of reports on "board games," on October 10th, 2002, reported "on loans" by some of our largest companies.

Toronto-Dominion Bank chairman, Charles Baillie, who is stepping down December 31st, 2002, is of the opinion that we do not need as extensive a law as America's "Sarbanes-Oxley Act." He also said he was moving on whilst the times were good – another John Roth?

Under a caption, EASY MONEY, the Globe & Mail again on page B7, 2002, lists 15 companies that give large loans to insiders on generous terms; a practice banned in the United States. I cite only a few:

Martin Rea International Inc.: $15.8 million dollars, given to three executives interest-free, to buy shares;

Empire Co. Ltd.: $4.4 million dollars, interest-free, of which $1.8 million dollars was given to C.E.O. Paul Sobey.

Sobey Inc.: $16 million dollars, interest-free, given to top executives to buy shares.

Sobey Inc.: $2 million dollars given to C.E.O. Glenn Murphy.

Shoppers Drug Mart: $7.3 million dollars, interest-free loans, given to senior executives to buy shares;

Shoppers Drug Mart: $1.8 million dollars, interest-free loan to C.E.O. Glen Murphy.

The article ends with the admonition that we have a problem here, and new rules (laws) are necessary.

Optimistically, my interests in varied subjects and activities have not diminished dramatically. I face each day as it comes, with days I fill with reading, writing, attending medical appointments, and visiting family and friends. Had I been younger, I would have joined our great Roman Catholic Monk Hood to help our poor. Instead, I am establishing a Staniszewski Foundation for the infant poor and scholarships for needy university students.

I am eternally grateful to have had a father and mother who had us baptized and eventually brought up in the Roman Catholic faith of their Polish parents. Religion was a vital part of our lives and imbued me with a certain character. My brother John and I served the church as altar boys. I came across a D'Arcy McGee High School Report where I scored 87 in religion and 100 in geography. I had similar scores at college in

Montréal. This exposure to religious instructions paid off in my later years in life.

A Toronto Law School teaches "Ethics." Morality and the highest moral principles of civilization cannot be crammed into hour-long classes to law students in a two-three month course. A big part of the religion my parents taught me was to help people in need and share whatever one has for the good of all.

A 16th century explorer once uttered, "It is the Lord God that gave the land to Cain, Let us all be on guard not to allow our Canada to slip out of our hands."

Yet, Mulroney and the party that followed in 1993 embraced "Free Trade" with the U.S.A. "NAFTA added Mexico," that had been dictatorially ruled for 70 years and had recently elected a president with no connections with the past dictatorial party.

Recently, these fiascos occurred: The U.S. blockage of Prince Edward Island potatoes; the twenty-seven (27%) percent duty imposed on Canada's soft wood lumber. This duty is collected and sent by U.S. officials to the U.S. corporations who are in the soft wood lumber. What folly; can't our Minister Pettigrew get off his derriere and put an end to this and the "Free Trade" and "NAFTA" agreements.

If he cannot do so, let Chrétien replace him with a man who has guts and the government repudiate these agreements! A committee in Ottawa is studying a plan for a custom's union with U.S.A. and Mexico. That's what Bismarck of Germany did with all the smaller principalities...and thus welded one potent, imperialist Germany.

I was distraught to learn that the T.D. Canada Trust Bank's retiring chairman, Charles Baillie disclosed that the bank (my bank) had lost $2.9 billion dollars in loans that weren't collectible. Bank chairman Baillie is aggressively against Canada's adopting the recent American law, "Sarbanes-Oxley," which injects criminal prosecution on fraudulent acts of corporate Board and top executives.

Since my last operation of August 2001, after gruelling months of cancer treatments, I now live comfortably, as if on an instalment plan. My October 2002 colonoscopy was clear, but only time will tell. I marvel how my current doctors seem to be extending my life.

In February 2003, I was presented "The Queen's Golden Jubilee Medal" by Dwight Duncan, Member of the Provincial Legislature. The Queen's Jubilee Medal was awarded to hundreds of individuals across our great country for their significant contribution to Canada, to their community, and to fellow Canadians. As I wind down my life, I am proud that I could make a difference through my small but well-meaning contributions.

As of the publishing of this book, my health has seem to taken a turn for the worse and it comforts me to know that I am leaving the legacy of my "Skirmishes" both good and bad, with the readers of this book. I sincerely and with remorse ask my family to forgive me for any wrong that I may have done them.

Top Left: "The Knight's Cross of the Order of Merit" from the
Free Republic of Poland (2002)

Top Center: "Polish Gold Cross of Merit" from the Polish
Government in Exile (1985)

Below: "Ceremonial Polish Air Force Officer's Sword, with
Commander in Chief Inscription and Sheath (2002)

Bottom Left: "The Queen's Jubilee Medal" (2003)

Bottom Right: "The Maltese Cross" (1967)

Hon. Paul I. B. Staniszewski

BUST OF HON. PAUL I. B. STANISZEWSKI, PRESENTED TO THE UNIVERSITY OF WINDSOR IN 1992. DISPLAYED IN THE UNIVERSITY OF WINDSOR'S LEDDY LIBRARY.

CANADA

PRIME MINISTER · PREMIER MINISTRE

Ottawa, Ontario
K1A 0A2

May 16, 1995

Dear Mr. Staniszewski:

Thank you for your most recent letter concerning your efforts to promote federalism in the province of Quebec.

The unity of Canada is, by definition, a matter of concern to all Canadians. I am in daily receipt of ideas and suggestions as to how to we should approach the separatist threat in Quebec. Mr. Villemaire's efforts are a welcome addition to this outpouring of patriotism.

I am sure that you would agree that the recent "virage" on the part of the separatists is validation of that famous old saying: "You can fool all of the people some of the time and some of the people all of the time. But, you can never fool all of the people all of the time." Despite Premier Parizeau's various twists and turns, the basic desire among Quebecers to stay in Canada is not being diverted.

Please accept my warmest regards.

Sincerely,

Jean Chrétien

The Honourable Paul I.B. Staniszewski
516 Michael Drive
Tecumseh, Ontario
N8N 4M9

LETTER FROM CANADIAN PRIME MINISTER JEAN CHRÉTIEN TO
HON. PAUL I. B. STANISZEWSKI (1995)

Vatican--15 November 2002

Honourable and Dear Barrister,

I sincerely thank you for receipt of your gift of money, which will be used for the needs of the church.

With eternal thanks for your generosity, I send you my sincerest regards and pray that you will remain under the protection of our Holy Mother.

I Bless You

John Paul II

Barrister
Paul I. B. Staniszewski
TECUMSEH, ON
N8N 4M9
CANADA

(TRANSLATION OF POPE JOHN PAUL II's LETTER)

TRANSLATED LETTER FROM THE VATICAN'S POPE JOHN PAUL II TO
HON. PAUL I. B. STANISZEWSKI (2002).

In recognition of:

The Honourable Paul I.B. Staniszewski

When help was needed most...

You delivered.

When tragedy struck the United States on September 11th, 2001 you rallied support and brought comfort to a nation. You made a world of difference.

Thank you.

Canadian Red Cross

Anywhere. Anytime.

American Red Cross

LETTER TO HON. PAUL I. B. STANISZEWSKI FROM THE RED CROSS FOR HIS SUPPORT AFTER SEPTEMBER 11TH, 2001

Dr's A. & R. Kicinskis from Poland and Paul having picture taken at the
street
named after him by the mayor of Windsor Mike Hurst.

PAUL BEING AWARDED RED CROSS CERTIFICATE FROM
SENATE OF CANADA
BY REV. MONSIGNOR L. A. WNUK P.A.

Hon. Paul I. B. Staniszewski

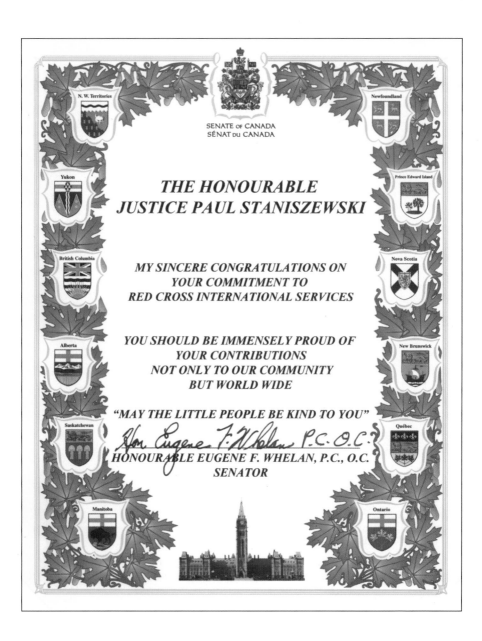

SENATE OF CANADA
SÉNAT DU CANADA

THE HONOURABLE
JUSTICE PAUL STANISZEWSKI

MY SINCERE CONGRATULATIONS ON
YOUR COMMITMENT TO
RED CROSS INTERNATIONAL SERVICES

YOU SHOULD BE IMMENSELY PROUD OF
YOUR CONTRIBUTIONS
NOT ONLY TO OUR COMMUNITY
BUT WORLD WIDE

"MAY THE LITTLE PEOPLE BE KIND TO YOU"

HONOURABLE EUGENE F. WHELAN, P.C., O.C.
SENATOR